UNIVERSITY OF NORTH CAROLIN.

DEPARTMENT OF ROMANCE L.

NORTH CAROLINA STUDIES
IN THE ROMANCE LANGUAGES AND LITERATURES

Founder: URBAN TIGNER HOLMES

Editor: FRANK A. DOMÍNGUEZ

Distributed by:

UNIVERSITY OF NORTH CAROLINA PRESS

CHAPEL HILL
North Carolina 27515-2288
U.S.A.

NORTH CAROLINA STUDIES IN THE
ROMANCE LANGUAGES AND LITERATURES
Number 302

MAPPING THE LANDSCAPE, REMAPPING THE TEXT

SPANISH POETRY FROM ANTONIO MACHADO'S
CAMPOS DE CASTILLA TO THE FIRST AVANT-GARDE
(1909-1925)

MAPPING THE LANDSCAPE, REMAPPING THE TEXT

SPANISH POETRY FROM ANTONIO MACHADO'S
CAMPOS DE CASTILLA TO THE FIRST AVANT-GARDE
(1909-1925)

BY

RENÉE M. SILVERMAN

CHAPEL HILL

NORTH CAROLINA STUDIES IN THE ROMANCE
LANGUAGES AND LITERATURES
U.N.C. DEPARTMENT OF ROMANCE LANGUAGES

2014

Library of Congress Cataloging-in-Publication Data

Silverman, Renee M., author.
  Mapping the Landscape, Remapping the Text : Spanish Poetry from Antonio Macha-
do's Campos de Castilla to the First Avant-Garde (1909-1925) / Renee M. Silverman.
  pages cm. – (North Carolina Studies in the Romance Languages and Literatures ; 302)
  Includes bibliographical references.
  ISBN 978-1-4696-1522-6
  1. Spanish poetry – 20th century – History and criticism. 2. Ultraism (Literary move-
ment) – Spain. 3. Creationism (Literary movement) – Spain. 4. Avant-garde (Aesthetics)
– Spain – History – 20th century. 5. Experimental poetry, Spanish – History and criti-
cism. I. Title.

PQ6085.S55 2013
861'.6209-dc23   2013045427

Cover: José Corral, Vista panorámica de Madrid desde la torre de la Iglesia de
    Santa Cruz, 1929, Photograph, Museo de Historia, Madrid, Spain. Permission
    has been granted by the Museo de Historia to reproduce the image.

© 2014. Department of Romance Languages. The University of North Carolina
    at Chapel Hill.

ISBN 978-1-4696-1522-6

IMPRESO EN ESPAÑA

PRINTED IN SPAIN

ARTES GRÁFICAS SOLER, S. L. - LA OLIVERETA, 28 - 46018 VALENCIA (SPAIN)
www.graficas-soler.com

For Gerard L. Spielman

TABLE OF CONTENTS

ILLUSTRATIONS

ACKNOWLEDGEMENTS

THIS book would simply not be but for the contributions of many people and institutions. I would like to express my sincerest gratitude to María Asunción Gómez and Juli Highfill for reading a draft version of the book and making extremely perceptive comments regarding its style and substance. I also wish to convey my deepest appreciation for Tobin Siebers, whose intellectual and professional guidance, generosity with his time, and kindness over the years have been absolutely invaluable.

I am very grateful to Frank Domínguez, the Series Editor of the North Carolina Studies in the Romance Languages and Literatures (University of North Carolina at Chapel Hill Press), and to Anne Abell, Encarnación Cruz, and Greg Severyn, Managing Editors at NCSRLL, for their attentiveness, graciousness, and high professional standards. It has been a true privilege and an enormous pleasure to work with all four Editors. I owe a considerable debt not only to the various Editors at NCSRLL, but also to the two anonymous readers who evaluated the manuscript. This book is far better for their insights and suggestions for revision, for which I thank them both profusely.

It is essential for me to acknowledge the support that I have enjoyed as an Assistant Professor at Florida International University: I am most grateful to the Office of the Provost for generous financial assistance to offset the cost of publishing this book, the College of Arts and Sciences for a Summer Faculty Development Grant (2010), and to the Wolfsonian-Florida International University Museum for a Fellowship there (2009). Many thanks are due to the Chair of the Department of Modern Languages at Florida International University, Pascale Bécel, for her sustainment of my research, as well as to Ricardo Castells (Modern Languages) for his sound advice about publishing my work. I am particularly indebted to Rebecca Friedman (History/European Studies) for her mentorship. I would also like to express my gratitude to Sebastiaan Faber and Tim Scholl of Oberlin College, where I taught for one year. Finally, I wish to thank the Northeast Modern Languages Association and the judges of its Book Award committee, which recognized this project with an Honorable Mention (2012).

An important part of the research for this project at an earlier stage was made possible by the Horace H. Rackham School of Graduate Studies and the Department of Comparative Literature at the University of Michigan, which awarded me the Rackham Humanities Candidacy and Dissertation Fellowships, as well as the Rackham Predoctoral Fellowship. I am likewise grateful to the Fulbright U.S. Student Program, Institute of International Education (IIE), for an academic year grant (2002-2003) to carry out doctoral research in Madrid, Spain, and an extension of this grant to pursue further archival work on poet Gerardo Diego in Santander, Spain. I wish to extend special thanks to Manuel Fernández-Montesinos for his invitation to be based at the Fundación Federico García Lorca (Madrid, Spain) during my Fulbright year, and to Andrew A. Anderson for introducing me to Sr. Fernández-Montesinos. I particularly appreciate José Luis Bernal's (Universidad de Extremadura, Cáceres) insights into Gerardo Diego's poetry and Yopie Prins's (University of Michigan) comments regarding my work on Diego during this initial period.

I am extremely grateful to Elena Diego for permission to quote from the unpublished correspondence of Gerardo Diego, and to Miguel de Torre Borges for allowing me to do the same with the unpublished correspondence, manuscripts, and documents of Guillermo de Torre. Both Elena Diego's and Miguel de Torre Borges's consistent good will towards me and my work is much appreciated. I wish to thank Vicente García-Huidobro and the Fundación Vicente Huidobro for permission to quote from Vicente Huidobro's unpublished correspondence, and L&M Services, B.V. for allowing me to quote from unpublished letters by Robert Delaunay and Sonia Delaunay-Terk, in addition to other documents authored by Robert Delaunay. It is with sincere appreciation that I acknowledge the permission granted by the Centro Cultural Generación del 27 to reproduce images from their facsimile edition of

Guillermo de Torre's *Hélices* (2000); I am especially grateful to the Center's Director, José Antonio Mesa Toré, for his generosity, and to Eduardo Herrero, for his aid. I am indebted to the librarians and staff at the Biblioteca Nacional de España, the Fundación José Ortega y Gasset, the Fundación Gerardo Diego (Andrea Puente in particular), the Bibliothèque Nationale de France, and the Bibliothèque Kandinsky, Musée Nationale d'Art Moderne (Paris, France) for their help and expertise regarding my archival research, as well as for their guidance with respect to securing permissions. I am similarly appreciative of the assistance afforded me by the staff at the Residencia de Estudiantes and the Hemeroteca Municipal de Madrid. For graciously furnishing me with the images that illustrate this book, I thank the following institutions, all of which I hold in high esteem: the Centro Cultural Generación del 27; the Museo del Prado; the Museo de Historia (Madrid, Spain); the Guggenheim Collection of Venice/Solomon R. Guggenheim Foundation, New York; the Wilhelm-Hack-Museum (Ludwigshafen am Rhein, Germany); Art Resource, Inc. (New York); and the Musée National d'Art Moderne (Paris, France). I owe a special debt to Ana Costa Novillo of the Museo de Historia (Madrid, Spain) for her help in securing permission to reproduce the photograph by José Corral which appears on the cover of this book and as Fig. 2.1. Last but not least, thanks are due to Michelle James of Florida International University for her help with the technical aspects of putting the book manuscript together.

An earlier version of the nucleus of this book's Chapter 4 was published as an article, "Gerardo Diego's *Heterocronismo* and the Avant-Garde: *Imagen* and *Manual de espumas*," *Hispanic Review* 77.3 (Summer 2009): 339-67 (Copyright © 2009 University of Pennsylvania Press. All rights reserved.) I revised and expanded the article considerably for the book chapter. I would like to thank the Editors, editorial board, and reviewers of the *Hispanic Review*, whose comments on my work have proved to be intellectually crucial, as well as the University of Pennsylvania Press, which publishes the journal. I am grateful to Irene Chytraeus-Auerbach and Elke Uhl, the Editors of the volume *Der Aufbruch in die Moderne. Herwarth Walden und die europaeische Avantgarde*, in which appears my article, "*La Prose du Transsibérien et de la petite Jehanne de France* (1913): Abstraction, Materiality, and an Alternative *Simultaneisme*"; they and the volume's publisher, LIT Verlag, have graciously permitted me to use a modified version of the paragraphs in the article in which I analyze Blaise Cendrars's text to *La Prose du Transsibérien et de la petite Jehanne de France*, a long poem and art object by Cendrars and Sonia Delaunay-Terk.

Finally, I wish to express my gratitude for the generous and patient love that I have received from my parents, Joan and Donald Silverman, my grandparents, my husband Rafael Moro Aguilar, and my son Rafi. I thank them all from the bottom of my heart.

INTRODUCTION

O N the cover of Guillermo de Torre's (1900-1971) avant-garde poetry volume *Hélices* (1923), the neutral blacks, browns, and beiges of the wood-engraved print (*xilografía*) by Rafael Barradas emphasize the graphic structure of the image (see fig. 0.1, p. 259).[1] Dominating the right-hand side is a large figure wearing the uniform and cap of the urban worker. Its right arm folds across the waist, while its left arm gestures commandingly towards a cluster of smaller figures at lower left. With a sharp-angled bill, its cap echoes the forceful left-arm signal. Below the principal figure's extended arm, the group of minor figures labors; their bodies slant dramatically forward and back, as if pushed and pulled by the sheer force of effort. Deep V-shapes created by black lines contouring the smaller figures repeat the upside-down triangle between the body of the big figure and its outstretched arm, simultaneously becoming the triangle's compositional extension and generating an ethos of physical work: in our apprehension the image snaps into focus as being "about" construction. Similar to the art form of *xilografía*, Barradas's design foregrounds the act of making, and establishes a metaphorical relationship between such making and the "architecture" of the avant-garde poetic text. I propose the concept of a *textual architecture* to reflect

---

[1] A *xylograph* is an engraving on wood or, as in this particular work by the Uruguayan artist Rafael Barradas (1890-1929), the impression made from one. *Xilografía* (xylography) was popular with the Spanish avant-garde and could frequently be found in its journals, especially those linked with the *Ultraísmo* movement. Barradas and Norah Borges (1901-1998), Jorge Luis Borges's sister and Torre's future wife, were among *xilografía's* most successful interpreters. See the original 1923 edition of *Hélices* published by Mundo Latino.

this constructive paradigm–a paradigm that governs Torre's work and the vanguard *Ultraísmo* (1918-1925) movement which he led.

Mapping the Landscape, Remapping the Text: Spanish Poetry from Antonio Machado's Campos de Castilla *to the First Avant-Garde (1909-1925)* likewise turns on the idea of construction, in the sense of building the architecture of the poetic text, and drawing the blueprint of subjectivity and identity. At the book's core is a double analogy that expresses, first of all, how the architectonics of the poetic text mirror the drafting of identity, and second, the way in which poetry's architecture can be compared to the structure of subjectivity. I contrast the turn-of-the-century plotting of identity squarely in the Spanish landscape with its cosmopolitan remapping at the hands of the first avant-garde (1909-1925).[2] My choice to refer to a *first Spanish avant-garde* is meant to suggest the existence of an initial vanguard wave in Spain, typified by several concerns: one, dismantling the turn-of-the-century textual "construction" that situated identity in spaces coded as national or regional; two, the "reconstruction" of poetic form as a means of transforming the conception of subjectivity and identity; and three, Spain's repositioning, relative to the geography of Europe and its avant-gardes, from periphery to center. These mappings and remappings, the main interests of the present study, depend on the treatment of perspective and perception. I tease apart the layers of signification wrapped up in both perspective and perception as concepts, as they relate to the structuring of subjectivity and identity. By subjectivity I mean, alternatingly, the articulation of the self that is the subject of the text, the experience of the viewing (or perceiving) subject, and the shared auto-definition that remains

---

[2] The avant-garde made a definitive irruption into Spain in 1909 when Ramón Gómez de la Serna published his translation of F. T. Marinetti's "Futurist Manifesto" in the journal *Prometeo*. That year came to be emblematic of the beginning of the first avant-garde in Spain while, from my perspective, 1925 marks the end of the beginning. John Crispin characterizes the so-named "Generation of 1925's" aesthetic in terms of assimilating various European modern and avant-garde movements (to which I would add the modern and avant-garde movements of Latin America) with the popular and the Renaissance tradition of the *culto* gloss on the popular. For him, the synthesis of the avant-garde and the modern with the popular and the traditional was intended to create a supra-national art that could compete with anything that other countries had to offer (215). The same interest in synthesizing the vanguard and popular remains characteristic of the "Generation of 1927," in particular the work of Federico García Lorca (1898-1936). (I treat the problematics of literary "generations"–with special regard to the "Generation of 1898"–in Chapter 1.)

integral to collectivity. How Spain's contested identity is negotiated, perspectivally and perceptually, in the textual landscape, as well as in which ways the articulation of subjectivity is affected by changes in the form of the poetic text, constitute the ultimate types of construction and reconstruction here under examination.

I begin my critical intervention, in Chapter 1, by reconsidering the mapping of Spanish identity in Antonio Machado's (1875-1939) *Campos de Castilla* (1912; 1917) before moving on to analyze, in Chapters 2 and 3, the way in which the avant-garde uproots the identity that Machado plants in the land. In *Campos de Castilla*, Machado paints a veritable landscape before our eyes, depicting, in the poem "Campos de Soria," "el campo ondulado" of the central Spanish region of Castile in all the glorious hues of a springtime sunset:

> tornasoles de carmín y acero,
> llanos plomizos, lomas plateadas,
> circuidos por montes de violeta,
> con las cumbres de nieve sonrosada. (CXIII lines 25, 33-36/134)

With its "sueño alegre de infantil Arcadia," the image of the countryside evokes the Arcadian landscape tradition–withdrawal from the world into an idyll–only to run up against ruin–a juxtaposition that Machado intends as a clarion call for national renewal (18/134). Writing in the shadow of Spain's long imperial decline and the "Disaster" of 1898, the poet draws upon landscape, as it was couched in nineteenth- and turn-of-the-century discourses and representations of identity, for the ethical purpose of recovering the country's sense of direction.[3] *Campos de Castilla* fits with the body of literary and philosophical texts that is characterized by a regenerationist perspective on Spain's malaise. Since this corpus of texts responds to the crisis symbolized by the year of the Disaster, its authors are conventionally identified as the "Generation of 1898," despite the considerable political, philosophical, and stylistic differences among them.[4]

---

[3] By the "Disaster" of 1898 is meant the Spanish-American War, Cuban independence, and the loss of Puerto Rico and the Philippines as colonies.

[4] Azorín invented the label "Generation of 98," linking a time in literary history with social criticism and protest, as well as a regenerationist stance, all of which were strengthened and given renewed urgency by the Disaster. He first employed the term in a series of four articles which were published in 1913 under the title "La Generación de 1898," and which were later incorporated into the volume *Clásicos y modernos*.

It is particularly against the quintessentially Spanish (*lo castizo*) in the Generation of 98 that the first Spanish avant-garde reacted, yet we should remember that some members of the Generation of 98, such as Miguel de Unamuno (1864-1936), actually had cosmopolitan inclinations–but for motives that diverged from those of the vanguard. It is also the case that the avant-garde, true to its nature, rebelled against various strong currents of the time. These would include *modernismo* and Juan Ramón Jiménez's (1881-1958) "pure poetry" (or, as he termed it, "poesía desnuda"), aspects of which could be considered "cosmopolitan" or "universal."[5] My contrast of Machado's *Campos de Castilla*, as opposed to other texts from the Generation of 98, with the first avant-garde, is designed to illuminate the vanguard's transformation of the relation of perspective and perception to subjectivity. The metaphor of "textual landscape," which evokes the visual and sensorial properties of the text, as well as the genre of landscape in poetry and painting, reveals one of the most significant reasons for my juxtaposition of *Campos de Castilla* with the avant-garde. Since perspective and perception are foundational with respect to subjectivity, comparing *Campos de Castilla* to the vanguard's very different textual landscapes provides insight into not only the way in which the representation of perspective and perception changes, from Machado to the first avant-garde, but also how such metamorphoses in the representation of perspective and perception affect subjectivity.

Campos de Castilla begs the question of how Machado situates the collective in the landscape–a landscape that is at once tied to the remembered, seemingly eternal past and reimagined as part of a renovated national future. (That this common identity is located in

---

[5] It bears remembering that Jiménez was a father figure to the first avant-garde as well as to the Generation of 1927 when it was still emerging. (He later broke with several of his disciples from the Generation of 1927.) Jiménez's work can be found in some of the first avant-garde's journals, such as *Horizonte* and *Reflector*, which were associated with *Ultraísmo* (Bonet 352). For a discussion of Jiménez's relationship with both the first avant-garde and the Generation of 1927, see also Andrés Soria Olmedo, "Juan Ramón Jiménez, crítico del vanguardismo." In *La nueva literatura*, Rafael Cansinos-Assens (1883-1964) emphasizes the purity and intimacy of Jiménez's poetry (153-70). Regarding Juan Ramón Jiménez's "pure poetry," or *poesía desnuda*, see Bernardo Gicovate, "El concepto de la poesía en la poesía de Juan Ramón Jiménez," Alvaro Salvador Jofré, "La dialéctica vestido/desnudo en la poesía de Juan Ramón Jiménez," Adolfo Sotelo Vázquez, "Miguel de Unamuno y la forja de la poesía desnuda de Juan Ramón Jiménez," and John C. Wilcox, "'Naked' versus 'Pure' Poetry in Juan Ramón Jiménez, with Remarks on the Impact of W. B. Yeats."

Castilian terrain as opposed to another area–perhaps one with a different self-conception–continues to be problematic, although it should be recognized that Machado, a native son of Andalusia, did not privilege Castile in all of his works.) The idea of recollection and landscape's prompting of memory proved compelling for Machado. His standpoint developed out of the educational philosophy of the *Institución de Libre Enseñanza* (hereafter *ILE*), where he had been a student; for him just as for the *ILE's* founder Francisco Giner de los Ríos, remembrance meant recalling the true identity of the *pueblo*, and bringing identity to mind was seen as a way of finding a new orientation for a rudderless Spain.[6] Significantly for this book, *Campos de Castilla* pivots on the way in which landscape awakens memory, and how remembrance can lead to the rediscovery of collective identity.

Yet at roughly the same time as the 1912 publication of *Campos de Castilla*, an altogether different model of the textual landscape was emerging, born of Italian, French, Spanish, and Latin-American parentage under the sign of Cubism and Futurism: we have only to think of the Italian Futurist F. T. Marinetti's (1876-1944) *parole in libertà*, Guillaume Apollinaire's (1880-1918) calligrammes, and the Chilean Vicente Huidobro's (1893-1948) visual poems and *poesía pintada*.[7] Such visual poetry can best be described as nondiscursive and presentational, and since it is organized by ellipsis and parataxis, the lettering and the white space on the page acquire equal importance for signification and reader reception. As a consequence, consciousness of the object status of the page and the formal qualities of

---

[6] Francisco Giner de los Ríos (1859-1915) founded the *Institución Libre de Enseñanza* with his brother Hermenegildo in 1876. In Chapter 1 of this book, I trace the *ILE's* origins in the philosophy of the German Karl Christian F. Krause (1781-1832) and discuss its ties to Spanish *Krausismo*, of which Giner and Julián Sanz del Río (1814-1869) were leading exponents.

[7] *Campos de Castilla*, Antonio Machado's third book of poetry, first appeared in the spring of 1912. It was published by Renacimiento, which Gregorio Martínez Sierra directed. However, what we refer to today as "Campos de Castilla" is not the same as the 1912 edition. The 1912 version comprises eighteen poems, if we are to group the "Proverbios y cantares" under one title; *La tierra de Alvargonzález* occupies almost half of the space, and "Campos de Soria," approximately ten percent. The 1917 "edition" is, in reality, not an edition *per se*, but rather a section of the *Poesías completas* (1917), the content of which includes the poems from 1912 plus forty additional ones. (The number of "Proverbios y cantares" expanded from twenty-eight to fifty-four in 1917.) It is this 1917 section of the *Poesías completas* that is now considered to be *Campos de Castilla*, yet it was not even titled as such at the time of publication (Ribbans, Introduction, *Campos de Castilla* 13-14).

the poem is raised, encouraging the reader's engagement with the text in fresh ways (Bohn 3-5). The perceptual simultaneity character-istic of Cubism and Futurism is intended to produce this desired sort of reader-text interaction. Common not only to Cubism and Fu-turism, Apollinaire and Huidobro, but also to the Parisian move-ment *Simultaneisme* (about which I will say more shortly), the repre-sentation of perceptual simultaneity as parallel to both a dramatically increased interplay between reader and text, and a "modern" type of simultaneous psychic processing of sensation should be understood as a crucial aspect of the avant-garde's pro-ject. At the same time, it is necessary to recognize the divergences among Cubism, Futurism, and *Simultaneisme* with respect to the part played by perceptual simultaneity. While *Simultaneisme* may be defined by the representation of perceptual simultaneity, and where-as Cubism aims to depict various perspectives at once, spatializing time and the impressions of the psyche, the portrayal of simultane-ous perception in Futurism is largely a means to an end: it accentu-ates the speed that typifies every element of modern urban life, in-cluding the innovations in technology, science, and transportation that were fairly worshipped by the Futurists.

I compare Machado's translation of perspectival techniques from landscape painting to poetry with the visual arrangement of the textual landscape in the avant-garde–centering at the same time on how and why they bring about divergent results. While Macha-do employs perspective to fix subjectivity and identity in the *castizo* countryside, the vanguard uses it instead to reconfigure them. This reordering metamorphoses perception on the level of representa-tion; learning to process the architectonics of avant-garde poetry then permits the reader to interrogate the relationships among identity, landscape, and textual construction as posited by Macha-do. Torre's inclusion of miniature calligrammes and scattering of poetic lines on the page in "Paisaje plástico" (*Hélices*), for instance, alters the way in which verbal language ordinarily signs and gener-ates meaning, causing it rather to function like visual language (see fig. 0.2). His transformation of our grasp of the space of the text al-lows us to break free of the spell cast by landscape, whose power comes from the representation of perspective and perception—a representation which, productive of remembrance and a sense of collective belonging, would situate us squarely within particular, de-marcated boundaries.

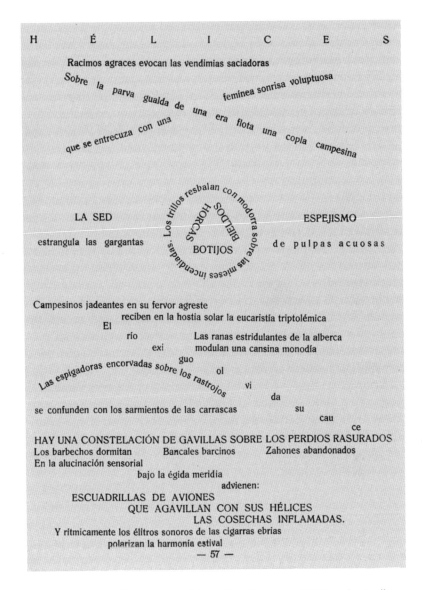

Fig. 0.2. Guillermo de Torre, Detail from "Paisaje plástico," *Hélices*, by Guillermo de Torre (Málaga: Centro Cultural de la Generación del 27, 2000).

The first Spanish avant-garde rebelled against the location of identity within (national or regional) borders, and broke the bond that Machado forged between people and place. For the avant-garde's remapping of the text as architectonic "landscape" ran parallel to the cosmopolitanism that it deployed to counter turn-of-the century notions of essential identity. It should be noted that the two most prominent tendencies in the first avant-garde, *Ultraísmo* and *Creacionismo*, both concentrated on poetry, maintained different relationships to cosmopolitanism. Whereas *Creacionismo's* cosmopolitanism was an outgrowth of its spearhead Huidobro's personal internationalism and bilingualism, Torre made the cosmopolitan key to the formal innovation and Europeanizing, urban aesthetic that he regarded as central to *Ultraísmo*.[8] Torre's cosmopolitanism manifests itself in his persistent detachment of the subject from the textual landscapes of *Hélices* and decentering of perception, each of which strategies he converts into the poetic equivalent of freedom of movement, association, and identification without reference to origins. To properly distinguish between *Ultraísmo* and *Creacionismo* is also to compare *Ultraísmo's* embrace of practically all vanguard movements–hence the name *Ultra-ismo*–with *Creacionismo's* very specific aesthetic as conceived by Huidobro.

In order to find methods of transforming the representation of perspective and perception, Torre looked to José Ortega y Gasset (1883-1955), the Spanish philosopher and champion of the avant-garde. He also took inspiration from the French vanguard, notably the theorist and cinéaste Jean Epstein (1897-1953), and *Simultane-*

---

[8] Under Torre's stewardship, *Ultraísmo* came to integrate a range of influences, from *Creacionismo*, Cubism, Italian Futurism, and *Simultaneisme* to Walt Whitman and cinema. Huidobro moved from Santiago de Chile to Europe, and then traveled often from Paris to Madrid, writing in Spanish and French, and publishing the journal *Creación/Création* (1921-1924) in both tongues (Bonet 179). For a detailed account of Huidobro's relationship with the first Spanish avant-garde, and the several extended visits that he made to Madrid between 1916 and 1921, see especially Gloria Videla de Rivero's 1997 article "Huidobro en España." Rafael Cansinos-Assens's (1883-1964) 1919 telling of the Huidobro-in-Europe story provides helpful perspective ("Vicente Huidobro y el Creacionismo"). With respect to bilingualism and translation in *Creacionismo*, consult Javier Pérez Bazo, "Tres poemas franceses de Gerardo Diego y el problema de la traducibilidad del texto creacionista," and Francesca Vázquez, "Traductología de vanguardia." Gerardo Diego authored an article on bilingualism in poetry ("Bilingüismo poético") in 1962. Miguel Gallego Roca's *Poesía importada. Traducción poética y renovación literaria en España (1909-1936)* will prove useful regarding the role of translation in Spain's literary avant-garde.

isme, which was conceived by the artists Robert Delaunay (1885-1941) and Sonia Delaunay-Terk (1885-1979), and the poets Blaise Cendrars (1887-1961) and Apollinaire. In *Hélices*, as well as in his articles and manifestos, Torre's defamiliarization of perspective and fragmentation of perception impedes the subject's–and by extension the reader's–identification with any commonality. He thus throws into doubt the linkage of territory and people intrinsic to Machado's framing of the landscape, and challenges the way this connection produces an apparently stable identity. I call this metamorphosis in the representation of perspective and perception *perceptual cosmopolitanism*.

Torre's perceptual cosmopolitanism stands as a striking corrective to Machado's turn inward onto the Castilian landscape, but he remained blind to the consequences of separating subjectivity and identity from communal space. To address the limitations of his cosmopolitan paradigm, in Chapter 4 I turn to Gerardo Diego (1896-1987), who developed a unique textual architecture that manages to integrate the collective and the past while continuing to be avant-garde. By returning to musico-poetic lyric in the volumes *Imagen* (1922) and *Manual de espumas* (1924)–instances of his idiosyncratic *Creacionismo*–Diego provides an alternative to the reduction of subjectivity and disintegration of identity that go hand-in-hand with Torre's pulling up of roots. By reclaiming lyric, he restores the expressivity and communicativeness associated with a strongly articulated subjectivity and collective identity. Interlaced into his poetry are precisely those lyric structures that are simultaneously poetic and musical–the refrain (*estribillo*), chorus, syntactic parallelism, and call and response–and which have the capacity to bind subjects together in a community. Their rhythmic and iterative nature has the effect of jogging memory, where memory is conceived as the very foundation of subjectivity and identity.

I draw on Paul de Man's idea that modernity and modern literature can be conceptualized in terms of the Nietzschean struggle between remembrance and forgetting. We are confronted by a similar duality when we examine Walter Benjamin's essays "The Image of Proust" (1929), "The Work of Art in the Age of Mechanical Reproduction" (1936), and "On Some Motifs in Baudelaire" (1939).[9] This

---

[9] See Paul de Man, "Literary History and Literary Modernity." It should be kept in mind that Benjamin's views on form and genre, as well as on perception and memory evolved over the ten-year span between "The Image of Proust" and "On Some Motifs in Baudelaire."

divide between memory and oblivion is a driving force behind the imperative–keenly felt by the first Spanish avant-garde–to choose the amnesia and disoriented subjectivity that comes with defamiliarizing perception over the grounded feeling that recollection elicits. However, defamiliarization is not the only viable option for constructing perspective and perception in the vanguard text, nor is "shock" (Benjamin's parlance) the only possible form of perceptual experience. Rather, Diego's reintroduction of memory offers the avant-garde a third option, distinct from the way in which remembrance generates collective identity in Machado's *Campos de Castilla*, and different from how, in Torre, transforming perspective and perception leads to a dissociated state of being. Although the construction of Diego's poetry accords, at least on the surface, with the predominant avant-garde modes of the time, it nonetheless summons the collective and the past. In *Imagen* and *Manual de espumas*, Diego produces a coherent subjectivity, at once gesturing metapoetically towards the temporal heterogeneity of memory, and going back to tradition through musico-poetic lyric and its characteristic structures. Exchange among subjects occurs within these structures, which permits him to weave common memory with lyric's thread. And in doing so, he turns the detritus of the collective past into the building blocks of the text, creating an architectonic model for avant-garde poetry that is firm yet flexible in its expressive possibilities–a model that I name a *musical architecture.*

FROM FRAMING THE LANDSCAPE TO PERCEPTUAL COSMOPOLITANISM

Machado's framing of the landscape in *Campos de Castilla* fashions and refashions his readers as a community, so that they might become responsive to turn-of-the-century Spain's deteriorated circumstances and assume responsibility for the country's regeneration. So as to put through such a change, which entails compelling the reader to recognize and thus identify with the *castizo* in the Castilian landscape, Machado transposes techniques from landscape painting–strategically setting up angles of vision, focusing the eye on certain areas of the representation, and adjusting the relationship among the "picture planes." Likewise, his vivid portrayal of sensation and sensory detail reinforces the reader's identification with the landscape, and revives the memories bound up with it. For example, in "A orillas del Duero" (*Campos de Castilla* XCVIII) the first-person subject recalls impressions elicited by a journey through the countryside, yielding a rich description of the land's contours. By apprehending Machado's delineation of the landscape, the reader shares in the subject's remembered experience. In the poem's first section (lines 1-32), each sensory detail acquires special meaning, alternatively recalling Arcadia and suggesting Castile's former strength as the bastion of the Reconquest. Not only are its features–the "redonda loma cual recamado escudo," "cárdenos alcores sobre la parda tierra," and "serrezuelas calvas por donde tuerce el Duero"–emblematic of the Castilian countryside and character, but also, the intensely sensory character of their description strikes a chord, putting remembrance into play ("A orillas del Duero" 16-17, 19/101-102). The remembrance prompted by Machado's depiction of sensory detail is simultaneously individual and collective. His double recollective "framing" becomes part and parcel of a yearning for an idealized past, which he then juxtaposes with images of Castile in its current state of ruin. By setting the feeling of belonging against a profound sense of loss, he means to awaken his readers to the stark reality of Spain's malaise and the desperate need for their involvement in its remedy.

Torre breaks with Machado's representation of landscape as collective identity by upending the perspectival and perceptual maneuvers which are characteristic of *Campos de Castilla*. To illustrate: in "Dehiscencia," the first poem and *ars poetica* of *Hélices*, Torre pictures a fecund Nature bursting with new life after the devastation of war.[10] The stream of evocative detail in Machado here becomes a hyperbolic barrage pouring out in extended tropes. Torre accompanies this sensory bombardment with a complete transformation of Machado's meditative representation of the countryside. In many poems of *Campos de Castilla*, the subject's distanced position is essential to quiet contemplation, which in turn stimulates remembrance. In "Dehiscencia," contrastingly, Torre creates a dizzying variety of perspectives by exaggerating the separation between the subject and the "landscape":

---

[10] Torre almost surely alludes to World War I (1914-1918). He gives the years 1918-1919 for the composition of the poems in the initial "Versiculario Ultraísta" section of *Helices*, in which "Dehiscencia" appears as the first text. (See the "Sumario" that prefaces the volume.)

Y es entonces cuando mi espíritu ha vislumbrado auguralmente
   la insólita fecundación:
Súbitamente, entre el paróxico danzar de los planetas,
la tierra estatifica su rotación.
Y la hesperidia abstracción amnésica de la poma terráquea
adquiere una sorprendente configuración floral. (21-25/11)[11]

The profusion of views produces an "abstracción amnésica" that
erases memory, for the fragmenting of perspective of which this
multiplicity is symptomatic disturbs the clarity of association vital
to recollection.

In further considering the significance of the subject's remove in
Torre, we should bear in mind the link that Ortega posits between
the defamiliarization of perspective and abstraction. He argues, in
La deshumanización del arte (1925), that what we customarily speak
of as "proximity" and "distance" with respect to "point of view"
actually describes different ways of seeing:

> . . . [N]o es la *cantidad* geodésica de distancia lo que influye deci-
> sivamente en el punto de vista del pintor, sino la *cualidad* óptica
> de esa distancia. Cerca y lejos, que métricamente son caracteres
> relativos, pueden tener un valor absoluto para los ojos. En efecto,
> la *visión próxima* y la *visión lejana* de que habla la fisiología no
> son nociones que dependan principalmente de factores métricos,
> sino que son más bien dos modos distintos de mirar. (189; em-
> phasis in the original)

For Ortega, switching from a "close up" to a "distanced" standpoint
has a defamiliarizing effect on the subject of representation: "Pues
bien: al pasar un objeto de la visión próxima a la lejana, se fantas-
magoriza. Cuando la distancia es mucha, allá en el confín de un re-
moto horizonte–un árbol, un castillo, una serranía–, todo adquiere el
aspecto casi irreal de apariciones ultramundanas" (*Deshumanización*

---

[11] The phrase "hesperidia abstracción amnésica de la poma terráquea" is part of
an extended metaphor that compares the poetic subject's sentiments with a cosmic
event, in which amid the dance-like movements of the planets, the Earth stops its
rotation. One aspect of this extended metaphor is a trope that compares the Earth
to fruit. Torre derives the non-standard adjective *hesperidia* from *hesperidio*, a Span-
ish noun meaning a fleshy fruit divided into sections on the inside with a thick skin
on the outside, such as a lemon or orange. *Hesperidia* is linked to *poma*, which sig-
nifies a fruit from a tree, usually an apple ("Hesperidio"; "Poma").

191). Torre realizes that defamiliarization is vital to abstraction, as well as how it can be used to create an innovative poetic language. In his 1920 article "Itinerario noviespacial del paisaje," Torre contrasts avant-garde abstraction with the proximate views that he attributes to Azorín, who gave the Generation of 98 its name.[12] He rejects Azorín's detailed realism, which hearkens back to nineteenth-century *costumbrismo*, because he comprehends how this type of focus can produce an empathetic reaction in the reader:

> De las interpretaciones azorinianas, pues, de sus veraces cuadros descriptivos, en el ciclo que alcanza desde 'La voluntad' a 'Los pueblos,' receptores impasibles, como nítidos espejos, de la realidad atmosférica, habríamos de arrancar para toda exégesis de concreción paisajista o descripción costumbrista de tipos y aspectos pueblerinos. ("Itinerario" 83)

By implementing Ortega's view of abstraction, Torre disrupts the way in which fixing on detail, in Azorín and Machado, leads to identification:

> Mas en nuestro apasionamiento abstracto, rehuímos el reflejo anecdótico y la localización provincianista. De ahí que nuestras excursiones divagatorias en torno al paisaje aludan a su *abstracto concepto intelectual* y no a su concreción realista. Así, pues, salgamos de Castilla, aunque en su dintorno espacial situemos las características del paisaje límpido y abstracto, henchido de perspectivas estéticas y sugerencias meditativas. (83; my emphasis)

Torre's dynamic construction of perspective contravenes the contemplative gaze that remains crucial to remembrance. For instance in "Al aterrizar":

> La ciudad multánime abre sus vísceras centrales y prolonga sus miembros periféricos, tentacularmente.
> La infinitud de edificios cristalinos–pueblos verticales–cupulados de estaciones agarófilas,
> seccionan transversalmente el dinamismo convulsivo de las claras avenidas rectilíneas.
> En su estuario vorticista naufragan las miradas tradicionales.
>
> (*Hélices* 5-8/13)

---

[12] Azorín was the pseudonym used by José Martínez Ruiz (1873-1967).

The poem's textual architecture, similar to urban space, is designed to disrupt all manner of "miradas tradicionales"–the kind that order Azorín's *costumbrista* evocations of villages and rural areas, as well as Machado's landscapes of memory. Rupturing these viewpoints by metamorphosing perspective and perception becomes Torre's method of escaping the bounds of the collective. As I suggest, in Torre, the defamiliarization involved in abstraction, beyond breaking down the borders of common identity, comes to constitute the textual equivalent of cosmopolitanism.

Torre's perceptual fluidity is the antithesis of the stable quintessence that Machado portrays through the Castilian landscape. Take, for example, his delineation of the city as a place where "el hombre pleonéxico, en vez de sentirse franciscanamente transfundido con cualquier elemento de la fauna o flora naturales, se siente fraternalmente interpenetrado por la plasticidad de los tranvías céleres, los *affiches* multicolores, las máquinas inundantes o cualquiera otra célula vibrante del organismo cosmopolita": we are no longer talking about rooting the textual subject or the reader in the space of the collective, but instead imagining how the boundaries dividing the self, other selves, and the external world can be dissolved altogether ("Itinerario" 90-91).[13] It is this disintegration that turns into a structural model for cosmopolitanism and for which cosmopolitanism, conversely, becomes metaphor. As Torre maintains in "Itinerario noviespacial del paisaje," the goal of the avant-garde poet should be to create "un paisaje espiritual dentro del paisaje objetivo," by which he adverts to the productive dissolution and reconstruction of the subject and the subject's perception, in relation to the textual landscape (86). He calls the permeability of the subject to the external world, and the potential for exchange between subject and object (or "I" and non-"I") "subjetivación intraobjetiva"–an idea that I trace from its origins in the German philosophi-

---

[13] The adjective "pleonéxico" ("pleonectic" in English) refers to greediness or avariciousness. It derives from the noun "pleonexia" (in Spanish and English), which is the same as in the post-classical Latin and the original ancient Greek ("Pleonectic"; "Pleonexia"). The phrase "máquinas inundantes" suggests the way in which machines of all types flood urban spaces; "inundantes" comes from the Spanish verb "inundar," which means to fill, saturate, flood, sweep over, or overwhelm. The idea is that machines and machinery penetrate the lives and psyches of urban dwellers, which remains in keeping with Torre's conception of perceptual fluidity and simultaneity.

cal concept of the *Einfühlung* [empathy], and the work of Theodor Lipps (1851-1914) and Wilhelm Worringer (1881-1965). In Torre, *subjetivación intraobjetiva* bridges the gap between the psyche and the exterior world, abstract (or "objective") and subjective sorts of representation, and subjective and objective perspectives. The crossing between subject and object, and the mutual interpenetration of the subject and external world through *subjetivación intraobjetiva* become the foundations of Torre's perceptual cosmopolitanism. Releasing the subject from its own confines, as well as freeing it to change its situation, in Torre's textual landscapes, parallels the metamorphic potential of the cosmopolitan.

In addition to *subjetivación intraobjetiva*, Torre patterns the representation of perception on the free-association which, according to Epstein, is intrinsic to the modern psyche, and which the theorist and cinéaste consequentially envisions as the proper structure for avant-garde poetry and film. Epstein holds that the abstract form of modern literature comes from the triumph of spontaneity in the authorial psyche's revolt against destructive controls; in *La poésie d'aujourd'hui, un nouvel état d'intelligence. Lettre de Blaise Cendrars* (1921) he describes the unfiltered workings of mind and pen as "la vie végétative," "spontanéité," "distraction," "fatigue mentale," and "accélération vitale." Yet for all Epstein's emphasis on the psychic existence of the author, he takes the position that a mechanical device–the camera–should supplement human sensory capability by helping the eye to integrate the fourth dimension of time into its perception of space. Such expanded powers, peculiar to what he terms, after Louis Delluc, "*photogénie*," allows the linking of objects in space and time–in his view the source of cinematic abstraction. In two articles, "Problemas teóricos y estética experimental del nuevo lirismo" and "El cinema y la novísima literatura," Torre advocates following Epstein's lead in throwing off all limitations on the representation of perception, and in translating this perceptual unshackling into the jettisoning of the grammatical and syntactical rules of literary writing.[14] And just as in Epstein, in Torre the em-

---

[14] The complete titles of Torre's articles on Epstein are: "Problemas teóricos y estética experimental del nuevo lirismo: 'La poesía de hoy' por el teorizante Ep stein" and "El cinema y la novísima literatura: sus conexiones." They appeared in the journal *Cosmópolis* in 1921. Torre later adapted these articles for inclusion in his 1925 *Literaturas europeas de vanguardia*.

brace of the mechanical as a prosthetic enhancement of the senses turns into a means of transforming both perception and perception's representation in poetic form.

Torre's relationship with the artists Delaunay and Delaunay-Terk, and the knowledge of *Simultaneisme* that friendship with the couple afforded him made an even greater impact on his reinvention of the representation of perception. Delaunay, *Simultaneisme's* theorist, defines the breakdown and reconstitution of visual perception in terms of the binary *destruction/construction*, which Torre renders, in an unpublished monograph on the painter, as *destrucción/reconstrucción*. In *Destrucción, reconstrucción: La pintura de Robert Delaunay* (1920) as well as two other texts, *El arte decorativo de Sonia Delaunay-Terk* (1921), and *Blaise Cendrars* (n.d.), he uses his keen understanding of *Simultaneisme* and the techniques involved in the Delaunays' art to devise a similar paradigm, which becomes the formal basis of perceptual cosmopolitanism.[15] Delaunay and Delaunay-Terk dissolve visual perception into its component parts, color and light, which they then refashion as form–the *"contrastes simultanés."* Torre converts his fragmented representation of perception–a poetic version of the *contrastes simultanés*–into a textual landscape that permits the protean movement of a cosmopolitan subject.

Torre's metamorphosis of perception makes the now, exploding with sensory possibility, the focus of his work, and his positing of a present-tense apprehension unfettered by any restriction effectively short-circuits the remembrance that is crucial to Machado's aims. However, in setting the subject at liberty from the landscape of memory, and in dissolving the boundaries separating the subject from the external world, Torre not only establishes a model for cosmopolitanism, but also creates a disquieting feeling of anomie. The severing of psychic connections to the collective and the past disintegrates the networks that are constitutive of the self, and cuts off the communicative channels that shape its relationship with others.

---

[15] In 1925, Torre published a version of *El arte decorativo de Sonia Delaunay-Terk* as an article in the journal *Alfar*.

RECOVERING MEMORY: GERARDO DIEGO'S MUSICAL ARCHITECTURE

It was Diego who restored the complex subjectivity and access
to the collective past that stayed missing from Torre and the early
Huidobro. Diego quickly took his place as Huidobro's most fervent
admirer and the most apt student of *Creacionismo* in Spain–along
with Juan Larrea and Pedro Garfías–yet at the same time he was
the first to react against Huidobro's emphasis on visual metaphors
and the spatial layout of the text.[16] Although Diego enthusiastically
accepted Huidobro's imperative for *creación* and *invención*, the to-
tal rupture with the anterior that Huidobro saw as key to the new
poetics did not sit nearly as well. In *Imagen* and *Manual de espumas*,
as well as in his posterior anthological and auto-anthological works,
Diego sought to write remembrance into the avant-garde, and the
avant-garde into remembrance.

In keeping with Diego's desire to recover the past, time becomes
the major constructive principle of *Imagen* and *Manual de espumas*.
Different from that of the early Huidobro, Diego's poetry derives its
force from the structures of versification, rhyme, and rhythm, in ad-
dition to avant-garde architectonics such as visual metaphor and ex-
perimental ways of arraying the lines on the page. The prominent
part played in Huidobro by visual metaphor, and his treatment of
the poetic image and the space of the page as three-dimensional is
matched in Diego by rhythm as textual structure. Diego's message is
that he intends to build his textual architecture using diverse meth-
ods, culled from all periods in the history of poetry, including but
not exclusive to those favored by the avant-garde.

Diego, like Huidobro, makes a point of jettisoning the *passé*,
however he diverges from the Chilean in the weight that he places
on rhythm and repetition as expression of the temporal. By turning
time into one of the primary buttresses in the architecture of his po-
etry, Diego recalls the source of rhythm in musico-poetic lyric.
Rhythm's constructive ability also evokes the way in which repeated

---

[16] I make particular reference to Huidobro's poetry volumes *El espejo de agua*
(1916), *Adán* (1916), and *Tour Eiffel, Hallali, Ecuatorial,* and *Poemas árticos* (1918).
Juan Larrea (1895-1980) and Pedro Garfías (1901-1967) were enmeshed in the
Creacionismo movement in Spain; Larrea was heavily involved, displaying a special
concern for *Creacionismo's* poetics.

patterns order popular lyric.[17] These iterations strengthen popular lyric's communicative functions, which serve to fortify intersubjective networks and preserve collective memory. Here I look to John Hollander's work on the refrain in musico-poetic lyric: he argues that in modern poetry, iterating the refrain at once forges bonds among "singers," and allegorizes subjectivity and communication among subjects (74). Such repetitions and the intersubjectivity that they sustain reinforce and reinvigorate common memory.

Recollection, in Diego, works along lines similar to the construction of memory as conceived by Henri Bergson (1859-1941): past and present are connected in a tapestry of perceptions woven across time. In *Imagen* and *Manual de espumas*, the repetition of rhythmic figures organizes the poetic text, and Diego's varying of the refrain resembles Bergson's conception of how impressions are articulated and rearticulated in memory. In "Estética" (*Imagen*), which Diego dedicates to Spanish composer Manuel de Falla (1876-1946), he constructs a flexible architecture that is as much temporal and expressively musical as it is spatial and architectonic:

> Estribillo   Estribillo   Estribillo
> El canto más perfecto es el canto del grillo
>
> Paso a paso
>   se asciende hasta el Parnaso
> Yo no quiero las alas de Pegaso
>
>   Dejadme auscultar
> el friso sonoro que fluye la fuente
>
> Los palillos de mis dedos
> repiquetean ritmos ritmos ritmos
> en el tamboril del cerebro
>
> Estribillo   Estribillo   Estribillo
> El canto más perfecto es el canto del grillo (1-12/187)

---

[17] I am aware of–and to a certain extent accept–J. G. Cummins's preference for the term "poesía de tipo tradicional" (poetry of the traditional type) over "poesía popular" (popular poetry), but in this study I use *popular poetry* in order to emphasize the roots of lyric language. Cummins's usage of *poesía de tipo tradicional* in *The Spanish Traditional Lyric* integrates courtly and other literary transformations of "popular" lyric (1). Equally important to consult are José María Alín's *El cancionero español de tipo tradicional* and Eduardo M. Torner's *Lírica hispánica: relaciones entre lo popular y lo culto.*

While the visual arrangement of the lines on the page is analogous to Huidobro's early volumes, the exaggerated insistence on rhythm, assonance, alliteration, and internal and end rhyme underscores the poem's difference from them. Diego's relaxing of Huidobro's solid architectonics is reflected in the architectural metaphor of the phrase "Dejadme auscultar / el friso sonoro que fluye la fuente": this is not your ordinary static construction, he is telling us, but a musical architecture whose sturdiness depends on its capacity for variation. The refrain as a basic element of Diego's musical architecture restores lyric time and the expanded possibilities of memory that go along with it, thereby creating an aperture for the return of remembrance to avant-garde poetry. The "ritmos ritmos ritmos," rapped out "en el tamboril del cerebro," are the fundamental undergirding of the poetic text and memory. Varying refrain-like structures in the course of their reiteration generates a temporal matrix comparable to individual memory, and its repetition produces the supports of collective recollection.

Diego's recognition of the way in which rhythmic and rhyme patterns awaken memory summons to mind Machado's idea of the relationship between rhyme, rhythm, time, and remembrance in poetry. For Machado, rhythm and rhyme situate poetic language in lived time, and in doing so, return to us the emotion of that time, and emotion, from his perspective, remains an essential quality of lyric. Diego, like Machado, regards the temporal aspect of rhyme and rhythm as lending structure to the poetic text, and both men conceive of this structure as being flexible and expressive rather than rigid and uniform. As Machado remarks in "Sobre el libro *Colección* del poeta andaluz José Moreno Villa":

> En efecto, uno de los oficios de la rima es hacernos sentir, por contraste, el fluir de los sonidos que pasan para no repetirse. Pero la rima que, con relación a los elementos irreversibles del verso, acentúa su carácter de permanencia, no es por sí misma ni rígida, ni uniforme, ni permanente. . . Es un cauce, más que una corriente; pero un cauce que, a su vez, fluye. Complicando sensación y memoria contribuye a crear la emoción temporal *sine qua non* del poema. (1366)

To exemplify how rhyme and rhythm jog memory, Machado analyzes the workings of assonance in the *Romancero* tradition. He points out that just as in the *romance* sound ("con su imagen fónica") locates poetic language in time, reviving the sentiments of anterior moments in history, in lyric the temporal elements of rhyme and rhythm reconnect the reader with the emotions of the past. Yet in lyric, the past is specific to the poet and the poet's subjectivity–"la historia emotiva de cada poeta" ("Sobre el libro *Colección*" 1368).

As a pianist well-versed in musical modernism, thanks to his friendship with Falla, Diego discerned the ways in which reiterated structures can perform in music and musico-poetic lyric.[18] Diego develops the refrain as musical architecture in *Manual de espumas*, expanding its role from musico-poetic structure to mnemonic device with the power to form connections among subjects. "Canción fluvial" is reminiscent of popular lyrics and their part in traditional communities:

> Mirad las lavanderas
> nutriendo de colores las limpias faltriqueras
>
> La espuma que levantan
> sube a la misma altura
> que esa copla que cantan (*Manual de espumas* 27-31/88)

Key repeated sections of the poetic text, composed of fragments whose iterations "rueda rueda / como el molino turbio / de la arboleda," are analogous to the refrains in lyrics sung in rural areas for the purpose of passing along necessary information ("Canción fluvial" 39-41/88). Handed down from generation to generation, such lyrics strengthen the intersubjective networks that make up a community's fabric.

Given Diego's interest in musico-poetic lyric, dedicating a poem like "Canción fluvial" to the Cubist painter Juan Gris (1887-1927)

---

[18] By "musical modernism," I mean a set of plural yet continuous and coherent currents in twentieth-century composition. First, the term refers to the idea commonly held among composers after 1900 that music must find means of expression that would emphasize the radical transformations that were characteristic of the age. Second, from the early 1890s on, musical modernism has signified formal experimentation as well as innovation in orchestration and tonality. Third, it suggests how anxiety about the social and cultural effects of modernity made the composer's subjective experience increasingly central to music; this aspect of musical modernism reflects the influence of Impressionism and Expressionism in painting. Lastly, musical modernism challenges the expected connection between music and narration (Botstein).

might seem paradoxical, particularly in light of the manifest attention paid in the text to lyrical structures such as the refrain. Similar to other poems in *Imagen* and *Manual de espumas*, "Canción fluvial" shows the influence of pictorial Cubism's architectonic treatment of space and Huidobrian visual metaphors:

> Por las praderas giratorias
> pasa sólo una vez el río taciturno
> cuando la noche toca su disco de gramófono
> y los pájaros cuelgan de los árboles mustios
> ("Canción fluvial" 1-4/87)

By paying homage to Gris and, through Gris, Huidobro (who arranged for Diego to meet the Cubist painter during a 1922 Paris residency), Diego reasserts his avant-garde credentials, evincing his mastery of vanguard poetry's architectonic structures. He thus makes clear that the avant-garde side of his poetry is in no way incompatible with its musical architecture.

In "Canción fluvial," Diego states his case by means of the contrariety between the references to Cubism and *Creacionismo*, and the title of the poem, which summons the fluidity of music and lyric. At first glance, the architectonic thrust of the phrases, "Por las praderas giratorias / pasa sólo una vez el río taciturno / cuando la noche toca su disco de gramófono / y los pájaros cuelgan de los árboles mustios"–a series of visual metaphors which refers to a record and its grooves spinning around a turntable–would appear to be discordant with the image of the birds, whose association with song indicates the musical and lyrical. Upon further examination, however, the seeming dissonance between the highly structured, nighttime "landscape" portrayed in the poem, remindful of Gris's schematic Cubist paintings, and the lyric "song" of the birds, resolves into a surprising harmony. By deliberately selecting the conventional metaphor in which the poet's voice is compared to a songbird, and by contraposing it with the image of the "disco de gramófono," Diego powerfully suggests how "voice," itself a metaphor for subjectivity and lyric expressivity, can work in tandem with avant-garde construction.

Shifting from landscape as the space of the collective and the common past to an abstract textual landscape from which identity has been displaced transforms our perspective on the world and our place in it. This significant change reshapes the way in which we are located–and locate ourselves–relative to the space of representation–whether we turn our gaze inward or outward, stay within prescribed boundaries, or find ourselves strategically placed to cross borders. Yet when the configuration of space, and the representation of perspective and perception restrict the poetic text to the now a situation is created in which new perceptions are unable to combine with old impressions in memory: something of subjectivity and the self's ability to relate to others is diminished. However, neither the perceptual free-association and cosmopolitanism of Torre, nor Huidobro's architectonics should be discarded from the avant-garde's repertoire–as Diego wisely recognized. On the contrary, the synthesis of vanguard construction and an expressive textual architecture inspired by musico-poetic lyric, in his poetry, becomes a means of transcending the limits of the first Spanish avant-garde.

CHAPTER 1

FRAMING THE LANDSCAPE:
ANTONIO MACHADO'S *CAMPOS DE CASTILLA*

Es el campo undulado, y los caminos
ya ocultan los viajeros que cabalgan
en pardos borriquillos,
ya al fondo de la tarde arrebolada
elevan las plebeyas figurillas,
que el lienzo de oro en el ocaso manchan.
Mas si trepáis a un cerro y veis el campo
desde los picos donde habita el águila,
son tornasoles de carmín y acero,
llanos plomizos, lomas plateadas,
circuidos por montes de violeta,
con las cumbres de nieve sonrosada.
–Antonio Machado, "Campos de Soria," *Campos de Castilla*

¡Álamos del amor que tuvisteis
de ruiseñores vuestras ramas llenas;
álamos que seréis mañana liras
del viento perfumado en primavera;
álamos del amor cerca del agua
que corre y pasa y sueña,
álamos de las márgenes del Duero,
conmigo vais, mi corazón os lleva!
–Antonio Machado, "Campos de Soria," *Campos de Castilla*

FRAMING the landscape, in Antonio Machado's (1875-1939) *Campos de Castilla* (1912; 1917), means the poet's ethically motivated positioning of the reader relative to the countryside that he portrays. The land is the central Spanish region of Castile, which Machado depicts in consonance with his regenerationist perspective on Spain's depressed circumstance at the turn of the nineteenth into the twentieth century. Of concern to him, in the collection of poems, is the national crisis of identity and orientation conventionally symbolized by the "Disaster" of 1898.[1] It is important to keep in mind, however, that this crisis was brought about over the course of time, not only by the violence of colonial wars, but also by government dysfunction, depopulation of the countryside, economic and social disparities, and a stagnant educational system. Machado's landscapes are a response to the internal psychological and intellectual consequences of this multi-layered problem, including Spain's perception of itself as lacking direction, being less developed than its neighbors, and remaining caught between a desire for Europeanization and a yearning for the autochthonous. In *Campos de Castilla*, to frame the rough heartland is to establish perspectives on its true nature and, by extension, on its people, and to forge visceral links between landscape and reader through a detailed depiction of its contours. The "frame" constitutes an entryway–a vantage point on the critical picture that Machado paints of Spain at *fin-de-siècle*. Machado's framing of the landscape invites the reader to cross the threshold of representation, thereby producing a feeling of identification with Spain's real character as well as responsibility for its deterioration.

By "frame," I refer to the concept known as the *parergon*–the "reflective hinge" that makes representation possible. Framing is meta-representation: since "content" (the *ergon*) actually comes from the frame (*par-ergon*), we can discuss neither the frame as apart from that which is framed, nor content as separate from the means of framing.[2] In *Campos de Castilla*, the frame consists of the

---

[1] Although Cuba's 1898 independence, and the loss of Puerto Rico and the Philippines loomed large in the national imagination, it must be remembered that Spain actually retained its colonies in Africa into the twentieth century.

[2] Jacques Derrida's argument that the *parergon* at once frames and is constitutive of the art object or text questions the age-old binary in aesthetics between inside and outside. His point is that this "frame" is part and parcel of representation (52, 60, 63). Derrida takes up the issue of the frame in order to problematize philosophical idealism, which was one of the main objects of Deconstructionist criticism. Regarding the significance of framing to perspective and perception, see also José Ortega y Gasset, "Meditación del marco," and Margaret H. Persin, *Getting the Picture: The Ekphrastic Principle in Twentieth-Century Spanish Poetry*.

ways in which Machado directs the reader's apprehension of the landscape. The visual construction of the countryside and the inclusion of evocative sensory detail, on the one hand, and rhetorical figure, on the other hand, establish point of view. I deliberately invoke the double meaning of framing as a way of seeing and relating the self to an idea, for Machado's framing of the landscape is conceived with an eye towards drawing in and persuading the reader:

> Es el campo undulado, y los caminos
> ya ocultan los viajeros que cabalgan
> en pardos borriquillos,
> ya al fondo de la tarde arrebolada
> elevan las plebeyas figurillas,
> que el lienzo de oro en el ocaso manchan.
> ("Campos de Soria," *Campos de Castilla* CXIII lines 25-30/134)

This framing produces the landscape as such–a "lienzo de oro." In combining spatial indicators, color, and detail into a coherent whole, we position ourselves in relation to Machado's depiction. Further, the poet uses the visual and aesthetic codes associated with landscape to jog the reader's memory of a past that would make the model for a brighter future. His Castilian countryside is by turns Arcadian–a remembered Arcadia that stands for Spain's origins–and the image of the decrepit and disoriented present. Calling up the past through landscape is Machado's method of getting back the country's sense of self, and such a recovery is meant to serve as a bridge to national renascence.

Integral to Machado's framing is his use of the rhetorical figure apostrophe (direct address), instances of which are quite numerous in *Campos de Castilla*. Apostrophe imagines the inanimate landscape, in the collection's poems, as a sentient being, treating it as if it were capable of response. The prosopopoeia (personification) implicitly involved in apostrophe makes the Castilian countryside embody the values that Machado believes to be genuinely Spanish, and which he regards as originating in the land. In accordance with its Greek meaning of "giving face," prosopopoeia can be considered to bestow human features upon the landscape, causing us to relate Castile's condition with our own and increasing our capacity for empathy. Machado's apostrophe of the land becomes an address of the reader: apostrophe emphasizes its own invocatory function as well as the lyric poet's role of engaging and convincing an audience.

We should note that landscape remains a primary focus of a critical nucleus of poems, albeit not all those in the collection. It is this group of landscape-oriented texts, notably "A orillas del Duero" (XCVIII) and the nine-section "Campos de Soria" (CXIII), that are here the object of investigation.[3] Machado wrote most of *Campos de Castilla* in the city of Soria–also the name of an eastern Castilian province through which the Duero River flows. In Soria, he met, married, and was too soon obliged to bury his young wife, Leonor: "Cinco años en la tierra de Soria, hoy para mí sagrada–allí me casé, allí perdí a mi esposa, a quien adoraba–, orientaron mis ojos y mi corazón hacia lo esencial castellano" (Machado, "Prólogo" 274). Machado came to locate "lo esencial castellano"–which signifies the fundamentally Spanish in *Campos de Castilla*–in the landscape. Yet in spite of the collection's moral nature, we should maintain a skeptical attitude about both the authenticity of this essence and its linkage with Castile.

Turning his eyes to Spain's quintessence, as articulated in the land's geographical traits, proved to be crucial to the development of Machado's social consciousness. The carefully wrought terrain of *Campos de Castilla* calls for the reader to regard Spain through the same critical lens as the poet–a lens that is shaped by the philosophical and ethical inquietudes that have traditionally been attributed to the "Generation of 1898." It was Azorín (José Martínez Ruiz; 1873-1967) who first associated the regenerationism that intensified in the wake of the "Disaster" of 1898 with what he conceived as a literary "Generation of 98."[4] For him, as he writes in the series of

---

[3] After "Retrato" (XCVII), the first poem and arguable *ars poetica* of *Campos de Castilla*, the collection consists primarily of a mix of lyric poems (often with narrative elements) and ballads (*romances*) such as "Un loco" (CVI), "Un criminal" (CVIII), and the multi-section *La tierra de Alvargonzález* (CXIV). The collection also comprises texts that memorialize Leonor, Antonio Machado's wife, after her premature death, as well as those that portray Spain's situation didactically, like "Poema de un día" (CXXVIII). A few of the texts depict the land and folklore of Andalusia–"La saeta" (CXXX) and "Los olivos" (CXXXII)–which as a native son of the southern city of Seville, Machado knew well. There are also the "Proverbios y cantares" (CXXXVI) and "Parábolas" (CXXXVII), in which the poet gives voice to his religious and moral convictions. Geoffrey Ribbans points out the relative independence of the *Elogios* poems, some of which, according to him, date from before 1907. (He refers specifically to the poems CXLVI, CXLVII, CLI, CLII [Introduction, *Campos de Castilla* 15].)

[4] Luis Granjel discusses Azorín's coinage of the term "Generación de 1898" and his authorship of the series of articles entitled "La Generación del 98" (17).

four articles that bestowed this name on a generation of authors, "estudiar la literatura" reveals the "modalidad media del sentir" of a given period ("Generación" 176). Yet even Azorín views the Generation of 98 as "la época que abarca de 1870 a 1898" rather than a single year, and he takes pains to situate the term that he invented in the history of Spanish literature. He argues that the Generation of 98 brought "el grito de pasión de Echegaray al sentimentalismo subversivo de Campoamor y a la visión de realidad de Galdós," factors which, according to him, created "un estado de conciencia que había de encarnar en la generación de 1898" (180). Miguel de Unamuno (1864-1936), Ángel Ganivet (1865-1898), Jacinto Benavente (1866-1957), Ramón del Valle-Inclán (1866-1936), Pío Baroja (1872-1956), Azorín, Ramiro de Maeztu (1874-1936), Machado and, occasionally, a few others have been variously linked with the Generation of 98.[5] To the list have also been added such painters as Aureliano de Beruete (1845-1912), Juan Espina y Capo (1848-1933), Joaquim Mir (1873-1940), Darío de Regoyos (1857-1913), Santiago Rusiñol (1861-1931), and Ignacio Zuloaga (1870-1945).[6] Notwithstanding legitimate doubts regarding the Generation of 98's validity as a concept, we should acknowledge that Machado and those grouped with this "generation" shared a preoccupation about Spain's turn-of-the-century malaise.[7] To accept relevant critiques of the idea of a "generation" as related to a particular *Weltanschauung* does not make denying the pervasiveness of crisis-related themes within the so-named Generation of 1898 a necessity. At the

---

[5] Donald Shaw affirms Guillermo Díaz-Plaja's two most important conclusions regarding the Generation of 98: one, the division of the Generation's membership into two *promociones* (the senior Miguel de Unamuno [b. 1864] and Ángel Ganivet [b. 1865], and the junior Pío Baroja [b. 1872], Azorín [b. 1873], Ramiro de Maeztu [b. 1874], and Antonio Machado [b. 1876]); and two, the similar organization of the *modernistas*, whom he considers as separate from the *noventayochistas*, into two age-groups (6). See Díaz-Plaja's *Modernismo frente a '98* and "El modernismo, cuestión disputada."

[6] Other painters who have been connected with the Generation of 98 include: Adolfo Guiard (1860-1916); Francisco Iturrino (1864-1924); Agustín Lhardy (1848-1928); José Gutiérrez Solana (1886-1945); and Joaquín Sorolla (1863-1923) (Jurkevich 35-36).

[7] Baroja denied involvement in the "Generation of 98." Pedro Salinas criticizes his rejection of it as a function of his conflation of the concepts of a "literary generation" and a "literary school" ("El concepto de generación," *Literatura española* 31). See also Granjel (30-33). There is also the issue of whether or not the Generation of 98 can be considered distinct from the coeval *modernismo*.

same time, it cannot be stressed enough that those who have been thus categorized were far from uniform in their politics, philosophical outlooks, educational backgrounds, or styles, even if the imperative for national regeneration can be identified in their work.[8]

While in the Generation of 98 Castile often became the ground for explorations of national identity as antidote to Spain's anomie–a controvertible undertaking–by no means was this the rule. Azorín, Unamuno, and Machado, for example, were hardly identical in their thinking about Castile; neither was the Castilian the only landscape depicted in their work.[9] Machado often portrayed the Andalusian countryside of his childhood in his poetry, and some of his evocations–"La saeta" and "Los olivos"–are included in the 1917 version of *Campos de Castilla*.[10] Machado's emphasis on Castile in *Campos de Castilla* took inspiration from different visions of it in works by Azorín and Unamuno, as well as in painters such as Carlos de Haes (1826-1898) and Beruete. The poet's fascination with the region is also due to the education that he received at the *Institución Libre de Enseñanza*,[11] and his personal experience in Soria.

As part of their concern for Spain's situation, Machado and many of his fellows explored the association of national (and regio-

---

[8] Salinas, arguing in favor of the Generation of 98's existence, derives the idea of literary "generations" from its roots in German criticism, from Wilhelm Dilthey to Hans Jeschke and Julius Petersen ("El concepto de generación," *Literatura española* 28).

[9] To take two notable examples: Unamuno's novel *Paz en la Guerra* (1897) depicts the geographical characteristics of the countryside around his native Bilbao, as well as the architectonic features of the city, so as to reflect the socio-political divides that are the novel's subject; and in Valle-Inclán's *Flor de santidad* (1904), the Galician landscape echoes the mysticism of Adega, the novel's protagonist (Seeleman 234). Unamuno began *Paz en la guerra* in Bilbao around 1888, and finished the novel in Salamanca, where he held the chair in Greek, in 1896 (González Egido 14).

[10] With respect to the topic of Andalusia and *Campos de Castilla*, consult Oreste Macrì's introduction to Antonio Machado, *Poesía y prosa*, vol. 1 (29).

[11] The *Institución Libre de Enseñanza* was a pedagogical organization, and center of middle and secondary education between the years 1876 and 1939 (García Suárez 3). It should be regarded as a product of the intellectual rebellion that came out of the Revolution of 1868. The Revolution's failure spurred liberal thinkers to throw into doubt traditional ideologies and societal norms through the reform of pedagogy and science. The positivism in which Krausism, the major philosophical influence on the *ILE*, was rooted changed ideas about aesthetics and the value of landscape. It was this shift which, in transforming attitudes about landscape (leading to an upsurge in excursionism, the scientific investigation of Spain's geography and geology, and artistic and literary representations of the countryside), impacted the Generation of 98 (Pena 14).

nal) identity with landscape by becoming a "generation of *excursionistas*" (Ramsden 141).[12] Description of the countryside is woven into such watershed novels as Unamuno's *Paz en la guerra* (1897), Baroja's *Camino de perfección* (1902), Azorín's *La voluntad* (1902), and Valle-Inclán's *Flor de santidad* (1904). In *La voluntad*, Azorín equates the landscape with the spirit of humankind; it is "nuestro espíritu, sus melancolías, sus placideces, sus anhelos, sus tártagos" (qtd. in Seeleman 236). Lyric meditations on place and landscape are part of Unamuno's 1907 volume *Poesías*, especially the sections entitled "Castilla," "Cataluña," and "Vizcaya." In "El mar de encinas" ("Castilla"), he lauds the *encina* ("ilex" or "holm oak") as the "floración secular del noble suelo / que, todo corazón de firme roca, / brotó del fuego // de las entrañas de la madre tierra," thus making the tree symbolic metaphor and metonymy for the passionate land from which it grows up (*Poesías* 38-41/215). Close, even minute, observation of landscape can similarly be found in several of Azorín's and Unamuno's non-fictional prose texts.[13] The publication of Azorín's *Castilla* (1912) and Unamuno's *Por tierras de Portugal y de España*, significantly, immediately precedes that of the first version of *Campos de Castilla*.

In *Campos de Castilla*, Machado imitates Azorín's descriptive style and attention to detail. Although the prologue of Azorín's *Castilla* could not be more brief–it is a scant two paragraphs in length–in it he gives the reader a clear indication of the volume's

---

[12] Machado thought of himself as an avid *excursionista*. In his "Autobiografía escrita en 1913 para una proyectada antología de Azorín," he declared, "Mi gran pasión son los viajes. Creo conocer algo algunas regiones de la Alta Castilla, Aragón y Andalucía" (284).

[13] The countryside is the express object of exploration in Azorín's *El alma castellana* (1900), *España* (1909), *Lecturas españolas* (1912), *Castilla* (1912), *Un pueblecito – Riofrío de Ávila* (1916), and *El paisaje de España visto por los españoles* (1917). The same is true of Unamuno's *España y los españoles* (I. 1897-1919), *Paisajes* (1902), *De mi país. Descripciones, relatos y artículos de costumbres* (1903), *Por tierras de Portugal y de España* (1911), and *Andanzas y visiones españolas* (1922). To the catalogue of landscape-focused works by Azorín can be added the posterior *El libro de Levante* (1929), *Valencia* (1941), and *Visión de España – Páginas escogidas* (1941). His *La ruta de Don Quixote* (1905), *Clásicos y modernos* (1913), *Al margen de los clásicos* (1914), and *Fantasías y devaneos. Política. Literatura. Naturaleza* (1920) all have to do, in one way or another, with landscape in Spanish literature and culture. Landscape plays a fundamental role in Unamuno's 1907 *Poesías*, particularly the verses in the sections "Castilla," "Cataluña," and "Vizcaya." *Rosario de sonetos líricos* (1911) evokes Unamuno's native city of Bilbao as well as the regions of Asturias and León.

thrust–"Se ha pretendido en este libro aprisionar una partícula del espíritu de Castilla" (n. pag.). He approaches detail as fleeting "particles" to be caught and thus controlled, remaining ever vigilant so as to prevent even the smallest prosaic feature from escaping his penetrating gaze. Azorín's obsession with detail feeds into the "preocupación por el poder del tiempo" that makes up the "fondo espiritual de estos cuadros"–a concern that also informs Machado's poetry (n. pag.). Each of the short narratives in the volume are akin to paintings or, to put it precisely, portraits that encompass the natural, architectonic, material, and human aspects of Castile. As Azorín asks rhetorically in "La tierra de Castilla" (*Fantasías y devaneos*; 1920): "¿No veis una íntima conexión, una secreta armonía entre este paisaje y la casa, el traje, el carácter, el gesto, el arte y la literatura de Castilla? ¿No es este paisaje el mismo espíritu de Quevedo–el más típico de los espíritus castellanos–, compendioso, austero, severo, rígido, altivo, indomable, inflexible?" (*Obras completas* 4: 121-22). In *Castilla*, the protagonists of classic works of Spanish literature, from the *Poema del Cid* to Cervantes's *La ilustre fregona*, are wrested from time and rendered anew as if painted or photographed likenesses of ordinary people; Azorín's evocations of them summon the *cuadros de costumbres* popular earlier in the nineteenth century. In a prefatory note to *Lecturas españolas*, whose "coherencia estriba en una curiosidad por lo que constituye el ambiente español–paisajes, letras, arte, hombres, ciudades, interiores," he brings the significance of this portraiture into focus, explicitly linking it with "una preocupación por un porvenir de bienestar y de justicia para España" (n. pag.).

The influence of *Castilla* on *Campos de Castilla* is reflected in the poem "Al maestro 'Azorín' por su libro 'Castilla'" (*Campos de Castilla* CXVII). Machado, in the manner of Azorín, gives us a location that could not be more commonplace–"La venta de Cidones está en la carretera / que va de Soria a Burgos"–or lives less exalted–"Leonarda, la ventera, / que llaman la Ruipérez, es una viejecita / que aviva el fuego donde borbolla la marmita" (CXVII 1-4/175). At the same time, the poet evokes his subjects with the assiduousness of the most earnest of portrait painters, depicting "Ruipérez, el ventero" through the constituent parts of his face–"cejas grises" and "dos ojos de hombre astuto" (5-6/175). Machado identifies the only other "character" besides Leonarda and Ruipérez simply as "un caballero" (9/175), portraying him by way of his habits and physical environment rather than by name. Just as in Azorín's *Castilla* and *Lecturas españolas*, Machado's descriptions display a strongly metonymic bent: delineating such facets of the gentleman's routine as his dress ("vestido va de luto"), the simple material of which his writing desk is made ("una mesa de pino"), and the way in which the lines "Cuando moja la pluma en el tintero, / dos ojos tristes lucen en un semblante enjuto" make the austerity and mundane sadness of his existence palpable (12, 9, 10-11/175). Machado's portrayal of the gentleman's surroundings turns into a reflection on the Castilian landscape and on how the natural melancholy of its terrain shapes human nature. By centering on the quotidian in human life, he sheds light on the eternal Castile of which Leonarda, Ruipérez, and the gentleman are merely fleeting expressions.

Machado's turn towards social consciousness in *Campos de Castilla* is tied to the way in which he suggests the qualities of the Castilian land and people. He intends each detail and characteristic attribute to reveal a facet of Spain's identity, depicting them so that they resonate with the reader's own notion of this selfhood. By 1912, the publication date of the first version of *Campos de Castilla*, Machado's engagement with the challenges around which his generation coalesced had become evident in his poetry, making the *modernismo* of the anterior *Soledades* (1899-1902) recede, if not entirely fade away.[14] Just as Machado's first phase, typified by the symbolism and *modernismo* of the *Soledades*, gave way to a socially engaged second period of which *Campos de Castilla* is emblematic, after a time of transition that encompassed the *Nuevas canciones* (1924; 1917-1930), his work turned broadly philosophical and pedagogical—a change that Machado marked by employing "Juan de Mairena" and "Abel Martín" as doubles for himself. Apart from Machado's social and philosophical meditations, his "Canciones a Guiomar," written while he was living in Segovia (1919-1931), included a lyrical vein through which he expressed his love for Pilar Valderrama, a married woman who accepted his attentions without returning them.

---

[14] Regarding the *modernismo* of the *Soledades* in comparison with *Campos de Castilla*, see José Luis de la Iglesia, et al., *Antonio Machado y la filosofía*; Antonio Sánchez Barbudo, *Estudios sobre Unamuno y Machado*; and Bernard Sesé, *Claves de Antonio Machado*. Machado claimed in retrospect that he reacted against French Symbolism, which exerted a major influence on *modernismo*: "Recibí alguna influencia de los simbolistas franceses, pero ya hace tiempo que reacciono contra ella" ("Autobiografía" 283).

My conception of *modernismo* in Spain is fairly consonant with its definition, by Guillermo Díaz-Plaja, Pedro Salinas, and Dámaso Alonso, in terms of language and technique; they distinguish *modernismo* from the Generation of 98 which, according to them, is a *Weltanschauung* rather than a movement with a peculiar style.[15] At the same time, I do not discard Juan Ramón Jiménez's retrospective consideration of *modernismo* as an attitude.[16] Certainly, Spanish *modernismo's* embrace of French Symbolism and Parnassianism, and its Latin-American origins in the poetry of Rubén Darío (1867-1916) indicates an international and universal bent–an "attitude" of sorts. As Jiménez has pointed out, there is a return to idealism and universalism in *modernismo*, as well as a purity and a liberty that derives from Friedrich Nietzsche (Owre 321).[17]

Campos de Castilla retains much of *modernismo's* stylistic vocabulary: chiaroscuro, the chromatic, synaesthesia, musicality, and a refined symbolism.[18] Yet Machado's growing discomfort with *modernismo*, inseparable from the anxieties produced by his gravitation towards social issues instead of aesthetic concerns, did not start with *Campos de Castilla*. Neither did these preoccupations originate during Machado's stay in Soria, but rather intensified while he was there, and in fact, his worries can be traced as far back as 1903 (Ribbans, Introduction, *Campos de Castilla* 23).[19] In 1905, to the

---

[15] Consult the following sources: Guillermo Díaz-Plaja, "El modernismo, cuestión disputada"; Pedro Salinas, "El concepto de generación literaria aplicado a la del 98"; and Dámaso Alonso, *Poetas españoles contemporáneos*.

[16] See Juan Ramón Jiménez, *El modernismo: notas de un curso (1953)*.

[17] At the same time, *modernismo* can be specific to a particular region, country, or author. We should also recall that the concerns of *modernismo*, especially the Latin-American variety, go beyond language and technique.

[18] Written between 1899 and 1902, the *Soledades* first appeared in 1903. *Soledades. Galerías. Otros poemas.* was published in 1907. Between 1903 and 1907 the powerful influence of *modernismo* on Machado becomes reduced. The *Galerías* are marked by an introspective mood (Ribbans, Introduction, *Soledades. Galerías. Otros poemas.* 20-21).

[19] Ribbans argues that beginning in 1903, Machado's letters to Unamuno show the poet's growing distaste for the art-for-art's-sake in literature (Introduction, *Campos de Castilla* 23). In 1906, Machado published an essay that evinced signs of frustration with this attitude, with specific reference to the *modernista* poets, while at the same time praising the beauty of Juan Ramón Jiménez's *Arias tristes*. He writes, ". . . yo no puedo aceptar que el poeta sea un hombre estéril que huya de la vida para forjarse quiméricamente una vida mejor en que gozar de la contemplación de sí mismo. Y he añadido: ¿no seríamos capaces de soñar con los ojos abiertos en la vida activa, en la vida militante?" (qtd. in Sesé 38).

surprise of several of his fellow poets, Machado decided to stop lea-
ding what had been a bohemian literary life in Madrid and earn his
living in the provinces teaching French, a job that could only be
earned by passing a difficult series of state exams. He took the re-
quired tests in 1906, obtaining a teaching post in Soria that year.[20]

Machado's metamorphosis into a socially committed poet can
be attributed in no small part to Unamuno, with whom he corres-
ponded.[21] Machado attests to the weight that Unamuno's ideas ca-
rried with him in his "Autobiografía escrita en 1913 para una pro-
yectada antología de Azorín"–"Admiro a Costa pero mi maestro es
Unamuno" as he writes–and in an anterior letter to the philosopher
(284). In the letter, penned in 1904, the poet wrestles openly with
doubts about his artistic aims:

> No quiero que se me acuse de falta de sinceridad porque eso se-
> ría calumniante. Soy algo escéptico y me contradigo con frecuen-
> cia. ¿Por qué hemos de callarnos nuestras dudas y nuestras vaci-
> laciones? ¿Por qué hemos de aparentar más fe en nuestro
> pensamiento, o en el ajeno, de la que en realidad tenemos? ¿Por
> qué la hemos de dar de hombres convencidos antes de estarlo?
> Yo veo la poesía como un yunque de constante actividad espiri-
> tual, no como un taller de fórmulas dogmáticas revestidas de
> imágenes más o menos brillantes. ("Fragmentos" 9)

His reappraisal of the values associated with the aesthetics of *mo-
dernismo*, as well as his new focus on social issues, becomes appa-
rent in the same correspondence:

> Pero hoy, después de haber meditado mucho, he llegado a una
> afirmación: todos nuestros esfuerzos deben tender hacia la luz,
> hacia la conciencia. He aquí el pensamiento que debía unirnos a

---

[20] In his "Autobiografía escrita en 1913," Machado recounts that, "En 1906 hi-
ce oposiciones a cátedras de francés y obtuve la de Soria, donde he residido hasta
agosto de 1912, con excepción del año 10, que estuve en París, pensionado para es-
tudiar filología francesa" (283). He made the decision with strong encouragement
from Francisco Giner de los Ríos of the *ILE* (Sesé 40). Machado moved in 1907 to
take up his teaching position (Serrano Poncela 23-24).

[21] See Ribbans, Introduction to *Campos de Castilla* (23), and Aurora de Albor-
noz, *La presencia de Unamuno en Antonio Machado* (23-29). Albornoz notes that
while the influence of Unamuno on Machado was certainly significant, their rela-
tionship cannot be considered the only factor in Machado's conversion to social
commitment (27).

todos. Usted, con golpes de maza, ha roto, no cabe duda, la espe-
sa costra de nuestra vanidad, de nuestra somnolencia. Yo, al me-
nos, sería un ingrato si no reconociera que a usted debo el haber
saltado la tapia de mi corral o de mi huerto. Y digo: Es verdad,
hay que soñar despierto. No debemos crearnos un mundo aparte
en que gozar fantástica y egoístamente de la contemplación de
nosotros mismos; no debemos huir de la vida para forjarnos una
vida mejor, que sea estéril para los demás ("Fragmentos" 9-10).

Machado's phrasing–"nuestra vanidad," "nuestra somnolencia," and
"soñar"–simultaneously reflects Unamuno's view of the causes of
Spain's crisis and questions what the poet came to see as the solip-
sistic tendency of *modernismo's* poetic meditations. Demonstrating
his break from *modernismo*, Machado criticizes its attention to the
aesthetic: "Nada más disparatado que pensar, como algunos poetas
franceses han pensado tal vez que el misterio sea un elemento esté-
tico. Mallarmé lo afirma al censurar a los parnasianos por la clari-
dad en las formas. La belleza no está en el misterio, sino en el deseo
de penetrarlo" ("Fragmentos" 10). The way out from his artistic
morass, as he tells Unamuno, is to "soñar despierto"–to dream wi-
de-awake. The *paisajismo* of *Campos de Castilla* turns into, as an
outcome of these shifts in Machado's philosophical outlook and po-
etic style, a "vía de entrada crítica en la Historia, y no evasión esteti-
cista" (Blanco Aguinaga 319-20). Machado layers the representa-
tion of an idealized authentic past and images of Spain's
present-time decline in the landscapes of *Campos de Castilla*. The
paths that the landscape provides for exploring the connections
between past and present become gateways to understanding
Spain, which according to Machado's redefined notion of authors-
hip, remains one of its chief responsibilities: "Escribir para el pue-
blo es escribir para el hombre de nuestra raza, de nuestra tierra, de
nuestra habla, tres cosas inagotables que no acabaremos nunca de
conocer" (qtd. in Albornoz, *Presencia* 330).

Machado's rooting of Spain's essence in the land relates to Una-
muno's twin concepts of *casticismo* and *intrahistoria*, which Unamu-
no elucidates in *En torno al casticismo* (1902). Unamuno deriva *lo
castizo* from the adjective *casto*, or pure, as applied in botany and
zoology to signify "purebred." Yet at the same time, he is careful to
distinguish between purity in the world of biology, to which he ma-
kes frequent recourse in his metaphors, and the cultural purity that

he aims to explain. Unamuno holds that the proper conceptualization of *lo castizo*–what is truly and authentically Spanish–does not exclude foreign influence, as the unthinking traditionalism that he roundly criticizes would do.[22] It is essential to recall that Unamuno embraced the universal and the cosmopolitan as much as he did *casticismo* and *intrahistoria*, since he found the *castizo* and international influence to play complementary roles in the regeneration of Spain. He goes so far, in *En torno al casticismo*, to suggest Spain's opening towards Europe as a solution to the country's stagnation: "Quisiera sugerir con toda fuerza al lector la idea de que el despertar de la vida de la muchedumbre difusa y de las regiones tiene que ir de par y enlazado con el abrir de par en par las ventanas al campo europeo para que se oree la patria" (165). For him, Spain's redemption depends upon the circulation of cosmopolitan ideas:

> Ojalá una verdadera juventud, animosa y libre, rompiendo con la malla que nos ahoga y la monotonía uniforme en que estamos alineados, se vuelva con amor a estudiar el pueblo que nos sustenta a todos, y abriendo el pecho y los ojos a las corrientes todas ultrapirenaicas y sin encerrarse en capullos casticistas, jugo seco y muerto del gusano *histórico*, ni en diferenciaciones nacionales excluyentes, avive con la ducha reconfortante de los jóvenes ideales cosmopolitas el espíritu colectivo intracastizo que duerme esperando un redentor! (167-68; emphasis in the original)

Unamuno's posture is consistent with a certain cosmopolitan and universalizing strain within the Generation of 98, which does not preclude an intense preoccupation with *casticismo*.

Since *lo castizo* is the substance of national identity, and because this national identity becomes key to Spain's reorientation, determination of the country's future direction turns on the issue of *casticismo*. The nucleus of tradition that is *lo castizo* finds expression in *intrahistoria*, which Unamuno sets against the history of larger-than-life leaders and grand-scale events (49). In *El porvenir de España*

---

[22] The "casticismo del lenguaje y del estilo"–the *casticismo* of language, art, and literature–constitutes the "revelación de un pensamiento castizo"–the mentality unique to a people and place (*En torno al casticismo* 36). It is nothing more or less than the life-blood that courses through the people, sustaining the collective and letting stream forth–in "literatura plebeya" and "coplas de ciegos" for example–what lies naturally within (*En torno al casticismo* 163).

(1898-1912), a series of essays in which he and Ganivet engage in dialogue about Spain's fundamental character and the impact of this character on the country's future, Unamuno argues that it is *intrahistoria* that reveals the spirit of a nation. History, on the contrary, covers spirit over, burying it under the weight of surface-level occurrences:

> La historia, la condenada historia, que es en su mayor parte una imposición del ambiente, nos ha celado la roca viva de la constitución patria; la historia, a la vez que nos ha revelado gran parte de nuestro espíritu en nuestros actos, nos ha impedido ver lo más íntimo de ese espíritu. Hemos atendido más a los *sucesos* históricos que pasan y se pierden, que a los *hechos* sub-históricos, que permanecen y van estratificándose en profundas capas. (*Porvenir* 990; emphasis in the original)

From Unamuno's perspective, to center on *intrahistoria* is to excavate all the myriad layers of national spirit, bringing Spain's true identity to light along with them.

The binary history-*intrahistoria* recalls the antitheses that form the basic structures in the thought of Georg W. F. Hegel, whose mark on *En torno al casticismo* is apparent.[23] Hegel conceives what he terms the *Volksgeist* as a substance on which the spirit of a people nurtures itself at any given moment in time, an idea that persists in Unamuno. The *Volksgeist* consists of all that composes the *Gesamtheit*, the spirit that is the totality of nature, soil, air, water, in short, everything about the place in which a people exists, as expressed in its homegrown cultural, political, and social institutions. It is the encounter of diverse manifestations of such a substance at various points in history that generates the synthesis that is universal spirit–the *Weltgeist* (Ribas 24-25, 30). The dialectical movement by virtue of which Hegel's *Volksgeist* develops becomes, in Unamuno–to paraphrase the philosopher's peculiar metaphoric language–the force that carries the sediment of *lo castizo* through the depths of the sea, or being, of a particular people: "Esa vida intrahistórica, silenciosa y continua como el fondo mismo del mar, es la

---

[23] In Albornoz's view, "podríamos decir que la antítesis historia-intrahistoria es una manifestación concreta de la estructura antitética del pensamiento de Unamuno que, acaso deliberadamente, convierte los conceptos de historia e intrahistoria en opuestos" ("Presencia" 119).

sustancia del progreso, la verdadera tradición, la tradición eterna, no la tradición mentira que se suele ir a buscar al pasado enterrado en libros y papeles, y monumentos, y piedras" (*En torno al casticismo* 50).[24]

The cultural poverty that Unamuno names as one of turn-of-the-century Spain's major problems, comes, in his analysis, from the drying up of sources of inspiration–"No hay frescura ni espontaneidad, no hay juventud." In his eyes, Spain had turned into "un pantano de agua estancada" and "un páramo espiritual de una aridez que espanta" because the "corrientes vivas internas en nuestra vida intelectual y moral" had ceased to flow (*En torno al casticismo* 154). He laments what he sees as Spanish society's vacuousness and vulgarity: "Extiéndese y se dilata por toda nuestra actual sociedad española una enorme monotonía, que se resuelve en atonía, la uniformidad mate de una losa de plomo de ingente ramplonería" (151). Unamuno traces such a drought in creativity to the way in which traditionalist reaction against Europeanization worked to suffocate *lo castizo*, since the truly *castizo* emerges through contact with outside ideas; the traditionalists' mistaken emphasis on internal, or national, "history" ignores the fact that the vital reality of *intrahistoria* is formed in response to influences from abroad. Spain's weak "espíritu colectivo," while stemming from insufficient self-knowledge, is not simply the result of failing to engage in introspection, but rather this introspection's misguided focus on national history:

> Y así sucede a los pueblos que en sus encerronas y aislamientos hipertrofian en su espíritu colectivo la conciencia *histórica* a expensas de la vida difusa intrahistórica, que languidece por falta de ventilación; el pensamiento *nacional*, trabajando hacia sí, acalla el rumor inarticulado de la vida que bajo él se extiende. Hay pueblos que en puro mirarse al ombligo nacional, caen en sueño hipnótico y contemplan la nada. (164; emphasis in the original)

The overemphasis on the internal and the historical that is traditionalism's hallmark deprives the *castizo* of fresh air from abroad—essential to maintaining its spontaneous expressiveness and vibrant fluency.

---

[24] In contrast to Hegel, the dialectic in Unamuno occurs as the productive interchange between History and *intrahistoria* rather than between the *Volksgeister* of different peoples (Ribas 26, 30).

In a way similar to *En torno al casticismo*, the focus on the quotidian in *Campos de Castilla* is intended as a means of reconnecting readers with Spain's forgotten self-identity. In "A orillas del Duero" and "Campos de Soria," Machado juxtaposes *intrahistoria*, which inheres in the countryside's natural cycles and their effect on ordinary people, with the remnants of Spain's formerly grand history. On one level, in "A orillas del Duero," the reader glimpses the distant memory of military victory over the Moors and colonial conquest from the perspective of Spain's ruined state:

> La madre en otro tiempo fecunda en capitanes
> madrastra es hoy apenas de humildes ganapanes.
> Castilla no es aquella tan generosa un día,
> cuando Myo Cid Rodrigo El de Vivar volvía,
> ufano de su nueva fortuna y su opulencia,
> a regalar a Alfonso los huertos de Valencia;
> o que, tras la aventura que acreditó sus bríos,
> pedía la conquista de los inmensos ríos
> indianos a la corte, la madre de soldados,
> guerreros y adalides que han de tornar, cargados
> de plata y oro, a España, en regios galeones,
> para la presa cuervos, para la lid leones.
>
> (*Campos de Castilla* XCVIII 49-60/102-103)

Machado compares Spain to a mother once "fecunda en capitanes" who can now only barely claim the lesser position of step-mother to "humildes ganapanes"; her formerly triumphant children have similarly fallen to occupy a lowly station. The bravery of Rodrigo de Vivar ("El Cid"), who returned Valencia's fertile lands to King Alfonso VI of Castile and Aragon, and the exploits of the conquistadors are the history of individual actors and dramatic transformations. In "Campos de Soria," Machado reduces the impressive edifices built by this history to rubble:

> ¡Muerta ciudad de señores
> soldados o cazadores;
> de portales con escudos
> de cien linajes hidalgos,
> y de famélicos galgos,
> de galgos flacos y agudos,
> que pululan
> por las sórdidas callejas. . . (85-92/136)

The hunting dogs of the privileged few have grown lean along with the rich's fortunes. They now teem through the city streets like the poor masses from which their masters formerly distinguished themselves. On the degenerated Spanish empire the sun has begun to set:

> El sol va declinando. De la ciudad lejana
> me llega un armonioso tañido de campana
> –ya irán a su rosario las enlutadas viejas–.
> De entre las peñas salen dos lindas comadrejas;
> me miran y se alejan, huyendo, y aparecen
> de nuevo ¡tan curiosas!... Los campos se obscurecen.
> Hacia el camino blanco está el mesón abierto
> al campo ensombrecido y al pedregal desierto.
>   ("A orillas del Duero" 69-76/103)

The image of the elderly women in mourning and at their rosary mirrors Machado's lament for old Spain, as articulated in the poem's refrain: "Castilla miserable, ayer dominadora, / envuelta en sus andrajos [harapos l. 68] desprecia cuanto ignora" (41-42/103).[25] Deepening the impression of the country's degraded state is the appearance of the weasels–animals that eat the eggs and young of others–which represents ruin. Chiaroscuro, produced by contrasting the whiteness of the country path and the light of the inn's open door against the darkened countryside, augments this atmosphere of desolate sorrow.

On another level, *intrahistoria's* manifestations can only truly be discerned by observing the slow changes that occur periodically in nature: the progression of seasons and years, and their impact on those who cultivate and live close to the land. In "Campos de Soria," Machado centers the reader's gaze on the "plebeyas figurillas" so that we see ourselves in their daily sojourn through the Castilian lands (29/134). Their presence is metaphor for the transient character of human existence and the eternal tradition carried on by common folk, as well as the conjunction between people and place. Machado turns the reduction of activity imposed by the lingering snow and cold of winter into an intimate evocation of home and hearth: "La nieve. En el mesón al campo abierto / se ve el hogar donde la

---

[25] The refrain of "A orillas del Duero" is repeated at lines 41-42 and 67-68, with one minor variation: Machado substitutes the word "harapos" for "andrajos" the second time around, at line 68.

leña humea / y la olla al hervir borbollonea" (51-53/135). His description of the countryside and the lives of those whose fates depend upon it is at once meticulously accurate and impressionistic:

> El cierzo corre por el campo yerto,
> alborotando en blancos torbellinos
> la nieve silenciosa.
> La nieve sobre el campo y los caminos,
> cayendo está como sobre una fosa. (54-58/135)

The poem's intensely sensory quality and precise representation of detail draw the reader into Machado's meditation on the eternal and indigenous. Synaesthesia ("la nieve silenciosa") lends an immediacy to the landscape: we are led deep into the endless white of the wintry landscape and made to feel its chill, compared in a simile to that of a grave–a foreshadowing of the death that Machado subsequently describes. His underlining of the sensory in his portrait of the harsh countryside's inhabitants reflects the way in which the natural world exerts force over their existence:

> Un viejo acurrucado tiembla y tose
> cerca del fuego; su mechón de lana
> la vieja hila, y la niña cose
> verde ribete a su estameña grana.
> Padres los viejos son de un arriero
> que caminó sobre la blanca tierra,
> y una noche se perdió ruta y sendero,
> y se enterró en las nieves de la sierra.
> En torno al fuego hay un lugar vacío,
> y en la frente del viejo, de hosco ceño,
> como un tachón sombrío
> –tal el golpe de un hacha sobre un leño–.
> La vieja mira al campo, cual si oyera
> pasos sobre la nieve. Nadie pasa. (59-72/135)

We see the tragic fate of the muleteer through Machado's evocative description of the house and those who live there. Poignantly expressive of loss are the empty fireside seat, the old man's vacant expression, and the hearing of phantom footsteps by his wife. The poet's diction and handling of color manifest the interpenetration between the natural and human worlds bound up in the idea of *in-*

trahistoria. The green-colored border ("verde ribete") that the young girl sews on her scarlet serge cloth evokes–ironically, given the wintry landscape and the absence of her father—the greenery of spring–the "verdes pradillos," "verde obscuro en que el merino pasta," and "verdes prados" (3/133, 16/134, 75/136). In the face of what at first seems to be unremitting perdition, hope for the future comes to the mind's eye of the young girl, which she vividly imagines as verdant fields and blooming flowers: "La niña piensa que en los verdes prados / ha de correr con otras doncellitas / en los días azules y dorados, / cuando crecen las blancas margaritas" (75-78/136). "Ribete," similarly, constitutes a paronomasia on the "ribera" ("bank") of the River Duero; each word comes from the Latin root *"ripa"* ("river," "stream"; "bank"; "riverbank"; "shore").

Machado's centering on the countryside in *Campos de Castilla* fits with a larger trend of exploring national identity through landscape.[26] This culture of landscape, as it evolved during the last third of the nineteenth century in Spain, shaped his poetic evocation of the country's autochthonous being. The conceptual development of landscape as expression of Spanish identity came in two primary waves: the first consisting of a group of intellectuals that emerged out of the Revolution of 1868 ("La Gloriosa"), and the second of members of the so-named Generation of 98. Both were linked by Francisco Giner de los Ríos (1839-1915), the spearhead of a reformist cadre of university professors who embraced Krausism and a modern, rationalist Christianity. He had become, along with Julián Sanz del Río (1814-1869), the leading exponent and interpreter of the philosophy of Karl Christian F. Krause (1781-1832).[27] Krause's conception of humanity as the synthesis of spirit and Nature under

---

[26] On the subject of Machado and landscape see the following sources: Carlos Beceiro, "Antonio Machado y su visión paradójica de Castilla"; Steven L. Driever, "The Signification of the Sorian Landscapes in Antonio Machado's *Campos de Castilla*"; Kevin Krough, *The Landscape Poetry of Antonio Machado. A Dialogical Study of* Campos de Castilla; Enrique Lafuente Ferrari, "Antonio Machado y su mundo visual"; Juan José Martín González, "Poesía y pintura en el paisaje castellano de Antonio Machado"; Marcos Molinero Cardenal, *Antonio Machado y Soria: ideología y estética, 1907-1939*; Bartolomé Mostaza, "El paisaje en la poesía de Antonio Machado"; José Antonio Pérez-Rioja, "Soria, en la poesía de Antonio Machado"; Adela Rodríguez Forteza, *La naturaleza y Antonio Machado*; and Reyes Vila-Belda, "Paisajismo e impresionismo en *Campos de Castilla*, de Antonio Machado."

[27] Julián Sanz del Río was already a university professor (*catedrático*) when he journeyed to Germany in 1843 to study the idealist philosophical current that ran from Kant, Hegel, and Fichte to Krause.

divine unity–a melding of subjective idealism (Kant and Fichte) and absolute idealism (Schelling and Hegel)–led him to envision questions of law and liberty as based on individual conscience, and reason as sufficient for knowledge of the divine. The Spanish Krausism of Sanz and Giner became a movement that promoted freedom of conscience, a reverence for science and, above all, the use of education to reform Spanish culture and society (De Jongh 11-12, 15).

Dismissed from his university professorship for refusing to hew to the approved state curriculum and to strict Catholic doctrine, Giner founded the *Institución Libre de Enseñanza* with his brother, Hermenegildo, in 1876.[28] He regarded transforming the educational system as fundamental to the country's reorientation, which in his view depended on recovering its genuine national identity; for him, this identity was located in the landscape. Machado's framing of the terrain around Soria and the Duero River in *Campos de Castilla* should be considered a product of the education that he received at the *ILE*. The artistic and scientific analysis of the land that he learned there colors his descriptive and symbolic language, and it likely planted in him the seed of the idea of landscape as national character.[29]

---

[28] According to José Antonio García-Suárez, Giner was relieved of his teaching duties for his solidarity with the other main promoters of Krausism in Spain–Sanz del Río, Fernando de Castro, y Nicolás Salmerón. The three men were stripped of their university posts in 1868, when the conservative campaign against the Krausists intensified (90). In keeping with the progressive intellectual currents of the day, Giner looked to advances in science and education in order to arrive at practical political and cultural policies–alternatives to the polarizing ideologies that marked the period framing the Revolution of 1868 (Pena 14). The *ILE's* pedagogical philosophy was grounded in positivistic determinism, especially Hippolyte Taine's notion of *race, moment et milieu.*

[29] The *ILE's* outlook informed–and was informed by–the realist landscape painting of the time, which explains why the school placed so much emphasis on the observation of detail. For example in Giner's essay "El paisaje," lengthy passages are devoted to evoking the peculiarities of the countryside around Madrid, such as granite formations (363-64):

> Todo el mundo, verbigracia, distingue el pintoresco dentellado con que se recortan sobre el azul del cielo las Pedrizas del Manzanares, en la vecina sierra carpetana, y el suave modelado de los cerros que rodean á Madrid. Aquéllas son de granito, éstos de diluvio cuaternario. El granito, por su composición y estructura, presenta una cierta resistencia, así en cantidad como en dirección, á los agentes atmosféricos; merced á lo cual no se deja destruir sino en un cierto sentido, de donde nacen á su vez determinadas formas. Doquiera que aflora al descubierto, el agua, al resbalar sobre sus masas, las redondea, produciendo en las pequeñas esas superficies ásperas, rugosas, cubiertas de líquenes, que interrumpen la

Antonio and his brother, the poet Manuel Machado (1874-1947), began attending the school in 1883 (Sesé 27). In his "Autobiografía escrita en 1913," Machado describes conserving his "gran amor" for his teachers, Giner and Manuel Bartolomé Cossío, the esteemed art historian and pedagogue (283).[30] Giner and Cossío implemented a new mode of visual and aesthetic education based on the close analysis of art works, designed to promote a new way of seeing and thereby conceiving the world. Cossío led expeditions to Madrid museums to encourage what Giner called, in an article for the *Boletín de la Institución Libre de Enseñanza* (hereafter *Boletín*), "la crítica espontánea de los niños" ("Crítica espontánea" 41). The aesthetic awareness and judgment of students was honed through Cossío's artistic excursions, as part of a program of experiential learning. As one student recalled of his methods:

> [No] se proponía que supiéramos muchas cosas, sino que aprendiéramos a ver; esto es, despertar, avivar el espíritu de observa-

---

continuidad de la tierra vegetal, y en los grandes cantos, la configuración peculiar de las 'piedras caballeras,' monolitos á veces enormes y que en ocasiones oscilan como otros tantos monumentos megalíticos naturales, hasta que la radiación del calor que las dilató durante el día, las contrae por la noche, las hiende, las raja en mil grietas, que luego, al hincharse dentro de ellas el hielo, estallan, desprendiendo gigantescas esquirlas, y éstas, apiladas unas sobre otras, forman ese agudo dentellado de las cimas graníticas de nuestra cordillera; dentellado, sobre todo, visible allí donde se entrelazan dos tipos de granito: uno más resistente, otro más quebradizo y más blando. (363-64)

Giner mentions in a note that "El paisaje" was written around 1885, before the inauguration of the Segovia railway (370). Machado's enthusiasm for painting and landscape, made manifest in daily visits to the Prado Museum while he lived in Madrid, and in his verses dedicated to artists, received its first youthful stimulation from the *ILE*.

[30] Giner was a good friend of Machado's father. Antonio Machado y Álvarez (1846-1893), known also as "Demófilo," was a noted left-leaning lawyer and intellectual who introduced the discipline of folklore to Spain (Ribbans, Introduction, *Soledades. Galerías. Otros poemas.* 28, 25). The poet wrote a moving tribute to Giner in the *Boletín* of the *ILE* on the occasion of his teacher's death. Of what he learned from Giner, Machado recalls the following: "Lo que importa es aprender a pensar, a utilizar nuestros propios sesos para el uso a que están por naturaleza destinados y a calcar fielmente la línea sinuosa y siempre original de nuestro propio sentir, a ser nosotros mismos, para poner mañana el sello de nuestra alma en nuestra obra" ("Don Francisco Giner de los Ríos" 296). Machado's metaphor of cleaving to a sinuous line of thought has interesting resonances in light of Giner's and Manuel B. Cossío's innovative incorporation of art history and the study of landscape into the curriculum at the *ILE*.

ción instintivo y convertirlo de instintivo en reflexivo y analítico llegando a formar el juicio crítico razonado.

Es el principio general, intuitivo, que conforma su visión de la Pedagogía, aplicada al proceso de la educación estética; saber ver, saber juzgar, y saber gozar con la belleza. (qtd. in Ortega Morales 244)

Since Giner thought of history and tradition as finding expression in and through the countryside, landscape painting took on a special function different from that of other forms of visual art (Ortega Morales 237-38; Vila-Belda 285).[31] From the perspective of Giner and his associates, landscape as a genre represented the antithesis of history painting with its focus on individual actors and occurrences; landscape painting became a way of jettisoning this history and starting afresh with the study of folk customs and the countryside in which they grew up (Ortega Morales 239). Giner's affirmation that, "podría decirse en algún modo que la pintura de paisaje es el más sintético, cabal y comprensivo de todos los géneros de la pintura," relates to the distinction that he makes between "campo" and "paisaje," in which landscape ("paisaje") includes not only the physical and biological properties of the land ("campo"), but also the "obra del arte humano, y hasta el hombre mismo, cuya presencia anima con una nueva nota de interés el cuadro entero de la Naturaleza" ("El paisaje" 361). Landscape painting attains significance in his eyes because he envisions "landscape" as a synthetic work of art that brings together Nature and the human. Constitutive of the landscape, according to Giner, are "la tierra y el agua en sus formas; el mundo vegetal, con sus tipos, figuras y colores; la atmósfera con sus celajes; el hombre con sus obras; los animales y hasta el cielo con sus astros y con el juego de tintes, luces y sombras." He aestheticizes all aspects of the land; the mineral part of the earth, for instance, "El suelo, la costra sólida del planeta," merits its own "'estética geológica'" ("El paisaje" 362-63). The art of the landscape painters José Jiménez Fernández (1846-1873), Espina, Agustín Lhardy, and Beruete, who involved themselves in the *ILE*,

---

[31] The philosophy of the *ILE* remains indebted to Krausism, which can be described as eminently aesthetic in its pedagogy. Giner followed Krausist thought, in that he conceived education as a means of perfecting the human and the social (Ortega Morales 298).

developed in response to these ideas (Ortega Morales 238). Berue-
te, a founding member of the school, helped to formulate its con-
ception of landscape as geology and history (Castro Cardús 3; *Siglo
XIX*, 91).[32]

The *Boletín's* descriptions of field trips reflected the way in
which the *ILE* partnered geography, geology, and orography with
aesthetics, art history, philosophy, and literature.[33] Since Giner
thought that the exercise of geographic science, extended by the in-
fluential A. de Humboldt to history and aesthetics, would assist in
the rediscovery of national identity, the pages of the *Boletín* were fi-
lled with articles on the geology and orography of Spain and Portu-
gal (Pena 14-15).[34] Professor Francisco Quiroga published a three-
part study entitled "Estructura uniclinal de la Península Ibérica" in
1881 and, from that year forward, space was devoted to Professor
B. Lázaro's precise dissertations on Spain's botanical life.[35] Editors
accompanied notice of the projected summer schedule for 1881
with an extensive description of the previous year's excursions, the-
reby advertising the educational and health benefits that could be
reaped from such activities:

> . . . [L]os alumnos hacen largas caminatas; toman baños de mar y
> de río; practican ascensiones; trazan croquis de terrenos con cur-
> vas de nivel; herborizan y recogen colecciones de minerales; visi-

---

[32] Aureliano de Beruete educated his son, Aureliano de Beruete y Moret (1876-
1922), the future art historian, critic, and director of the Prado Museum, at the *ILE*
(Pena 14; Castro Cardús 6-7).

[33] See also Gayana Jurkevich's helpful genealogy of ideas about landscape in
Spain in Part I, Chapter 1 of *In Pursuit of the Natural Sign: Azorín and the Poetics of
Ekphrasis* ("Defining Castile: *Institucionismo*, the Generation of '98, and the Ori-
gins of Modern Spanish Landscape" [27-53]). She takes up Taine's influence on the
ILE's philosophy on page 28. Experiencing the natural landscape "con claridad y
sencillez" was recommended from an early age, so as to facilitate "la adquisición de
nuevos conocimientos" and open "tan ancho camino á los estudios posteriores," as
an article on the *ILE's* teaching practices explained (Lázaro, "El arte" 163). On the
subject of ekphrasis, see also, in addition to Persin, Emilie L. Bergmann's *Art In-
scribed: Essays on Ekphrasis in Spanish Golden Age Poetry*, Jean H. Hagstrum, *The
Sister Arts: The Tradition of Literary Pictorialism and English Poetry from Dreyden to
Gray*, James A. W. Heffernan's *Museum of Words: The Poetics of Ekphrasis from
Homer to Ashbery*, and Murray Krieger's *Ekphrasis: The Illusion of the Natural Sign*.

[34] The September 30, 1883 edition, for instance, advocated graphic and experi-
ential methods of teaching descriptive geography (Torres Campos).

[35] I direct the reader to the following articles in the *Boletín de la Institución Li-
bre de Enseñanza*: "Historia de la flora ibérica (I)," Año X, núm. 217, 28 de febrero
de 1886: 51-54; Año X, núm. 218, 15 de marzo de 1886: 76-79; (conclusión) Año X,
núm. 219, 31 de marzo de 1886: 89-93.

tan y estudian monumentos arquitectónicos y otras obras de arte, minas, fábricas, puertos y faros; estudian sistemas de cultivo, extracción de minerales y elaboración de primeras materias; se ejercitan en el difícil arte de observar y en el trato de gentes de diversas clases sociales; se acostumbran á vivir en una relativa independencia; desarrollan su individualidad;–constituyendo así un precioso complemento de la educación recibida y de las nociones aprendidas durante el curso. ("Excursiones proyectadas" 86)

In an 1885 article on the school's geological field trips, Giner discussed two excursions through the countryside outside Madrid–opportunities for experiencing the landscape *"in situ"*–that served to *"ilustrar*, por vía de ejemplos, las lecciones teóricas" ("Excursiones geológicas" 131, 133; emphasis in the original). Detailed logs, particularly of travels through the surrounding areas of Madrid and other quarters of Castile, authored by Giner and the geologist Quiroga, became a regular part of the *Boletín* around this time.[36] Exploration of the land entailed contact with the common folk whose lives were inextricably linked with it. To learn the difficult art of observation and of dealing with people from diverse social classes–to paraphrase Giner–was to engage in an *intrahistoria* of sorts, contextualizing popular customs in their natural setting.

Giner's concentration on the Castilian landscape, which he called Spain's "espina dorsal," and the Guadarrama was the consequence of his view of Castile as representative of the whole of Spain ("El paisaje" 365; Ortega Morales 280-87).[37] The *Boletín* mirrored Giner's interest in Castile and the Guadarrama: for example, the June 15, 1885 edition contained an article that detailed the attributes of Spain's central plateau, along with the mountains of the Guadarrama (Calderón, "La meseta central de España: resumen de algu-

---

[36] See Giner, "Excursiones geológicas," Año IX, núm. 198, 15 de mayo de 1885: 131-34. Also consult Francisco Quiroga, "Excursiones geológicas en los alrededores de Madrid," Año IX, núm. 205, 31 de agosto de 1885: 248-51; an article of same title appears in Año IX, núm. 206, 15 de noviembre de 1885: 263-65.

[37] The *Guadarrama* is an area close to Madrid (to the northwest) whose geographical attributes include the Guadarrama Mountains (*Sierra de Guadarrama*), part of the Iberian Peninsula's Central Mountain Range (*Sistema Central*), and the Guadarrama River, a tributary of the Tagus (*Tajo*) River. Giner's characterization of Castile as Spain's "espina dorsal" is strongly reminiscent of *Sociedad para el Estudio del Guadarrama* founder José Macpherson's statement that the *Sierra de Guadarrama* constituted the "columna vertebral de la Península Ibérica" (Ortega Cantero 36).

nas investigaciones orográficas"); and an account of an excursion to the mountains of the Guadarrama appeared in the June 30, 1886 issue (Giner, "Excursión a la Sierra del Guadarrama"). The landscape of the Guadarrama, including its geological and botanical characteristics, took on cultural import for Giner, which he extended to the rest of the Castilian countryside (Ortega Cantero 34). In 1887, articles relating to the *Sociedad para el Estudio del Guadarrama* and authored by Quiroga began to find their way into the *Boletín*. Upon its founding in 1886, on the initiative of the *ILE*, the *Sociedad para el Estudio del Guadarrama* elected the distinguished geologist José Macpherson to be its director; the Society's founding protocols were signed by Beruete and Cossío.[38]

An eight-line untitled poem attests to the Guadarrama's–and Castile's–significance for Machado and the means by which landscape takes shape in *Campos de Castilla*. At the end of the text, Machado gives a real time and place for the travels that he portrays, specifying the year, 1911, and the route, the "Camino de Balsaín" in the rural heart of the Guadarrama:

> ¿Eres tú, Guadarrama, viejo amigo,
> la sierra gris y blanca,
> la sierra de mis tardes madrileñas
> que yo veía en el azul pintada?
>
> Por tus barrancos hondos
> y por tus cumbres agrias,
> mil Guadarramas y mil soles vienen,
> cabalgando conmigo, a tus entrañas.
>
> (*Campos de Castilla* CIV 1-8/118)

The essential and first-hand nature of Machado's experience of the land finds expression in his use of the pronoun *yo* and the possessi-

---

[38] See, in the *Boletín*, the following by Quiroga: "Sociedad para el estudio del Guadarrama. Otra excursión á Torrelodones (I)," Año XI, núm. 239, 31 de enero de 1887: 30-31; and "Sociedad para el estudio del Guadarrama. Excursión al cerro de Almodovar y á San Fernando (7 febrero 1887)," Año XI, núm. 241, 28 de febrero de 1887: 59-60. José Luis Barrera Morate discusses the founding of the *Sociedad para el Estudio del Guadarrama* in his 2002 biographical sketch of José Macpherson y Hemas (1839-1902) for the new *Boletín de la Institución Libre de Enseñanza*. Jurkevich points out that Beruete and Cossío were signatories to the Society's founding protocols (29).

ve adjective *mis*. What the poetic "I" sees in the horizon has been filtered through his visual sensibility, honed during "tardes madrileñas" and excursions while a student at the *ILE*: the gray and white mountains are "painted" onto the blue of the sky, becoming arranged into a "landscape." The figural makes its appearance as if in response to the past impressions described in the poem. From recalling the sight of "la sierra gris y blanca" comes the image of the "azul pintada," just as the personification of the "cumbres agrias" and "mil Guadarramas y mil soles" emerges from the remembered observation of geographic features. The way in which poetic language issues from the synthesis of sensation and memory becomes paradigmatic in the collection.

Decisive for Machado were the realist and impressionist[39] styles of landscape painting that were current in the nineteenth and early twentieth centuries. He absorbed realist methods of relating the different picture planes (background, middle ground, foreground) and using detail to guide the eye between these planes, so as to draw the viewer into the landscape. Impressionism modeled how incorporating knowledge of visual perception's workings into form and technique could increase the viewer's participation in representation. To take an example, placing small brushstrokes of contrasting hues side by side sets the retinal blending of colors in motion, thus making the depiction of natural scenes approximate the actual experience of them. Both realist and impressionist painting served as paradigms for Machado's location of the reader in the landscape–his way of producing identification with the Castilian countryside.

Two artists proved particularly significant: Haes and Beruete,

---

[39] French Impressionism arrived in Spain somewhat belatedly, after the movement's innovations had already been assimilated by the French art world and its public. Confusion between Spanish "Luminismo" and "Impresionismo" has remained problematic. Beruete commented on some of the differences between the "Luminismo" of Sorolla and the impressionism of the French variety. From Beruete's perspective, the French Impressionists focused more on matters of technique (such as the size and character of brushstrokes), while in Spain, the painters of "Luminismo" were oriented towards strong contrasts of light and shadow (Arias Angles 159-61). "Luminismo" was linked with Mariano Fortuny (1838-1874) as well as with Sorolla (Puente 88). Enrique Arias Angles identifies Beruete, Darío de Regoyos, Anselmo Guinea (1854-1906), Guiard, and the Catalan painters Francisco Gimeno (1858-1927), Eliseo Meifrén (1858-1940), and Joaquim Mir as, to one degree or another, impressionist (161).

who had a direct effect on the pedagogy of landscape (and landsca-
pe as national identity) at the *ILE*.[40] Although unlike Beruete, Haes
maintained no formal connection with the *ILE*, he was heralded as
a precursor to Giner for his championing of a landscape art groun-
ded in the outdoor observation of nature (Jurkevich 31). He habi-
tually made reference to the concrete traits of the land when he de-
veloped his themes in the studio, working from *plein air* studies
(Gutiérrez Márquez 80). Indeed the Belgian Haes was largely res-
ponsible for the critical appreciation of landscape and landscape
painting's enshrinement in Spanish educational institutions.[41] Haes
could disseminate his ideas widely, given that he held professors-
hips at the prestigious *Academia de Bellas Artes de San Fernando*
and at the *Escuela de Ingenieros de Caminos, Canales y Puertos*,
where he gave a course on architecture and the natural landscape
(Castro Cardús 3-4).[42] He encouraged the students who crowded
his Madrid studio and classes at the Academy, including the young
Beruete, to accompany him on excursions through the countryside
and to adopt his rational manner of interpreting the landscape (Or-
tega Morales 260-61, 265-66). During these journeys, Haes introdu-
ced his apprentices to *plein air* painting and sketching, of which,
along with landscape painting itself, he was Spain's first and fore-
most defender (Barón 45; *Siglo XIX*, 64; Calvo Serraller 51).

Characteristic of Haes's work is its geological specificity: in *Pai-
saje de planicie rocosa* (ca. 1859), crags at left cast a shadow on the
valley at right; and in *Desfiladero. Jaraba de Aragón* (1872), the sha-
dow of the high rocky hills at left falls on the sunlit ridges (right),
creating a strong contrast between dark and light tones. The place-
ment of the mountains in these paintings typifies the way in which
Haes creates perspectives and borders so as to order the various pic-
ture planes. His 1859 renderings of the Sierra Mountains around
Madrid in *Paisaje a la orilla de un río* and *Paisaje con una vacada en
un río* can be described in terms of the realism of their chromatic
range (ochres and browns), bucolic calm, and typically summer sce-

---

[40] Carlos de Haes was instrumental in getting landscape painting recognized in
Spanish academic circles as having value; he introduced *plein air* painting to Spain
in 1857 (Vila-Belda 283).
[41] The Chair of Landscape was established in 1844 and first held by the Spanish
Romantic painter Jenaro Pérez Villaamil (1807-1854).
[42] Haes taught at the *Academia de Bellas Artes de San Fernando* beginning in
1857 and at the *Escuela de Ingenieros de Caminos, Canales y Puertos* after 1860.

nery: trees in full foliage; light and shadow as filtered though the leaves; streams mirroring the afternoon light; and grazing livestock with their shepherds. In a similar vein, in an 1860 lecture read at the *Academia de Bellas Artes de San Fernando*, Haes recommends that landscape painters strive to represent the attributes of trees, flowers, rocks, and plants as they are in nature. Their variety of features make trees, in his eyes, the true protagonists of landscape painting: "Los árboles son las verdaderas figuras del paisaje," he asserts, "Cada uno tiene su fisionomía, cado uno su lugar favorito donde desplegar mejor su verdadero carácter" (Haes 345-46). In his studies of the Pyrenees Mountains–*Aguas Buenas* (*Pirineos*), *Cercanías de Aguas Buenas*, and *Pirineos franceses* (all ca. 1882)–Haes reflects the specificities of the region through his minute depiction of trees and tree trunks, as well as rivers and other naturally occurring pathways in the countryside (Gutiérrez Márquez 110).[43]

The fidelity to the natural environment in Machado's *Campos de Castilla*, especially the detailed rendering of rocks, trees, and plants, is analogous to the close attention to geological texture and vegetation in Haes's landscapes. In a similar way to the painter, in "A orillas del Duero," the poet differentiates among "desnudos peñascales," "cerros," *lomas*, "colinas," *montes*, "alcores," "serrezuelas calvas," "arcadas de piedra," and "altos llanos y yermos y roquedas." He identifies the "hierbas montaraces de fuerte olor" and the "romero, tomillo, salvia, espliego" with the sagacity of a local or one accustomed to close contact with the land (25, 10, 23, 17, 19, 31-32, 35/102). Machado describes the hills around the Duero River with exactitude–"colinas / obscuras coronadas de robles y de encinas"–and distinguishes the species of the trees displaying their leaves on the riverbanks as the poplar ("álamos") (11-12, 23-24, 28/102). Two poems in the collection, "Las encinas" and "El olmo seco," are devoted to trees native to the Castilian countryside.[44] In "Las encinas," Machado articulates the ilex's emblematic relation to Castile by cataloguing the kinds of terrain where it can be found–"laderas y altozanos, / serrijones y colinas / llenos de obscura maleza" (CIII 2-4/113).

At the same time, Machado converts the natural properties of the

---

[43] Ana Gutiérrez Márquez refers to two distinct studies of the Pyrenees, both of which are entitled *Aguas Buenas* (*Pirineos*).

[44] Another poem of a similar type, "Los olivos," portrays the olive groves that grace the Andalusian countryside.

landscape into a rich symbolic repertoire. To reflect the ilex's unobtrusive humility, which Machado praises, he at first contrasts it negatively, in an extended catalogue, with the impressiveness of other sorts of trees. He typifies the oak (*roble*) through metaphor as "la guerra," making it speak, in an instance of prosopopoeia, of "el valor y el coraje"; it is further personified as an athlete who "recalca y ennudece su robustez" (11-12, 19-20/113-14). Pines are as expansively grand as the sea, sky, and mountains ("El pino es el mar y el cielo / y la montaña"), and the palm, infinite as the desert, the sun, and faraway vistas, becomes identified with human desire: "La palmera es el desierto, / el sol y la lejanía: / la sed; una fuente fría / soñada en el campo yerto" (22-23, 24-27/114). In the aged trunks of the beechwoods can be read the legend ("la leyenda") of "una historia horrenda / de crímenes y batallas," and in the rustling leaves of the black poplars, we hear the sound of the river against its banks, as if it were a poet's lyre: "Los chopos son la ribera, / liras de la primavera" (28-31, 34-35/114). The metapoetic references to the bardic ("la leyenda") as well as the lyric's musico-poetic origins ("la lira") underscore the relationship between landscape and poetry that remains central to *Campos de Castilla*. In a gesture towards his own poetic, Machado attributes to apple, orange, eucalyptus, and cypress trees the sensory's capacity to imprint memory, without which neither landscape nor poetry, nor the collective memory that is the result of both of these things, would have the potency that they do:

> Tiene el manzano el olor
> de su poma,
> el eucalipto el aroma
> de sus hojas, de su flor
> el naranjo la fragancia;
> y es del huerto
> la elegancia
> el ciprés obscuro y yerto. (50-57/115)

However, it is the ilex that embodies the characteristics that Machado requires, although ironically, representing the *encina* and the right values of which it is emblematic taxes his powers of representation far more than trees of apparently superior qualities:

> ¿Qué tienes tú, negra encina
> campesina,

con tus ramas sin color
en el campo sin verdor;
con tu tronco ceniciento
sin esbeltez ni altiveza,
con tu vigor sin tormento,
y tu humildad que es firmeza?

En tu copa ancha y redonda
nada brilla,
ni tu verdiobscura fronda
ni tu flor verdiamarilla (58-69/115)

By means of the repeated negative syntactic structures in the apostrophe, Machado expresses the difficulty of capturing the quintessence of the ilex and Castile. Yet the seeming dearth of striking qualities belonging to the "negra encina / campesina" actually turns into the humility that is the source of the ilex's power and that of the poet-bard to sing of its virtues. He therefore chooses to depict this, its most valuable trait, purged of all superfluous elements:

Nada es lindo ni arrogante
en tu porte, ni guerrero,
nada fiero
que aderece su talante.
Brotas derecha o torcida
con esa humildad que cede
sólo a la ley de la vida,
que es vivir como se puede. (70-77/115)

The unbending core of the "parda encina," "siempre firme, siempre igual, / impasible, casta y buena" (79, 86-87/116), holds Machado's landscape together, becoming the center around which he maps Spain:

eterna encina rural
de los negros encinares
de la raya aragonesa
y las crestas militares
de la tierra pamplonesa;
encinas de Extremadura,
de Castilla, que hizo a España,
encinas de la llanura,

del cerro y de la montaña;
encinas del alto llano
que el joven Duero rodea,
y del Tajo que serpea
por el suelo toledano;
encinas de junto al mar
–en Santander– . . . (89-103/116)

Machado brings diverse regions, and the type of ilex which stands in metonymic relation to them, together in patchwork fashion to form a whole.

The realism that many of the poems in *Campos de Castilla* share with Haes's landscapes is tempered by a late-Romantic emotiveness reminiscent of Rosalía de Castro's (1837-1885) *En las orillas del Sar* (1884) and Jenaro Pérez Villaamil's (1807-1854) paintings:

Al olmo viejo, hendido por el rayo
y en su mitad podrido,
con las lluvias de abril y el sol de mayo,
algunas hojas verdes le han salido.

¡El olmo centenario en la colina
que lame el Duero! Un musgo amarillento
la mancha la corteza blanquecina
al tronco carcomido y polvoriento.

("A un olmo seco," *Campos de Castilla* CXV 1-8/171)

In one sense, Machado's description of the elm–the stain of the yellowed moss on its whitish bark and its rotten trunk–is faithful to nature. In another sense, it is metaphoric and symbolic: the sprouting of hopeful "hojas verdes" in the decaying, century-old tree powerfully suggests the way in which, for Machado, Spain's original spirit and strength can stave off ruin, renewing themselves in the face of the most hopeless conditions. In "Orillas del Duero," a shorter poem than the similarly titled "A orillas del Duero," Machado likewise employs geological and botanical particularity to evoke the melancholy and impoverished character of the Castilian land, as well as the beauty and value that it nevertheless retains. The "diminutos pegujales / de tierra dura y fría" and the "pedregales / desnudos y pelados serrijones" are home to the birds of prey ("águilas caudales") that decrepitude attracts, and plants whose rough texture mirrors their capacity for survival in harsh conditions ("malezas y jarales, / hierbas monteses, zarzas y cambrones"). Their hardscrabble nature represents the virtue that Machado ascribes to the Castilian character (*Campos de Castilla* CII 9-10, 13-17/110).

Besides changing the typical geographical specificity of Haes's painting into a metaphoric and symbolic vocabulary, Machado takes from the way in which his brand of realist painting employs light, color, and detail to guide the viewer's eye. In the 1870s, Haes began to make greater use of light and color to augment the realism of his landscapes: his palette and colors became brighter, and he painted more midday scenes with expressive and energetic brushstrokes. During this time, in which he traveled extensively in the north of Spain, he experimented with light's potential to give morphological definition to trees, rocks, and the geology of the land (Gutiérrez Márquez 96-97). In the oil-on-canvas *Canal de Mancorbo en los Picos de Europa* (1876) (see fig. 1.1, p. 260), emblematic of this period, variations in shades of gray create a play of light and shadow on the mountains at far center-right. The predominantly smoky tones of the mountains stand in keen contrast to the ochre of the crag set in front them, putting the jagged rock into relief and sharply demarcating the different picture planes. Placing lighter shades of gray at certain areas of the mountains shows the angle at which the strong sunlight shines, reflecting off sheer rocky surfaces: it is summer at midday. In contradistinction to the lightness of the colors at rear and right-center, the long shadow cast from center-left down through the middle darkens all of the hues, which makes for a sense of relative distance and elevation between the sunlit rocky mountains and the lower hills in shade. Underlining the mountains' height as opposed to the valley and hills are the diminutiveness of the figures of the cattle at pasture and the positioning of the stream close to the center of the composition, punctuated by swaths of deep brown and the white froth of rapids.

In a similar way to Haes, Machado juxtaposes opposite colors on the spectrum, and warm and cool tones to frame particular views. The ashen color of the hills depicted at the beginning of "Campos de Soria" indicates that they lie in the shade of the high bald mountains:

> Es la tierra de Soria árida y fría.
> Por las colinas y las sierras calvas,
> verdes pradillos, cerros cenicientos,

la primavera pasa
dejando entre las hierbas olorosas
sus diminutas margaritas blancas. (1-6/133)

The implied position of the mountains and hills, the result of light and shadow effects, locates the green meadows and white flowers at foreground, their brilliant color, we can infer, intensified by bright sun. In "A orillas del Duero," the horizontal blue patch of sky sets off the tall pointed mountains, brown earth of Castile, and hillocks, tinged red by the sunset–"Sobre los agrios campos caía un sol de fuego" (12/101). We follow the "buitre de anchas alas" on wing through the "puro azul del cielo," the bright blue of which contrasts with the deep earth tones of the countryside's geological features in the late-afternoon light:

Un buitre de anchas alas con majestuoso vuelo
cruzaba solitario el puro azul del cielo.
Yo divisaba, lejos, un monte alto y agudo,
y una redonda loma cual recamado escudo,
y cárdenos alcores sobre la parda tierra
–harapos esparcidos de un viejo arnés de guerra–,
las serrezuelas calvas por donde tuerce el Duero
para formar la corva ballesta de un arquero
en torno a Soria. . . . (13-21/101-102)

Creating the perspective necessary for our perception of the sharp mountain and round hills as far away are the location of the vulture, and the shape and color of the sky. The "pasajeros . . . carros, jinetes y arrieros" (29-30/102) that Machado places in the countryside become focal points, ordering the direction in which the reader's eye moves in negotiating the similarities and contrasts among colors. As a consequence, we linger on the "humilde prado / donde el merino pace y el toro, arrodillado / sobre la hierba, rumia," the presence of sheep and cattle signaling the bucolic simplicity that Machado holds up as ideal (25-27/102).[45]

---

[45] In Haes's *La canal de Mancorbo en los Picos de Europa*, he locates tiny cattle next to the stream at center, and in the earlier *Recuerdos de Andalucía, costa del Mediterráneo, junto a Torremolinos*, characterized by late-Romantic overtones, he specks the dusty path at foreground with two diminutive *campesinos*, one of them mounted on a mule, and a dog. See *El siglo XIX en el Prado* (68-69).

Just as the realistic detail and composition in *Campos de Castilla* can be considered comparable to Haes's painting, the collection's impressionism can be likened to Beruete's work, especially with regard to the portrayal of light and shadow, and the way in which the sensory becomes suggestive of mood. In comparison with Haes, Beruete trained his eye more intensely on Castile since, similar to Giner, he regarded the Castilian as quintessentially Spanish (Ortega Morales 269). Beruete's Castilian landscapes articulate his vision of the region's individuality and spirit, which he also conveys through pictorial references to the representation of its countrysides in Spanish painting, from El Greco and Diego Velázquez to Francisco de Goya (Pena 17-18).[46] In fact, Beruete became one of the principal exponents of the idea of landscape as a point of connection with tradition (Calvo Serraller 61; Arias Angles 167). Azorín dedicated *Castilla* "a la memoria de Aureliano de Beruete pintor maravilloso de Castilla silencioso en su arte" (n. pag.). And in a short piece titled with the full name of the painter, which consists of a fictional dialogue between two friends who are *aficionados* of his work, Azorín praises the way in which Beruete expresses the soul and spirit of Castile in his landscapes:

> Beruete fué un maravilloso paisajista. Las tierras de Toledo, de Segovia, de Cuenca, muestran su espíritu, el alma del paisaje, en sus lienzos. Poco a poco el maestro fué concentrando su amor a la tierra castellana. Cuando murió se hallaba en plena posesión de su técnica y de su idea. Había llegado ya a ese grado de simplificación, de tenacidad, a que sólo llegan los grandes artistas. Entre sus cuadros hay cuatro o seis (Ávila, Cuenca, Toledo) que marcan el grado máximo a que puede alcanzarse con la pintura. ("Aureliano de Beruete," *Obras completas* 7: 243-44)[47]

---

[46] Beruete assisted in establishing the *Colegio Internacional*, a precursor to the *ILE*.

[47] In Azorín's "Aureliano de Beruete," one of the two friends who participates in the fictional dialogue around which the piece is organized mentions the painter's death as having taken place approximately one year ago–"poco tiempo después de morir, el año pasado, en abril, se celebró una Exposición de sus obras" (*Obras completas* 7: 241). Azorín means the exhibition that Sorolla actually organized in his studio. (A date of publication for "Aureliano de Beruete" is not given in the *Obras completas*.)

Beruete's renderings of the Castilian countryside remain at once realist and evocatively impressionistic. This double nature is manifest in his depiction of Castile's unique coloring, and certainly, his use of light and color constitutes the most salient aspect of his art, in a way that recalls, yet remains distinct from, French Impressionism.[48] It also links him with the French Barbizon School, where he studied in his youth, since the hallmarks of Barbizon landscape painting are a naturalism rooted in the private contemplation of nature, and an attentiveness to mood and the countryside's underlying qualities (Rosenfeld and Workman 11).[49] Beruete translates the browns, ochres, and yellows of the Castilian earth with fidelity to paintings such as *El Tajo, Toledo* (1905); *Paisaje de Castilla* (1907); *La Casa del Sordo (Madrid)* (1907); *Castilla* (1907); *Madrid desde el Manzanares* (1908); *Las Huertas (Cuenca)* (1910); *Vista de Cuenca* (1910); and *Venta del Macho, Toledo* (1911). In several of these paintings, he combines naturalistic color with the short brushstrokes and light effects associated with impressionism.[50] Beruete suggests, in *Vista del Guadarrama desde el Plantío de los Infantes* (oil on canvas; 1910) (see fig. 1.2, p. 261), the angle of the midday sun by placing shadows directly under the trees at middle ground, and in the lowest areas of the valleys, where they would normally be cast by the tall mountains. Touches of golden and rosy hues on the trees, grasses, and plains of the valley, painted with short, overlapping brushstrokes, and the bright white highlighting on the snow of the mountains indicate

----

[48] Beruete, like his fellow landscape painter Martín Rico, regarded Impressionism with skepticism, at first rejecting its departures from conventional drawing and reliance on pointillist-style brush strokes. By 1905, however, he had come to recognize the movement's achievements in color and light and accepted (to a degree) its techniques. Despite the apparent similarity between the Impressionists' treatment of light and color and Beruete's, therefore, it is important to keep in mind that the Spanish painter arrived independently at his own methods (Arias Angles 159-60; Pena 14).

[49] Members of the Barbizon School were averse to what they regarded as the artifice of classical landscape painting, as well as to the conventions of landscape in late-eighteenth-century British art. The naturalism of Barbizon painting can be considered to stem from the type of artistic romanticism that was influenced by empirical science, as in the portraits of the insane by John Constable (1776-1837), and Théodore Géricault (1791-1824). This Romantic empiricism wanted to get to the heart of nature by means of the contemplation of its forms (Rosenfeld and Workman 11).

[50] Beruete brings together naturalistic color and the light effects of impressionism, namely in *Paisaje de Castilla*, *La Casa del Sordo*, *Castilla*, *Madrid desde el Manzanares*, and *Venta del Macho, Toledo*.

where the light is strongest. Particularly in *El Tajo, Toledo, Paisaje de Castilla, La Casa del Sordo*, and *Castilla*, Beruete heightens his depiction of the Castilian countryside's distinctive hues by representing the landscape at sunset, when the low sun brings out the red and purple tones in the earth and geological formations.

Beruete's impressionism extends to his manner of portraying the seasons of the year with light and color. In *Paisaje de Otoño. Madrid* (1910), he depicts the countryside near Madrid at the peak of fall. Employing short brushstrokes just as in *Vista del Guadarrama desde el Plantío de los Infantes*, albeit with a thicker impasto, he sets like and contrasting colors side-by-side in order to show where light and shadow hit. He reiterates specific shades in different places–the golden hues in the single tree at left foreground, on the ground at center, and in the group of trees at rear–thereby imposing order on the profusion of colors and aiding the viewer's eye in negotiating the picture planes. The blooming hawthorns of *Espinos en flor. Plantío de Infantes* (oil on canvas; 1908), represented through clouds of white brushstrokes, stand out from the dark tree trunks and branches, and the varied greens that make up the grasses and leaves. Along similar lines, in *Paisaje de invierno (Madrid)* (oil on canvas; 1911), the stark white of the birch trees is set off by silver highlighting, whose placement summons the low angle of the winter sun.

Machado delineates his landscapes with the impressionistic evocativeness of the late Beruete: the light and shadow, and contrasting colors of the countrysides in *Campos de Castilla* suggest time of day and season of the year, thus playing a formative role in the reader's apprehension of the various scenes. Such techniques endow Machado's landscapes with a strongly experiential and sensory aspect, making us feel as if we ourselves were encountering its properties in the course of their natural cycles. In "A orillas del Duero" and "Campos de Soria" we find the composition and detailing of the landscape's physical attributes, and the attentiveness to light that typifies Beruete's later paintings. In a way comparable to Beruete, Machado imitates the sunset's metamorphosis of mountains and hills, rocks, and low-lying stretches of ground. In "A orillas del Duero," the "cárdenos alcores sobre la parda tierra" reflect the striking reds of a "sol de fuego," and the river mirrors the silver tones of twilight ("las aguas plateadas del Duero" [17, 12, 32/101]). Likewise in "Campos de Soria," Machado captures the tones brought out by evening's waning light–"tornasoles de carmín y acero," "lla-

nos plomizos," "lomas plateadas," "montes de violeta," and "cum-
bres de nieve sonrosada" (33-36/134). The warm "carmín" makes
the cool steel and lead tones of the countryside stand out, and these
metallics underscore the reds and purples of the mountains at dusk.

The touches of sensory detail that Machado gives to "Amanecer
de otoño" recall Beruete's representation of the different seasons:

> Una larga carretera
> entre grises peñascales,
> y alguna humilde pradera
> donde pacen negros toros. Zarzas, malezas, jarales.
>
> Está la tierra mojada
> por las gotas del rocío,
> y la alameda dorada,
> hacia la curva del río.
>
> Tras los montes de violeta
> quebrado el primer albor;
> a la espalda la escopeta,
> entre sus galgos agudos, caminando un cazador.
> (*Campos de Castilla* CIX 1-12/127)

We focus on the gray shade of the rocky hills and blackness of the
bulls at pasture, which underscore the dim coloring of the autumn
countryside at daybreak. The flash of violet signaling the sunrise
centers our attention on the hunter and his slender greyhounds–the
embodiment of the interaction between humans and nature during
fall–and the golden shine taken on by the dewdrops heightens our
perception of the wet earth. Analogous to Beruete's light and sha-
ding techniques in *Espinos en flor. Plantío de Infantes* and *Paisaje de
invierno* (*Madrid*), in "En abril, las aguas mil" Machado employs
chiaroscuro to reproduce the look and feel of autumn:

> Lluvia y sol. Ya se obscurece
> el campo, ya se ilumina;
> allí un cerro desaparece,
> allá surge una colina.
>
> Ya son claros, ya sombríos
> los dispersos caseríos,
> los lejanos torreones.

> Hacia la sierra plomiza
> van rodando en pelotones
> nubes de guata y ceniza. (*Campos de Castilla* CV 24-33/120)

Consistent with the poem's impressionism are the internal and end rhymes, which imitate the rhythm of raindrops falling: "Son de abril las aguas mil. / Sopla el viento achubascando, / y entre nublado y nublado / hay trozos de cielo añil" (1-4/119).

In "A orillas del Duero" and "Campos de Soria," Machado follows the landscape-painting convention of situating small human and animal figures within a scene as focal points and indicators of relative size.[51] Yet the human figures in these poems serve another purpose besides directing attention: they are subjects to whom the described sensations and perceptions can be attached. We follow the travelers that Machado places in the landscape, half believing that our impressions come from these textual sources and half recognizing them as our own:

> Mediaba el mes de julio. Era un hermoso día.
> Yo, solo, por las quiebras del pedregal subía,
> buscando los recodos de sombra, lentamente.
> A trechos me paraba para enjugar mi frente
> y dar algún respiro al pecho jadeante;
> o bien, ahincado el paso, el cuerpo hacia adelante
> y hacia la mano diestra vencido y apoyado
> en un bastón, a guisa de pastoril cayado,
> trepaba por los cerros que habitan las rapaces
> aves de altura, hollando las hierbas montaraces
> de fuerte olor–romero, tomillo, salvia, espliego–.
> Sobre los agrios campos caía un sol de fuego.
> ("A orillas del Duero" 1-12/101)

In following the sensory trail left by the "I" (*yo*)–the first-person subject's impression of the redolence of the herbs and the bold colors of the hot July sunset–we come to adopt this subject's point of

---

[51] This device is recognizable from the neo-classical and baroque landscapes of Nicolas Poussin (1594-1665) and Claude Lorrain (c. 1600-1682), and the picturesque English countrysides of Constable and Thomas Gainsborough (1727-1788). It was also a facet of Barbizon and nineteenth-century Spanish painting, as exemplified by Haes, Martín Rico (1833-1908), Luis Rigalt (1814-1894), Ramón Martí Alsina (1826-1894), and Antonio Muñoz Degrain (1840-1924).

view. We lean on the "I" to gain our bearings just as the wayfarer supports his tired right hand on his staff.

The language of the traveler's account, in "A orillas del Duero," not only tells, but also shows the reader where the excursion takes place. By means of the spatial prepositions "por" and "por donde," "hacia" and "hacia adelante," "donde," and "sobre," we know exactly how to regard the landscape that is being painted before our expectant eyes–where to locate "las quiebras del pedregal," "los cerros," "las hierbas montaraces," "las serrezuelas calvas," and "desnudos peñascales." The verbs in the first thirty-five lines, "buscar," "trepar," "hollar," "divisar," "torcer," "formar," and the repeated "cruzar" likewise direct vision. Since these verbs remain strongly linked with visual perception and representation, they set the terrain around the Duero River and position the reader as a viewing subject. The subject's retelling of the journey illuminates and colors the picture of the Duero riverbanks, even as the landscape appears to delineate itself under our contemplating gaze:

> El sol va declinando. De la ciudad lejana
> me llega un armonioso tañido de campana
> –ya irán a su rosario las enlutadas viejas–.
> . . . .
> Los campos se obscurecen.
> Hacia el camino blanco está el mesón abierto
> al campo ensombrecido y al pedregal desierto. (69-76/103)

Setting the "camino blanco" side-by-side with the "campo ensombrecido" and "mesón abierto" focuses the eye, aiding the perception of other details. Each small item adds to a fragmentary track of verbal-visual references through which the significance of the landscape can be grasped. Fixing on the "enlutadas viejas" with their rosaries, for example, we associate their dress and attitude with mourning, which represent symbolically and metaphorically the spiritual grief brought on by Spain's degraded condition.

Unlike in "A orillas del Duero," in the first part of "Campos de Soria," the countryside is described in the third-person, and the traveler recedes into the landscape after an initial mention in line 10. At the same time, the presence of the wayfarer and the shepherds, who shield themselves from the cold of early spring, helps us to imagine ourselves as inside the landscape. Our natural tendency to seize on human perspectives makes them figures of subjectivity in the poem:

> Es la tierra de Soria árida y fría.
> Por las colinas y las sierras calvas,
> verdes pradillos, cerros cenicientos,
> la primavera pasa
> dejando entre las hierbas olorosas
> sus diminutas margaritas blancas.
>
> La tierra no revive, el campo sueña.
> Al empezar abril está nevada
> la espalda del Moncayo;
> el caminante lleva en su bufanda
> envueltos cuello y boca, y los pastores
> pasan cubiertos con sus luengas capas. (1-12/133)

We arrive at an impression of winter just before spring in Soria by means of the sensations that it engenders in the traveler and she-pherds; our perception is filtered through the way in which "el ca-minante lleva en su bufanda / envueltos cuello y boca" and "los pastores / pasan cubiertos con sus luengas capas." The details of the scene coalesce around their sensory experiences, from the sight of the "verdes pradillos" and "diminutas margaritas blancas" to the smell of "las hierbas olorosas." In a way comparable to "¿Eres tú, Guadarrama, viejo amigo?" sensation–and the recollection of sensa-tion–gives rise to figural language.

In the second section of "Campos de Soria," the landscape turns into an idyll. We are far from the cares of the world among the "chopos lejanos del camino," and surrounded by pleasant sen-sations (19/134). The chill has gone from the air, and spring advan-ces towards summer, turning the fields a deep green–pastures for the peaceful grazing of sheep. These are the familiar attributes of Arcadia, which Machado now calls by its name:

> Las tierras labrantías,
> como retazos de estameñas pardas,
> el huertecillo, el abejar, los trozos
> de verde obscuro en que el merino pasta,
> entre plomizos peñascales, siembran

el sueño alegre de infantil Arcadia.
En los chopos lejanos del camino,
parecen humear las yertas ramas
como un glauco vapor–las nuevas hojas–
y en las quiebras de valles y barrancas
blanquean los zarzales florecidos,
y brotan las violetas perfumadas.

("Campos de Soria" 13-24/133-34)

Machado locates the reader in the Arcadia of antiquity as well as Romantic versions of the Arcadian tradition. The landscape in "Campos de Soria" is analogous to the *locus amoenus* in Vergil's *Eclogues*, in that Machado like Vergil means this idyll to contrast with another, less natural, and therefore unhappier, life.[52] Machado's recreation of Arcadia as critique of Spain's disoriented condition at the turn of the century also parallels Vergil's questioning of the validity of pastoral existence in the context of Roman politics. Neither Vergil nor Machado turns completely away from the world in nostalgia, but rather, they use Arcadia to censure it (Alpers 354).

The Arcadian landscapes of *Campos de Castilla* recall those of William Wordsworth, for Machado's idylls just as Wordsworth's meld the observation of Nature with the transforming power of the poetic psyche. In both Machado and Wordsworth, poetry first flutters its wings with attentiveness to the sensible world and then takes flight with the imagination (Heffernan, *Wordsworth's Theory* 7, 15). *Campos de Castilla*, in a similar way to Wordsworth's *The Prelude* and *Lyrical Ballads*, remains grounded in sensory experience while acquiring the metaphorical, symbolic, and allegorical significations that only the poet can provide. Machado combines the poet's inner world with the objective and observable one, and this is why the collection is so richly pictorial, replete with little touches and broad strokes that appeal to the eye. "Somos víctimas . . . de un doble espejismo," Machado writes in the 1917 "Prólogo de *Páginas escogidas*," by which he means the problem of balancing between the real that can be sensed and the subjective:

---

[52] As Paul Alpers notes, one of Arcadia's major evocations in Vergil comes through the soldier and poet Gallus who, tormented by love lost, imagines the land where his beloved has fled as beset by war and wretched storms. The other is the juxtaposition between Tityrus's happy pastoral existence and Meliboeus's misery due to his exile from his farm (354).

> Si miramos afuera y procuramos penetrar en las cosas, nuestro mundo externo pierde en solidez, y acaba por disipársenos cuando llegamos a creer que no existe por sí, sino por nosotros. Pero, si convencidos de la íntima realidad, miramos adentro, entonces todo nos parece venir de fuera, y es nuestro mundo interior, nosotros mismos, lo que se desvanece. ¿Qué hacer entonces? Tejer el hilo que nos dan, soñar nuestro sueño, vivir; sólo así podremos obrar el milagro de la generación. ("Prólogo" 274)

He advocates negotiating between the internal and external–"tejer el hilo" that joins them in the psyche–neither retreating completely into the imagination nor depending solely on observation of the outside world.

In an essay about *Campos de Castilla* shortly after its publication, Azorín remarked on "la *objetivización* del poeta en el paisaje que describe [Machado]," by which he meant the synthesis of the objective world with the internal one of the poet (123; emphasis in the original):

> [P]aisaje y sentimientos–modalidad psicológica–son una misma cosa; el poeta se traslada al objeto descripto, y en la manera de describirlo nos da su propio espíritu. Se ha dicho que 'todo paisaje es un estado de alma' y á esta objetivización del lírico se alude en dicha frase. Al grado máximo de esa objetivización llega Antonio Machado en sus poemas. Nada de reflexiones ó incisos é intromisiones personales hay en esos versos; el poeta describe minuciosa é impersonalmente la Naturaleza. Sus paisajes no son más de una colección de detalles. Y sin embargo, en esos versos sentimos palpitar, vibrar todo el espíritu del poeta. ("Paisaje en la poesía" 123-24)

Azorín refers to the kind of exteriorization of the self known as the *paysage d'âme*–a "landscape" that reflects the poet's inner existence. However, as Geoffrey Ribbans perceptively argues, we cannot simply label *Campos de Castilla* a *paysage d'âme* and leave it at that (Introduction, *Campos de Castilla* 36-37). According to him, "Poetas de tal 'estado de alma' eran Verlaine, el Juan Ramón [Jiménez] de *Arias tristes* y el Machado de 'Del camino' y de las galerías"; different from these texts, the poems of *Campos de Castilla* are not entirely the product of the "fusión entre la emoción que provoca la naturaleza y el espíritu del poeta" (Introduction, *Campos de Castilla* 37). Rather, Machado's landscapes constitute a mix of the close study of nature and subjective interpretation. What Azorín identifies as objectification actually stems from the realism and positivism that Machado absorbed from the *ILE*, and painters such as Haes and Beruete. This "objective" is modified by Machado's impressionism, as well as a certain romanticism and symbolism.

Bound up with the realism and impressionism of Machado's landscapes, the sensory becomes coin in *Campos de Castilla's* economy of memory. In "Recuerdos," the vividness of the represented sensations brings them near to the experiences stored in the reader's psyche, in this way stimulating recollection:

> ¡Oh Soria, cuando miro los frescos naranjales
> cargados de perfume, y el campo enverdecido,
> abiertos los jazmines, maduros los trigales,
> azules las montañas y el olivar florido;
> Guadalquivir corriendo al mar entre vergeles;
> y al sol de abril los huertos colmados de azucenas,
> y los enjambres de oro, para libar sus mieles
> dispersos en los campos, huir de sus colmenas;
> yo sé la encina roja crujiendo en tus hogares,
> barriendo el cierzo helado tu campo empedernido;
> y en las sierras agrias sueño . . .
>
> (*Campos de Castilla* CXVI 1-11/173)

The poem's impressionism is heightened by synaesthesia–the melding of the landscape's bright colors with the scent of jasmine flowers and "frescos naranjales / cargados de perfume." Yet what the reader really responds to is the communication of the sensory across a temporal divide. The title of the poem, and the brief temporal and spatial indication at the end of the text ("En el tren.–Abril 1912" [174]) tell us that these evocations are not instantaneous responses, but rather impressions that have been previously sifted through memory.

Machado recapitulates the process through which memory combines with and orders present-time sensation. This concept of memory as integral to perception at any given time, as Nigel Glendinning points out, is eminently Bergsonian (69). Although whether and to what extent Bergson influenced *Campos de Castilla* (or any of the poet's other work) remains open to debate, we do know that

Machado's attended the philosopher's lectures during his 1910-1911 stay in Paris and expressed a knowledgeable interest in his theories.[53] Bergson's investigation into the way in which the pure memory of the mind intersects with the pure perception of the body led him to theorize, in *Matière et mémoire* (*Matter and Memory*; 1896), that "the continuous thread of memory" joins perception with a vision of the real: memory forges links with present-time sensory perceptions such that it becomes woven together as a whole (69). As we have seen, this idea is reflected in "Recuerdos" as well as in other poems of *Campos de Castilla*.[54] A similar image of memory as thread appears in "En estos campos de la tierra mía" (*Campos de Castilla* CXXV), in which Machado laments the inability of his recollective powers, dimmed by long years spent in Castile, to fully evoke the adored Andalusia of his childhood. The sway that his impressions of the Castilian landscape exert over him stems from their relative immediacy in comparison with his Andalusian remembrances:

> En estos campos de la tierra mía,
> y extranjero en los campos de mi tierra
> –yo tuve patria donde corre el Duero
> por entre grises peñas,
> y fantasmas de viejos encinares,
> allá en Castilla, mística y guerrera,
> Castilla la gentil, humilde y brava,
> Castilla del desdén y de la fuerza–,
> ¡oh, tierra en que nací!, cantar quisiera.
>
> ("En estos campos de la tierra mía" 1-10/185)

Nevertheless, it is the recollection of these less temporally distant countrysides that releases a torrent of sensory images from the deepest reaches of Machado's past:

---

[53] According to Segundo Serrano Poncela, Machado attended Henri Bergson's class at the College of France, taking advantage of a scholarship given to him by the *Junta de Ampliación de Estudios*, although different from Jean Bratton and Nigel Glendinning, he has the year as 1910 (*Antonio Machado* 43). In his "Autobiografía escrita en 1913", Machado himself refers to 1910 with respect to his time in Paris. In his biography of Machado entitled, *Ligero de equipaje: la vida de Antonio Machado*, Ian Gibson briefly discusses the poet's attendance of Bergson's classes in Paris (230). See also Bratton, "Antonio Machado y el lenguaje de la intuición" (8) and Glendinning, "The Philosophy of Henri Bergson in the Poetry of Antonio Machado" (50).

[54] Gary Gutting treats the crossing of pure memory and pure perception as a major concept in *Matière et mémoire*, as opposed to *L'Évolution créatrice*, in which Bergson defines pure memory and duration (64).

Tengo recuerdos de mi infancia, tengo
imágenes de luz y de palmeras,
y en una gloria de oro,
de lueñes campanarios con cigüeñas,
de ciudades con calles sin mujeres
bajo un cielo de añil, plazas desiertas
donde crecen naranjos encendidos
en sus frutas redondas y bermejas;
y en un huerto sombrío, el limonero
de ramas polvorientas
y pálidos limones amarillos,
que el agua clara de la fuente espeja,
un aroma de nardos y claveles
y un fuerte olor de albahaca y hierbabuena;
imágenes de grises olivares
bajo un tórrido sol que aturde y ciega,
y azules y dispersas serranías
con arreboles de una tarde inmensa . . . (11-28/185)[55]

In the "agua clara de la fuente" Machado recovers the image of
"grises olivares" baking in the "tórrido sol" of Andalusia's hilly
countryside. Indeed all the poet's memories have been converted
into images–"Tengo recuerdos de mi infancia, tengo / imágenes de
luz y de palmeras"–in the mirror of his psyche, and in accessing this
deep well, he releases a *mise en abyme* of recollections. He recogni-
zes the crucial role of remembrance in joining past and
present–"mas falta el hilo que el recuerdo anuda / al corazón, el an-
cla en su ribera, / o estas memorias no son alma" (29-31/185). Me-

---

[55] While Machado's diction recalls "La plaza y los naranjos encendidos" from
his earlier *Soledades* (1899-1907), here the imagery becomes starker and more som-
ber. I quote the short poem in its entirety:

La plaza y los naranjos encendidos
con sus frutas redondas y risueñas.

Tumulto de pequeños colegiales
que, al salir en desorden de la escuela,
llenan el aire de la plaza en sombra
con la algazara de sus voces nuevas.

¡Alegría infantil en los rincones
de las ciudades muertas!...
¡Y algo nuestro de ayer, que todavía
vemos vagar por estas calles viejas! (Machado, *Soledades.
Galerías. Otros poemas.* III 1-10/86)

mory's thread connects his perceptions of the world, spinning them out over time.

In "Retrato," the first poem and *ars poetica* of *Campos de Castilla*, Machado's recollection of his childhood home in Seville affirms the innocence, authenticity, and independence that are foundational to his vision of himself as a poet:

> Mi infancia son recuerdos de un patio de Sevilla,
> y un huerto claro donde madura el limonero . . .
> . . . .
>
> Hay en mis venas gotas de sangre jacobina,
> pero mi verso brota de manantial sereno;
> y, más que un hombre al uso que sabe su doctrina,
> soy, en el buen sentido de la palabra, bueno. (XCVII 1-8/99)

The identification of the self with a particular place is tied to the way in which sensory memory forms our idea of who we are. Recalling Seville relates to Machado's assertion and recovery of cherished values. Perception and sensation, however, are not only formative with respect to subjectivity, but are also a method of expressing this selfhood, as "Recuerdos" and "En estos campos de la tierra mía" would suggest. Sensation becomes the communicative vehicle for the experiences that are the rudiments of subjectivity–the means by which they can be shared.

Despite their sensory evocativeness, Machado's remembered idylls and Arcadian dreams cannot always sustain their own fiction. Decay resurfaces, in "A orillas del Duero" and "Campos de Soria," accompanied by a dramatic alteration in tone. In "A orillas del Duero," this change, from the descriptive to the lyric and elegiac, coincides with the image of the Duero River's crossing of Castile. Both the river's passage and the shift that it indicates are mirrored in the flowing appearance of the lines of *alejandrinos*:

> –Soria es una barbacana,
> hacia Aragón, que tiene la torre castellana–.
> Veía el horizonte cerrado por colinas
> obscuras, coronadas de robles y de encinas;
> desnudos peñascales, algún humilde prado
> donde el merino pace y el toro, arrodillado
> sobre la hierba, rumia; las márgenes del río

lucir sus verdes álamos al claro sol de estío,
y, silenciosamente, lejanos pasajeros,
¡tan diminutos!–carros, jinetes y arrieros–   30
cruzar el largo puente, y bajo las arcadas
de piedra ensombrecerse las aguas plateadas
del Duero.
      El Duero cruza el corazón de roble
de Iberia y de Castilla.
¡Oh, tierra triste y noble,
la de los altos llanos y yermos y roquedas,   35
de campos sin arados, regatos ni arboledas;
decrépitas ciudades, caminos sin mesones,
y atónitos palurdos sin danzas ni canciones
que aún van, abandonando el mortecino hogar,
como tus largos ríos, Castilla, hacia la mar! (21-40/102)

Parallel to the way in which "Castilla" is part for the whole of "Iberia" (and here the spiritual heart of Spain), the Duero stands in metonymic relation to Castile. Machado attributes Castilian strength and fortitude to Spain by means of the symbolic metaphor in which he compares "el corazón . . . de Iberia y de Castilla" to the solidity of an oak tree (*roble*). The juxtaposition of metaphor, a trope that depends on similarity, and metonymy, which is based on contiguity, can be likened to the adjunction of the different methods of framing in *Campos de Castilla*.[56] The descriptive and visual frame of the landscape, articulated through a first-person "I" or third-person subject, is joined and made complete by the rhetorical figure of apostrophe. At line 34, Machado switches from simply describing the land to directly addressing it, using the second-person possessive adjective to refer to its features–"*tus* largos ríos, Castilla" (my emphasis). With the apostrophe, Machado moves from evoking the natural beauty of the landscape to lamenting the cessation of its proper cultivation, which is akin to eliminating it as the source and bearer of autochthonous tradition.

    According to Jonathan Culler, apostrophe can be conceptualized on several different levels. Since it tropes the communication between orator and addressee in the lyric of antiquity, it becomes

---

[56] In "Two Aspects of Language and Two Types of Aphasic Disturbances," Roman Jakobson associates metaphor with relations of similarity and metonymy with those of contiguity (129-33).

the invocation of invocation. Apostrophe is an intensifier, as well as the mark of passion and the will to render the universe a world of sentient forces, and it produces the poet's voice as prophetic and transcendent of time.[57] In *Campos de Castilla*, apostrophe invokes the exhortation that lies just behind Machado's description of the countryside, metapoetically referring to the persuasion that is his purpose. His address of the landscape, which treats it as if it were capable of response, is suggestive of the way in which lyric invocation cultivates and convinces the audience. Machado thus emphasizes that he is interpellating his readers–calling on them in order to make them answer for Spain's condition. The series of rhetorical questions that follow the apostrophe, in "A orillas del Duero," demand the commitment that comes with a reply:

> Castilla miserable, ayer dominadora,
> envuelta en sus andrajos desprecia cuanto ignora.
> ¿Espera, duerme o sueña? ¿La sangre derramada
> recuerda, cuando tuvo la fiebre de la espada?
> Todo se mueve, fluye, discurre, corre o gira;
> cambian la mar y el monte y el ojo que los mira. (41-46/102)

Machado's likening of Castile's passive state to his readers' is designed to lead them to doubt the morality of inaction in the face of crisis. He means the audience to extend his portrait of inertia to their own collective unresponsiveness:

> Filósofos nutridos de sopa de convento
> contemplan impasibles el amplio firmamento;
> y si les llega en sueños, como un rumor distante,
> clamor de mercaderes de muelles de Levante,
> no acudirán siquiera a preguntar ¿qué pasa?
> Y ya la guerra ha abierto las puertas de su casa.
>
> Castilla miserable, ayer dominadora,
> envuelta en sus harapos desprecia cuanto ignora. (61-68/103)

---

[57] For Jonathan Culler, since apostrophe's freeing of inanimate objects from the confines of their material condition parallels the ability of the poet's voice to survive beyond time and death, the reader's surrender to apostrophe translates into acceptance of each of these fictions (145, 149, 152-54). The transcendence of the poet's voice through apostrophe can also be compared to the way in which a bard's lyrics, by means of variation, revive and renew national tradition. As Culler puts it, apostrophe constitutes the "figure of vocation"; in/vocation becomes vocation in a pun on the vocative (in the sense of direct address) and vocation (142).

The "Filósofos nutridos de sopa de convento" dismiss pressing matters as a worldly "rumor distante"–distractions from seemingly spiritual concerns that mask disengagement.

Machado's use of the plural informal *vosotros* form in the apostrophes of sections seven through nine of "Campos de Soria" imbues his clarion call with the urgency of familiarity. His selection of *vosotros* also effectively shifts the identity of the addressee from the countryside to his readers, thus redirecting his plea for national renewal from the land to all who dwell in it. In this way, apostrophe's attribution of agency to Castile–the calling out of subjectivity from the land–serves to implicate Machado's readers as a community in their country's malaise. Since to accept this enmeshment means to assume responsibility for Spain's regeneration, the apostrophe can be understood as generating the engaged collectivity that he desires. Machado then makes an express turn, at line 141, from directing himself to the countryside to addressing its people:

> ¡Oh, sí, conmigo vais, campos de Soria,
> tardes tranquilas, montes de violeta,
> alamedas del río, verde sueño
> del suelo gris y de la parda tierra,
> agria melancolía
> de la ciudad decrépita,
> me habéis llegado al alma,
> ¿o estabais en el fondo de ella?
> ¡Gentes del alto llano numantino   141
> que a Dios guardáis como cristianas viejas,
> que al sol de España os llene
> de alegría, de luz y de riqueza! ("Campos de Soria" 133-44/138)

Machado interpellates his readers by implicitly comparing them, just as the "Gentes del alto llano numantino" with the "cristianas viejas," who, from the time of the Reconquest, came to constitute the nation's bedrock in the popular imagination. In so doing, he exhorts his readers' active participation in Spain's rebuilding.

Remembrance constitutes the first step towards national renascence. Apostrophe's engraving of the land's natural features in memory becomes a means of recovering the authentic identity that has been obscured by the passage of time. Machado's catalogue of the countryside's attributes–a way of simultaneously preserving and prompting memory–opens a path to a return to origins:

¡Colinas plateadas,
grises alcores, cárdenas roquedas
por donde traza el Duero
su curva de ballesta
en torno a Soria, obscuros encinares,
ariscos pedregales, calvas sierras,
caminos blancos y álamos del río,
tardes de Soria, mística y guerrera,
hoy siento por vosotros, en el fondo
del corazón, tristeza,
tristeza que es amor! ¡Campos de Soria
donde parece que las rocas sueñan,
conmigo vais! ¡Colinas plateadas,
grises alcores, cárdenas roquedas!...
("Campos de Soria" 99-112/137)

Machado maps Castile's terrain for posterity, tracing the "colinas plateadas" and "cárdenas roquedas" like the river that shaped them with its "curva de ballesta." The poet's recollection imbues the landscape's rocks with so much life that they seem to dream as he does of yesterday–the time of Castile's at once spiritual and bellicose strength. Setting the clock back to this idealized anterior moment immortalizes it for future generations:

¡Álamos del amor que tuvisteis
de ruiseñores vuestras ramas llenas;
álamos que seréis mañana liras
del viento perfumado en primavera;
álamos del amor cerca del agua
que corre y pasa y sueña,
álamos de las márgenes del Duero,
conmigo vais, mi corazón os lleva! (125-32/138)

Poplars become as poets' lyres, turning sensory impressions of the landscape–"el sonido de [las] hojas secas" and "el son del agua, cuando el viento sopla"–into the music of lyric; they are Machado's instrument for preserving the past in his song (120-21/138). The poet's lyric remembrance and the collective memory that it engenders constitute the most perfect expressions of *casticismo*:

> He vuelto a ver los álamos dorados,
> álamos del camino en la ribera
> del Duero, entre San Polo y San Saturio,
> tras las murallas viejas
> de Soria–barbacana
> hacia Aragón, en castellana tierra.
> Estos chopos del río, que acompañan
> con el sonido de sus hojas secas
> el son del agua, cuando el viento sopla,
> tienen en sus cortezas
> grabadas iniciales que son nombres
> de enamorados, cifras que son fechas. (113-24/137-38)

The sights and sounds of the landscape return us to the time of "las murallas viejas / de Soria" and, conversely, revisiting the poplars on the banks of the Duero through memory restores them to the present moment. Carved into the bark of the trees and written on the page we read the legend of Machado's prescript for national regeneration: recollection will transform the landscape into a once and future Arcadia.

Framing the landscape, in *Campos de Castilla*, constitutes Machado's way of convincing the reader to adopt his regenerationist perspective on Spain's turn-of-the-century circumstance. His placement of detail and configuration of the countryside, influenced by realist and impressionist landscape painting, are meant to guide the eye and draw the reader into the representation. In response to these "visual" cues, Machado expects the reader to identify with the landscape that he depicts, which stands for Spain and its essential character. This process of recognition is also predicated on the way in which his use of striking detail and representation of the sensory jog memory. The awakening of the reader's individual sensory memory, combined with persuasion on the level of rhetorical figure, above all in the form of apostrophe, becomes productive of common remembrance–remembrance of an idealized past rooted in the countryside.

Machado's positing of landscape as the collective, and his location of subjectivity and identity in the land would find itself, not much later than the publication of *Campos de Castilla*, questioned by the first Spanish avant-garde. However Machado, it should be emphasized, counters this questioning by interrogating the poetics and aesthetics of the avant-garde. He remains deeply skeptical of vanguard poetry's conceptual and intellectual thrust–the reason for its reliance on metaphor–which in his view displaces the expressive subjectivity and emotion proper to lyric.[58] Such vanguard movements as *Ultraísmo* would detach the subject from the space of representation, as well as separating place from its geographic and cultural origins. These tactics turn the means and the consequences of Machado's framing–locating the reader in the landscape as collective space–upside down. In uprooting the subject, and by transforming the representation of perception so as to interrupt recollection, the avant-garde would loosen ties to *castizo* Spain, throwing open its borders to Europe and the cosmopolitan.

---

[58] Regarding Machado's questioning of the avant-garde, see his "Sobre el libro *Colección* del poeta andaluz José Moreno Villa." Despite the debates between them, Machado was generally respected by the avant-garde as a literary patriarch. To take an example, Rafael Cansinos-Assens's portrait of Machado in *La nueva literatura* honors his contribution to Spanish poetry (139-54).

CHAPTER 2

MAPPING THE SPANISH AVANT-GARDE: GUILLERMO DE TORRE AND *ULTRAÍSMO*

A signal aspect of the transition from Antonio Machado's *Campos de Castilla* to the first Spanish avant-garde is the changing significance of place and space, and the way in which this significance is determined by the representation of perspective and perception.[1] The vanguard *Ultraísmo* movement's reconfiguring of perspective and perception on the textual level becomes a means of both transcending the boundaries of Machado's collective landscape and throwing Spain's borders open.[2] Guillermo de Torre

---

[1] The first Spanish avant-garde grew and flourished between 1909, the year in which Ramón Gómez de la Serna published his translation of F. T. Marinetti's "Manifesto of Futurism" in the journal *Prometeo*, and 1925, with the appearance of José Ortega y Gasset's *La deshumanización del arte* and Guillermo de Torre's *Literaturas europeas de vanguardia*. With the dictatorship of Miguel Primo de Rivera, beginning in September of 1923, the liberal spirit that made possible the development of the vanguard in Spain diminished.

[2] The *Ultraísmo* movement is generally considered to have begun in 1918 and ended in 1925–a termination point marked by the publication of Torre's *Literaturas europeas de vanguardia*. Vicente Huidobro's visit to Madrid and his participation in Rafael Cansinos-Assens's *tertulia* at Café Colonial contributed to *Ultraísmo's* start. The publication of the first Ultra manifesto came out of the meeting of Huidobro and Cansinos's group (Bonet 605; Videla, "El Ultraísmo" 25-40). With respect to the birth of *Ultraísmo*, see Manuel de la Peña's 1925 account, *El ultraísmo en España*. See also José María Barrera López's *El Ultraísmo de Sevilla*; José Luis Bernal's *El Ultraísmo. ¿Historia de un fracaso?*; José Luis Falcó's *El Ultraísmo: teoría, y práctica poética*; Torre's *Ultraísmo, existencialismo y objetivismo en literatura*; and Gloria Videla's *El Ultraísmo: estudios sobre movimientos poéticos de vanguardia en España*.

Ultraísmo's loose association of members included (at one time or another between 1918 and 1925): Torre; Xavier Bóveda (1898-1963); Rogelio Buendía

89

(1900-1971)–poet, critic, and *Ultraísmo's* self-appointed leader–replaces *Campos de Castilla's* contemplative perception with a perceptual simultaneity whose rapid perspectival shifts destabilize the sense of belonging that Machado's linkage of subjectivity and place creates. The perceptual and perspectival freedom that Torre makes the basic paradigm of his work at once undermines the premises behind Machado's collective *castizo* landscape and establishes a vision for cosmopolitan exchange.

Torre bears the first Spanish avant-garde's standard of transformative renewal. His poetry volume *Hélices* was published in 1923–a time when the memory of World War I was still fresh in European collective consciousness.[3] Yet in the volume Torre really pays homage not to World War I, but to the positive effect that the war had on Spain's growth: the expansion of industry and trade, and the influx into the country of artists, writers, and musicians who wished to escape the hostilities. "Dehiscencia," the first poem in *Hélices*, portrays the renaissance that came after the Great War.[4] From "De-

---

(1891-1969); Rafael Cansinos-Assens (1883-1964); José de Ciria y Escalante (1903-1924); César Comet; Antonio M. Cubrero; Gerardo Diego (1896-1987); Pedro Garfías (1901-1967); César González-Ruano (1903-1965); Jaime Ibarra; Juan Larrea (1895-1980); Rafael Lasso de la Vega (1890-1959); Ernesto López Parra; Tomás Luque; Eugenio Montes (1897-1982); Luis Mosquera (1890-?); Eduardo de Ontañón (1903-1989); Manuel de la Peña; Miguel Pérez Ferrero (1905-1978); Ramón Prieto y Romero (?-1930); Eliodoro Puche (1885-1964); the brothers Francisco Rello (1904-1921) and Guillermo Rello (?-?); Vicente Risco (1884-1963); Humberto Rivas; José Rivas Panedas (1893-1944); José María Romero (1893-1936); Miguel Romero Martínez (1888-1957); Lucía Sánchez Saornil (who wrote under the pseudonym Luciano San-Saor [1895-1970]); Adriano del Valle (1895-1957); and Isaac del Vando-Villar (1890-1963) (Bonet 605). The dates of birth and death are unknown for César Comet, Antonio M. Cubrero, Jaime Ibarra, Ernesto López Parra, Tomás Luque, Manuel de la Peña, and Humberto Rivas. Rafael Cansinos-Assens should be considered one of the fathers of *Ultraísmo* (Bonet 136). Juan Manuel Bonet rightly includes Gerardo Diego and Juan Larrea in his list of Ultra-affiliated poets. However, I consider Diego and Larrea to be far too idiosyncratic to be identified fully with any one movement.
    [3] Although Spain remained neutral during World War I, there were bitter debates between those that supported the Allies (*aliadófilos*) and the partisans of the Central Powers (*germanófilos*).
    [4] I consulted both the original 1923 version of *Hélices* and the 2000 facsimile edition. References will be to the 2000 edition. In the table of contents prefacing the ten-part *Hélices*, Torre notes that he wrote "Dehiscencia" between 1918 and 1919; it therefore stands to reason that the Great War, which ended with the November 11, 1918 armistice, would constitute a referent, even though Spain remained neutral during the clash of arms. Torre's "Sumario" for *Hélices* is as follows:

hiscencia's" war-torn landscape emerges an open "espacio opaco"–a *tabula rasa* on which the future is to be written:

> Verticilo iridiscente de la roja rosa cósmica.
> Su trémula corola irradia estelarmente un haz de tensos filamentos
>   bermejos como reóforos eréctiles.
> Y en sus pétalos vibrátiles, truncos bajo el aura asolatriz de la
>   guerra,
> resaltan vívidas estrías sangrantes.
> ¡Mágica constelación alucinante en la convexa dermis celeste!
>
> Las llamaradas ignívomas, que ascendían desde los agros bélicos,
> –¡oh la gleba violada acerbamente!–
> se han extinguido en el espacio opaco.
> Y hay un rojo crepitar final de estrellas incendiadas,
> prendidas en el boscaje multifónico.
> Mientras, espigas de paz frutecen en los lagos de sangre.
>
> (lines 1-11/11)[5]

The rapturous tone and long, expressive lines of "Dehiscencia" evoke the post-war renascence as well as the exuberance of the first Spanish avant-garde. From the "excrecencias trágicas–piras de cadáveres, sangre y llantos," Torre creates a blooming landscape–a springtime of unlimited possibility into which ruins "desaparecen sordamente ante un / magno arco iris resurrecto" (12-13/11). The trope of botanical reproduction–"la insólita fecundación"–represents the flowering not only of peace but also of art and literature–"Los estambres del terráqueo ovario se abren núbilmente en sus anteras recogiendo la fóvila seminal, voluptuosamente... / Y después de la introyección presagiadora adviene un dinámico éxtasis henchido y au-

---

Versiculario Ultraísta (1918-1919)
Trayectorias (1919-1920)
Bellezas de hoy (1919-1920)
Palabras en libertad (1919)
Puzzles (1920)
Inauguraciones (1920-1921)
Kaleidoscopio (1922)
Poemas fotogénicos (1921-1922)
Frisos (1920-1921)
Hai-Kais (1920-1921) (7)

[5] A *reóforo* ("rheophore") is a current-conducting wire. *Ignívomo/a*, or ignivomous in English, means "fire-spewing" ("Rheophore"; "Ignivomous").

gural" (21, 28-29/11). "Reóforos eréctiles" and "pétalos vibrátiles" stimulate civilization's regrowth, which culminates in the reaping of "espigas de paz" (2-3, 11/11). Torre's poetic sowing bears an abundant harvest; its ripe fruit attests to the artistic blossoming brought about by war-induced modernization and migration, as well as by the reconstruction that followed the grand-scale conflict.

The flames of the avant-garde were fanned by international figures and, in response to their presence in Spain, a sense of openness to outside influences came to characterize *Ultraísmo*.[6] Torre in particular became a cottage industry of cosmopolitanism. He formed highly productive relationships with the Parisian painters and founders of *Simultaneisme* Robert Delaunay (1885-1941) and Sonia Delaunay-Terk (1885-1979), for instance, during their residence in Spain and Portugal (1914-1920).[7] His extensive list of correspondents included, in addition to the Delaunays: French theorist and cinéaste Jean Epstein (1897-1953); the Chilean poet and founder of the *Creacionismo* movement, Vicente Huidobro (1893-1948); Fernand Louis Berckelaers; Polish poet Tadeusz Peiper; French author and art critic Jean Cassou; Dominique Braga; the French modernist Paul Morand; Belgian author Paul Dermée; Italian Futurist poet Mario Dessy; and the French authors Nicolas Beauduin and Philippe Soupault.[8] As a consequence of the contacts that he made,

---

[6] To World War I, we can add the 1917 Russian Revolution as one of the causes of the Spanish cultural scene's internationalization.

[7] Blaise Cendrars and Guillaume Apollinaire founded the *Simultaneisme* movement along with Robert and Sonia Delaunay. The Delaunays' international contacts ranged from the Portuguese Futurists associated with the journal *Orpheu* to the Russian vanguard and the Cubists. They also included members of the Barcelona art world and the German *Der Blaue Reiter* group. Delaunay-Terk was herself cosmopolitan: of Ukrainian-Jewish extraction, she was adopted as a small child by relatives who were wealthy Saint-Petersburg estate-holders. As a young woman, she married first the German author, art collector, dealer, and critic Wilhelm Uhde, then the French Delaunay.

[8] Torre corresponded with the Delaunays from 1920 to 1937. The other members of the international vanguard to whom I refer are: Vicente Huidobro (1893-1948); Fernand Louis Berckelaers (pseudonym Michel Seuphor [1901-1999]), who was the editor, with Jozef Peeters, of the Belgian journal *Het Overzicht. Half-Maandelijks Tijdschrift: Kunst, Letteren, Mensheid* (1921-1925); Tadeusz Peiper (1891-1969); Jean Cassou (1897-1986); Dominique Braga; Paul Morand (1888-1976); Paul Dermée (1886-1951), editor of *L'Esprit Nouveau, Revue Internationale D'Esthétique* (1920-1925); Mario Dessy, Italian Futurist poet and editor of the Milan *Poesia, Rassegna Internazionale*; Nicolas Beauduin (d. 1960); and Philippe Soupault (1897-1990), who edited the journal *Littérature* (1919-1924) alongside André Breton and

Torre became well-versed in the avant-garde movements of Europe and the Americas.[9] Torre's role as *Ultraísmo's* theorist informs the pedagogical character of *Hélices* and *Literaturas europeas de vanguardia*, his 1925 retrospective of the first Spanish avant-garde. He intends these two works as Spain's Baedeker guides to the vanguard, illustrating such movements as *Creacionismo*, Cubism, Dada, *Simultaneisme*, and Italian Futurism, as well as other important influences like the American poet Walt Whitman (1819-1892), Jorge Luis Borges (1899-1986), Stéphane Mallarmé (1842-1898), and cinema.

One of primary purposes of *Hélices* was to import major modernist and avant-garde movements into Spain. Torre organizes each of *Hélices's* ten sections around particular movements, authors, and themes. Section 1, "Versiculario ultraísta," which begins with an epigraph from Whitman, suggests World War I and introduces the notion of a European and Spanish renascence through the avant-garde. Torre prefaces Section 2, "Trayectorias," with epigraphs from Arthur Rimbaud (1854-1891) and Blaise Cendrars (1887-1961); this section of the volume represents the modern psyche's hyperbolic perception of the city. He begins Section 3, "Bellezas de hoy," with his own words: "Los motores suenan mejor que endecasílabos," which nod to F. T. Marinetti's (1876-1944) "Manifesto of Futurism," in which the Italian Futurist writes, "We affirm that the world's magnificence has been enriched by a new beauty: the beauty of speed. A racing car whose hood is adorned with great pipes, like serpents of explosive breath–a roaring car that seems to

---

Louis Aragon. My description of Torre's correspondence is based on original archival research done at the *Biblioteca Nacional de España*, Madrid. It is important to note that Carlos García has published a number of editions of Guillermo de Torre's correspondence, among which are the following: *Correspondencia Juan Ramón Jiménez/Guillermo de Torre, 1920-1956*; *Correspondencia Rafael Cansinos Assens/Guillermo de Torre: 1916-1955*; *Escribidores y náufragos: correspondencia Ramón Gómez de la Serna-Guillermo de Torre, 1916-1963*; *Federico García Lorca-Guillermo de Torre: correspondencia y amistad*; *Las letras y la amistad: correspondencia (1920-1958), Alfonso Reyes-Guillermo de Torre*; and *Vicente Huidobro: epistolario: correspondencia con Gerardo Diego, Juan Larrea y Guillermo de Torre, 1918-1947*. I am indebted to Bonet's extensive *Diccionario de las vanguardias en España (1907-1936)* for biographical data relating to Latin-American vanguard figures, Robert Delaunay and Sonia Delaunay-Terk, and the Spanish and Catalan avant-gardes.

[9] In *Literaturas europeas de vanguardia*, Torre discusses art and literature from North and Latin America, including work by Huidobro, Whitman, Jorge Luis Borges, Norah Borges, Barradas, and the international cinema.

ride on grapeshot is more beautiful than the *Victory of Samothrace*" (*Hélices* 32; Marinetti 251). In "Bellezas de hoy," influences as diverse as French *Simultaneisme*, Borges, and Dadaism shape Torre's evocation of simultaneous perception. The fourth section, "Palabras en libertad" takes inspiration from Italian Futurism and Marinetti's "parole in libertà." Section 5, "Puzzles," looks at the polyglot character of the city, as well as its effect on the subject and the subject's perception. Section 6, "Inauguraciones," preceded by an epigraph from Guillaume Apollinaire's (1880-1918) *Calligrammes*, focuses on the visual arrangement of poetic lines on the page in the avant-garde–as for example in Huidobro. An epigraph from the Chilean poet's 1918 volume, *Ecuatorial*, starts "Pleamar," one of the poems in this part of the volume. In the seventh section, "Kaleidoscopio," Torre experiments with different methods of representing perception. Section 8 centers on the ideas and techniques introduced by Epstein. In Section 9, entitled "Frisos," Torre applies the concepts explored in the preceding sections of *Hélices* to the landscape tradition. In the tenth and final section, "Hai-Kais (Occidentales)," he looks at the connection between perceptual simultaneity and form through the lens of Ramón Gómez de la Serna's *Greguerías* (1917). Gómez de la Serna's (1888-1963) haiku-like *greguerías* at once bring a sense of the absurd and the sublime to the juxtaposition of perceptions that the city produces in the minds of its dwellers. The original cover of *Hélices* was designed by Uruguayan artist Rafael Barradas (1890-1929), who invented "Vibracionismo," an examination of perceptual simultaneity in relation to urban life.[10] The Spanish painter Daniel Vázquez Díaz (1882-1969) and Norah Borges (1901-1998), Torre's future wife and the sister of Jorge Luis Borges, contributed the majority of the illustrations, many of which use the wood-block printing technique known as *xilografía*.

The conception of *Ultraísmo's* ideal poet and critic, which Torre articulates in *Literaturas europeas de vanguardia*, at once reflects the cosmopolitanism of *Ultraísmo* and the avant-garde's typically rebellious posture.[11] He describes the movement as a "bloque

---

[10] Regarding Barradas and *Vibracionismo*, see Torre, *Literaturas europeas de vanguardia* (83).

[11] Emilia de Zuleta notes that, "El nuevo espíritu cosmopolita fue un fenómeno observado en las *Literaturas europeas de vanguardia*" (26).

colectivo" primed to "ejercer una acción conjunta y a mantener un estado de espíritu radical y renovador" (108). To this end, Torre gives the critic aligned with *Ultraísmo* the task of validating the movement's efforts at revolutionary inventiveness: "La crítica nueva ha de ser esencialmente afirmativa. La crítica de las tendencias vanguardistas europeas, analizadas en este libro, tiene como primordial una misión constructora" (35). It is this affirmative spirit of building that governs the innovation and cosmopolitanism of *Ultraísmo.*

Torre's internationalist attitude leads him to create a synthetic paradigm for his poetry. Integral to this constructivism are his reshaping of perspective and representation of perception, a crucial motive for which is the remapping of Spain relative to the European avant-garde:

> El Ultraísmo, por el momento–escribíamos en 1920,–no marca una hermética escuela sectaria ni una dirección estrictamente unilateral, como otros movimientos de vanguardia. Por el contrario, aspira a condensar en su haz genérico una pluralidad de direcciones entrecruzadas. De ahí que el *Vltra* [*Ultraísmo*] se nos presente como el vértice de fusión potente a donde afluyen todas las pugnaces tendencias estéticas mundiales de vanguardia, que hoy disparan sus intenciones innovadoras más allá de los territorios mentalmente capturados. (*Literaturas europeas* 75)

Torre locates the "Ultra" critic in the same lofty position as the subject in "Dehiscencia," who gazes down at the regenerating landscape: "La crítica identificada amorosamente con el sujeto, puede elevarse, desde su primitiva zona especuladora, a un plano de creación" (35). In designing the aerial perspectives in his work, he takes into account the way in which the subject's standpoint affects subjectivity and identity. Imagine, for example, the view from an airplane: distances become truncated and diverse landscapes are juxtaposed. The aerial perspective allows both eye and "I" (or subject) to "see" and therefore to "move" across borders. Torre's strategy contrasts with that of Machado, whose representation of perspective and perception in *Campos de Castilla* serves to situate the subject squarely in Spanish terrain. The way in which Torre's panoramas promote the subject's free movement is analogous to issuing the Spanish avant-garde a passport to cosmopolitan Europe:

> Pues uno de nuestros objetivos esenciales, en el espacio y en el
> tiempo, es llenar esa laguna de distanciación que siempre ha ais-
> lado a España haciéndola marchar en sus últimas evoluciones
> literarias extemporáneamente y a la zaga del movimiento mundi-
> al. (*Literaturas europeas* 75)

Torre calls for the poets of *Ultraísmo* to become "conscientes y
capaces de recoger desde España, como antenas sensibles, las corri-
entes líricas directrices del nuevo estado de inteligencia que va
cristalizando en todo el orbe intelectual" (*Literaturas europeas* 110).
In "Manifiesto vertical ultraísta" (1920), the Ultra poet takes on the
radio antenna's function of receiving, synthesizing, and retransmit-
ting information across national boundaries:

> VERTICAL: He ahí mi actitud literaria peculiarmente ultraísta:
> E VERTICAL: He ahí el erecto símbolo y la antena radiotele-
> R gráfica que irradia verbalismos sintéticos y conmociones de
>   última hora: VERTICAL: He ahí la línea del meridiano estético
> T que regula el horario de los intelectuales avanzados.
>   Jóvenes poetas: camaradas: erguíos verticalmente, firme-
> I mente erectos como antenas soñeras a bordo del trasatlántico ju-
> C venil en el océano ultraísta. ¿No percibís ya una metarrytmiza-
> A ción lírica y cómo nuestro proyector irradia hasta la región hi-
>   perespacial henchida de gases innovadores a una presión
> L sideral?
> VERTICAL: Actitud ultraísta: Antena polar: Poma astral: Y velivo-
> lantes, en torno a la abstracción perpendicular, una escuadrilla avió-
> nica de espíritus porveniristas que exultan impávidos en su tengen-
> cialidad solar. ("Manifiesto vertical")

Torre maintains a special interest in towers for the perspective that
they provide. In the poem "Torre Eiffel" (*Hélices*), Torre makes an
elaborate pun on his surname and the Tower, as well as referring to
the Parisian avant-garde by way of Robert Delaunay, to whom the
text is dedicated.[12] The *ex libris* illustration at the end of *Hélices*,

---

[12] Torre refers indirectly to the Eiffel Tower in the phrase "simultaneísmo
nunista." "Nunista" signifies what he calls "el Nunismo" of Pierre Albert-Birot, the
definition of which Torre gives in *Literaturas europeas de vanguardia*: "El nunismo,
sin llegar al paroxismo futurista, especula con los nuevos símbolos eléctricos y
maquinísticos del mundo irradiante y moderno. Y sin ambicionar, como el cubis-
mo, la cuadratura poemática, sostiene la pureza lírica de la obra cuyo fin está en sí

designed by Norah Borges (1901-1998), features a man wielding a
bow and arrow atop a tower; here Borges literalizes Torre's two last
names, *Torre y Ballesteros*, in the combined visual image of a tower
and crossbowman.

Torre's diction in "Manifiesto vertical ultraísta" and "Torre Eif-
fel" recalls radiotelegraphic transmission, of which the Eiffel Tower
was at the time emblematic. The Parisian tower became one of the
first structures to possess a radio antenna: it commenced its history
as a transmitter in 1904, only nine years after Guglielmo Marconi's
first successful experiment with telegraphy (Campbell xi, xiv, 4-7).
Beyond its communicative potential, wireless technology represents
the transformation of the modern subject's relationship with the ex-
ternal world; the continuous sensing activity of the radio antenna is
paradigmatic of a fine-tuned, far-reaching, and unceasing percep-
tion. In telegraphy, the *marconista*, or transcriber of coded data, be-
comes a site of synthesis between the human and machine (Camp-
bell 13). Torre's poet-antenna–a hybrid figure who takes on the
instrumental functions normally associated with radiotelegraphy's
mechanical devices–picks up signals from all corners of the globe,
resending them, in a "metarrytmización lírica," out to the world.
The radiotelegraphic tower constitutes a double metaphor for the
perspective gained from scaling heights and the upsurge in percep-
tual capability that accompanies modern technology. Torre's trans-
formation of perspective and the way in which it leads to perceptual
simultaneity, endowing the subject with the power to cross interna-
tional borders, constitutes his constructive paradigm for the avant-
garde poetic text. I term this paradigm *perceptual cosmopolitanism.*

The title of *Hélices*, which translates to English as "helixes" and
"propellers," expresses the workings of perceptual cosmopoli-
tanism: the text's construction becomes as a propeller, elevating
perspective and producing favorable circumstances for the forma-
tion of simultaneous perceptions. Just as a Cubist still life is not,
strictly speaking, "still," but instead a juxtaposition of perspectives
that at once depicts and stimulates optical comparison, Torre maps
textual landscapes that mirror the adjustable quality of the modern

---

misma, en la creación de una belleza autónoma y de una emoción automática,
allende la realidad objetiva y la simulación verbal" (203). Torre identifies Robert
Delaunay with the *Tour Eiffel* since it was emblematic of *Simultaneisme* as well as a
frequent subject of Delaunay's paintings.

eye (Krauss, *Picasso Papers*).[13] Torre's not-so-still lifes constitute a tactical shift from locating "I" and eye in the landscape of memory's bounded territory to deterritorializing the subject and its perception. "Un vuelo de miradas acribilla la noche // Cada relámpago / es un ojo de Argos / El viento nos golpea con sus puños": if Cubism–the modern version of the myth of Argus–and Torre's Cubist-inspired construction of perspective liberate "I" and eye by means of simultaneity, then certainly the subject connected with this free-wheeling perception must also gain autonomy ("Pararrayos," *Hélices* 1-4/47).[14] Jonathan Crary argues that with the rise of mass capitalism in the nineteenth century comes a "visual nihilism," an abstraction of vision that supposes an "autonomous perception severed from any external referent" (14). His idea has two major implications: first, the capitalist system distances psychic experience from the occurrences of daily life; and second, this same order relieves the eye from the burden of images that originate in *a priori* philosophical concepts. Torre's renovation of perspective and perception therefore enables him to break with the constructs behind Machado's *Campos de Castilla*.

Torre reverses the perceptual ordering that would restrict the subject's mobility, first by raising the eye above the textual landscape, and subsequently by eliminating all limitations on vision's range. In the first strophe of "Al aterrizar," in which Torre lifts the subject to a great height, the "I" ecstatically regards its own perceptual encounter with the images spread out below its gaze:

> Y he contemplado ávidamente, en un eufórico espasmo visual,
>   un hermoso panorama porvenirista,
> espejado en la consciente lámina de tu hélice,
> ¡oh velivolo augural!,
> que al retorno de tu raid extratelúrico, aterrizaste, trépido y
>   aleteante, en mi enhiesto hangar craneal... (*Hélices* 1-4/13)

There is a transition from the first to the third person in the second strophe, as the subject takes up its sky-high standpoint. This distancing of the subject from the textual landscape opens the "vís-

---

[13] See also Rosalind E. Krauss, ed. *October: The Second Decade, 1986-1996.*
[14] Argus was a monster with one hundred eyes in his head. The goddess Juno charged Argus with a strict watch on Io, with whom her husband, the god Jupiter, had been flirting.

ceras centrales" of the cityscape to view, generating a series of con-
trapositions akin to an aerial panorama or Cubist painting:

> La ciudad multánime abre sus vísceras centrales y prolonga sus
> miembros periféricos, tentacularmente.
> La infinitud de edificios cristalinos–pueblos verticales–cupulados
> de estaciones agarófilas,
> seccionan transversalmente el dinamismo convulsivo de las claras
> avenidas rectilíneas.
> En su estuario vorticista naufragan las miradas tradicionales.
> Y el fluir de la marea humana polirrítmica se yuxtapone al estridor
> maquinístico y al gesticular telegráfico.
> Se extravasan osmóticamente las percepciones sensoriales.
>
> (5-10/13)

Torre simultaneously dislocates the subject from the city, and syn-
thesizes the subject and the urban landscape in the images pro-
duced by perception.

In a similar way as in "Al aterrizar," in "Dehiscencia" a bird's-
eye perspective increases the force and reach of the subject's per-
ception:

> En el alba inmatura, emergida de las nébulas boreales,
> se irisan luminarias hendidoras de perspectivas virgíneas.
> ¡Los nacientes campos novidimensionales concentran el irradiante
> vértigo cinemático!
> ¡Energéticas auras multanimistas riman con las sístoles superatri-
> ces!
> ¡Todo se nimba, primigeniamente, de luces helicoidales y rayos
> intelectivos!
> El dilatado tegumento espacial distiende sus repliegues y exhala
> fragancias luminosas.
> ¡Y el Poeta al ascender en el horizonte, con ímpetu icariano,
> se lanza dardeante, entre las brumas rarificadas,
> a todos los vórtices sugeridores!... (30-38/12)

The subject's Icarian vision liberates its senses to form wild impres-
sions–extreme poetic images–in an "irradiante vértigo cinemático."
Its disjointed yet associative perception thus becomes the condition
for its uprooting from any historical or geographical situation that
may be posited as real. Torre's refusal to make the subject identify
with the landscape changes the philosophical and poetic grounding

of it in Machado's Castile: the blending of the subject and the external world in perception isolates the subject within its perceptual apparatus yet gives it total liberty to search out unmarked terrain.

Torre prefaces the initial "Versiculario ultraísta" section of *Hélices* with an epigraph from Walt Whitman's *Leaves of Grass*, staking his claim on Whitman's elevation of the poet's status and expansion of poetic subjectivity.[15] Dedicated to Whitman, "Canto dinámico" sings of the fresh relationship that Torre, like the American poet, envisions between the subject and the textual landscape:

> ¡Viajar! ¡Fluir! ¡Tránsito! ¡Ascensión!
> 'Dame la mano Walt Whitman'–como dice el Atlante, el buen
>   poeta gris, en su emocionante 'Saludo Mundial'–.
> ¡Oh, la incitante trayectoria perimundial!
>
> Mi gran anhelo tensamente dinámico:
> Seccionar el Orbe innúmero con mi cuerpo foliáceo, dionysiaca-
>   mente poseso.
> Avanzar con febriscencia horadante en un estuario poliédrico,
>   escoltado por la tromba astral.
> Sostener un circuito perenne de múltiple expansibilidad.
> Posar mis tarsos miriápodos en la gleba transmutativa y plural.
> Y alcanzar la transfusión cinética en el espasmo ascendente, al
>   perforar el tegmen hialino de las nubes sonámbulas. (*Hélices*
>   1-9/15)[16]

In "Song of Myself" (*Leaves of Grass*; 1855), the subject's polymorphic perception of the landscape is in tune with the expansive free-

---

[15] The epigraph to "Versiculario ultraísta" reads as follows: "'Las miriadas silenciosas / Los océanos silenciosos donde confluyen los ríos / Las innumerables entidades libres y distintas / Las verdaderas realidades son las imágenes'–Walt Whitman: *Leaves of Grass*" (10). The quotation comes from the poem "Eidólons," which Whitman places in the "Inscriptions" part of *Leaves of Grass*. In the original English, the lines that Torre chooses for the epigraph are: "The noiseless myriads, / The infinite oceans where the rivers empty, / The separate countless free identities, like eyesight, / The true realities, eidólons" (Whitman 53-56/42).

[16] I would define the difficult phrases "mi cuerpo foliáceo," "tarsos miriápodos," and "tegmen hialino" roughly in the following terms: "my foliated (composed of leaf-like layers, shaped like a leaf or in leaf-like form) body"; "myriapod (relative to or having the characteristics of Myriapoda, or centipedes, millipedes, pauropods, and symphylans) tarsus (a term for the seven small bones of the human ankle) bones"; and "hyaline (glassy, transparent like glass) tegmen (a plate of bone making up the roof of the human ear's tympanum)" ("Foliated"; "Myriapod"; "Tarsus"; "Hyaline"; "Tegmen").

dom that Whitman considered part of American culture. The ecstatic synthesis of "I" and landscape depends on perceptual simultaneity–a mode of experience that encompasses the democracy and chaos of his America. Torre's analysis of Whitman in his unpublished *Walt Whitman, poète cosmique*, centers on the freedom of the subject and the subject's perception to roam America's wide-open country: "Whitman représente l'autre Amérique, l'Amérique optimiste et toute moderne, l'Amérique de la vie intense, des gestes en plein air, de la fraternité déclamatoire et encombrante, l'Amérique impérialiste et humanitaire."[17] Whitman's significance for Torre stems from his linking of a mobile poetic subject with the perceptual dominion of vast spaces:

> Sólo temperamentos de alto voltaje como el de Whitman–¡gran reóforo lírico!–son aptos para exaltar simultáneamente todas las cósmicas perspectivas: así en el canto *Give me the splendid silent sun* de sus *Drum Taps*, plasma como un relieve eternal, y en ondulantes versículos, la libre fluencia de su espíritu multanimista.[18] ("Itinerario" 88)

Subjectivity is no longer about the recollection of a collective past; it is rather shaped by the unmoored "I's" perception of an unlimited geography.

The perspectival and perceptual organization of Torre's poetic texts resituates the subject from the national to the international, and from eternal landscapes to the fluid spaces of urban modernity. In "Ventilador," Torre contraposes a variety of cultural markers in his evocation of a sidewalk café. He grounds the series of metonyms that constitute these signs at an international "isla anclada" (3/89), which is metaphor for both the café and the cosmopolitan city:

---

[17] In consideration of Torre's handwriting–consistent with his customary penmanship during the late 1910s and early 1920s–and the time of his other writings on Whitman, I date the document from before 1925. As he does occasionally in his personal papers and unpublished manuscripts, Torre writes in French. He also gives his view of Whitman in *Literaturas europeas de vanguardia* (283-85, 381-89).

[18] Consult Torre, *Walt Whitman, poète cosmique*: "Le poète selon Whitman n'est qu'un 'reporter,' un écho – Le rôle du poète consiste à capter cette poésie épasse sur l'eau, sur la terre et dans le ciel –."

El café despliega sus alas
En las paredes   un río de colores
Una modelo rusa busca la cuadratura de sus gestos
Féminas sonrisas que enguirnaldan la atmósfera
y taladran la humareda verbal

La Rotonde	Vavin	Aïcha

Se encienden las palabras fosfóricas
sobre el mármol internacional
Vitrina cosmopolita
Adiós   mi bella Floriane de Montparnasse (*Hélices* 13-22/89)

Positioning the "I" in the café's polyglot space decenters the subject's identity at the same time as its perceptual and communicative abilities extend their reach:

En la exhalación de una hora he cazado
el último 'couplet' que aletea en mis manos
La media noche se deshoja en 'dancings'
El escotillón del metro cierra sus fauces
Los klaxons epilogan nuestras réplicas
Y otro ventilador al despedirme
enchufa su pulso en mi emoción ("Ventilador" 23-29/89)

The subject's concurrent approximation of and detachment from the textual landscape heighten the perceptual potency of the "I." This dynamized perception–and the combination of diverse references produced by it–disrupts the articulation of any single viewpoint. As composites, the images of the poem reflect the circumstances of the modern city-dweller.

The aerial perspectives of the poem "Torre Eiffel" likewise separate and bring together subject and cityscape. Torre relocates the Eiffel Tower from the Paris *Champs de Mars* to Madrid, deliberately confusing it with "el campanario de Santa Cruz" (6/33) a church bell-tower in the central *Plaza de Santa Cruz* (see fig. 2.1, p. 262):[19]

---

[19] In the early twentieth century, the bell-tower of Santa Cruz was linked with a peculiarly Madrid point of view. Located close to the geographical center of the city, it offered one of the best panoramas of 1920s Madrid's unfolding expanse.

> He aquí mi poema a la Torre
> Torre Eiffel
> Torre abstracta
> Torre del Mundo
> Yo la Torre de Madrid
> sobre el campanario de Santa Cruz ("Torre Eiffel" 1-6/33)

Torre's mixing of recognizably Parisian and Madrid views causes the poetic "I" to retreat into itself, and prevents the association of the images and impressions created from the height of the tower with a specific place or identity. It remains unclear whether the tower is subject, object, or both–or where it truly belongs. The poem's "Eclosión de los paisajes simultáneos" (22/33) destabilizes the tower's already uncertain identity, as well as the boundaries among subject, object, and image:

> Oh Torre avizor
> Tus ojos radiografían el cuerpo de París
>
>> Torre disfrazada y poliédrica
>> hija de Proteo
>> Cuántas caras nos has revelado
>> durante los días de guerra
>> y las noches oceánicas
>
> Torre del Occidente
> *Brújula de los vientos estéticos*
> *Línea del meridiano lírico*
>> Espectro del arco iris
>> Espectáculo de la novedad perpetua
> T   Flecha perpendicular
> O
> R   Directriz del espíritu nuevo
> R
> E   Pararrayos de la Belleza
>> ("Torre Eiffel" 61-75/35; emphasis in the original)

Having become a "Pararrayos de la Belleza," Torre's radiotelegraphic Tower places the subject and the poet–"Brújula de los vientos estéticos"–at the center of a perspectival, perceptual, and communicative space in flux.

In two apostrophes, Torre simultaneously addresses the *Tour Eiffel, Torre Eiffel* and, by means of the pun on his surname, himself: "He aquí mi poema a la Torre / Torre Eiffel / Torre abstracta / Torre del Mundo" (1-4/33); "Oh Torre avizor / Tus ojos radiografían el cuerpo de París" (61-62/35).[20] In another instance of direct address–"Escuchad el ritmo aviónico / del motor de mi Verbo / que canta y patina en el azul / y gira en torno a la Torre" (9-12/33)–the poet speaks to his readers as if they were listeners to the tower's radio broadcasts, exhorting them in the plural *vosotros* form to heed his call for transformation and multiplicity:

```
T S H
   Las antenas exultan
      Y las almas de las Torres
            a través de su carne metálica
         cambian sus palabras sintéticas
               de Polo a Polo
                                              a
                                        b
                              y      a r r i
                         o
                       t
                    s
                  e
                a
              Y
                     Mi espíritu se lanza
                     en el aire eléctrico

                        Torre
                  Hélice del tiempo
                  Gimnasta del espacio
            Cohete-señal
         de las intenciones ascensionales
         Bandera de triunfo al viento
         Reflector solar
                  de films inéditos ("Torre Eiffel" 43-60/34-35)
```

---

[20] According to Jonathan Culler, the figure of apostrophe complicates the circuit of communication in a given poem, as well as raising questions about who the addressee might be (135). It also serves as an indicator and signifier of emotion (138). Culler points out that the vocative aspect of apostrophe can be understood as establishing the self (or textual subject), and that this "I" suggests a "you"–an interlocutor or object. The implied animicity of the object, for him, constitutes an effort to figure the reconciliation between subject and object (142-43).

The singular *Torre Eiffel* changes to the plural "almas de las Torres," which emit "palabras sintéticas." This is similar to the way in which, earlier in the poem, Torre's mention of Proteus, the Greek mythological figure of metamorphosis, stands for the perceptual simultaneity of *Ultraísmo* as well as the movement's transformation of Spain's orientation with respect to the European avant-garde. His "Torre Eiffel" transmits a message of renascence altogether different from that of Machado's *Campos de Castilla*–telegraphing the heterogeneity that the "arco iris" represents metaphorically. Each of the poetic figures that at once effect and represent the transmutation of tower and signal–metaphor, juxtaposition, and apostrophe–parallel cosmopolitanism's exchange of viewpoints and codes. The *Tour-Torre-Guillermo de Torre* translates the Babel that it receives into an avant-garde Esperanto that ruptures with the form of conventional poetic communication.

Torre's representation of perspective and perception can be traced to two major sources apart from Cubism and *Creacionismo*: philosopher José Ortega y Gasset (1883-1955), and Jean Epstein. Torre knew Ortega personally, and he was familiar with the philosopher's work. In 1909, Ortega was named a professor at the recently established *Escuela de Estudios Superiores del Magisterio* and, in 1910, he assumed a chair in metaphysics at the University of Madrid. Between 1913 and 1915, especially, Ortega enjoyed great sway over those who studied at the *Residencia de Estudiantes*, the intellectual center of Spain's capital city (Llera 57; Durán 6-7). Each of the journals that he founded, *El Espectador* (in 1916) and the *Revista de Occidente* (in 1923), formed the thinking and attitudes of a generation, including the authors and artists affiliated with *Ultraísmo* and *Creacionismo*. In a letter dated January 4, 1922, Torre invited Ortega, whom he addressed as "Muy distinguido señor nuestro e ilustre amigo," to contribute to the journal *Cosmópolis* (Letter to Ortega).[21] In 1923, Ortega asked Torre to write for the *Revista de*

---

[21] *Cosmópolis* was published out of Madrid from 1919 through 1922. Torre's request of Ortega, which was written on the journal's letterhead, reads in part, "De Vd. agradeceríamos que nos honrase con la remisión de algún original literario, y éste lo publicaríamos en el primer número, si fuese posible, honrando, de tal manera, nuestra revista" (Letter to Ortega, January 4, 1922). Torre served as the secretary of *Cosmópolis* after the publication of no. 30 (June, 1921) (Bonet 175). In his editorial capacity at the Argentine newspaper *La Nación*, after his 1928 relocation to Buenos Aires with Norah Borges, Torre continued to request material from

Occidente and, by 1924, Torre was a regular reviewer (Llera 124; Zuleta 16). The *Revista de Occidente* demonstrated an intense interest in the Spanish avant-garde's development and also, as the journal's title indicates, in intellectual exchange with Europe and the Americas (Zuleta 13). Surely Torre's contact with Ortega and the *Revista de Occidente* molded his internationalist outlook and familiarized him with avant-garde movements outside Spain. Although Torre's *Literaturas de vanguardia* and Ortega's *La deshumanización del arte* were both published in 1925; the former manifests the influence of the latter work, fragments of which had been in prior circulation. Torre acknowledged Ortega's authority by sending him a signed "Manifiesto vertical ultraísta" bearing the admiring dedication, "A José Ortega y Gasset, lucífero de nuestro barroquismo estético" (Letter to Ortega, 1925; emphasis in the original).[22]

Torre forged an epistolary relationship with Epstein, and his interpretations of his French colleague's literary and cinematic theories were well received by their author in Paris. He wrote two articles on Epstein's work, "Problemas teóricos y estética experimental del nuevo lirismo" and "El cinema y la novísima literatura" for the journal *Cosmópolis*, which he later edited and included in revised form in *Literaturas europeas de vanguardia*.[23] At the time of their publication, these articles elicited an enthusiastic response from Paris:

> Mon cher Confrère, Je viens de lire la traduction *in extenso* de vos articules que vous avez bien voulu consacrer à me présenter au public espagnol.
>
> J'ai été vivement intéressé par vos très intelligentes remarques, et je puis dire que vos idées personnelles me paraissent très bien fondées et concordent d'ailleurs parfaitement avec les miennes. (Letter to Torre, October 10, 1921)

Ortega. Torre remained in Buenos Aires until 1932, when he returned to Madrid, working and residing there until the outbreak of the Spanish Civil War in 1936 (Zuleta 16-18). I consulted two letters from Torre to Ortega from the time period when Torre resided in Argentina; the letters, which are dated April 2, 1928 and September 25, 1929, are conserved at the Archivo José Ortega y Gasset, Fundación Ortega y Gasset, Madrid. In the 1929 letters, Torre requests submissions from Ortega.

[22] The document consists of a signed original of "Manifiesto vertical ultraísta" with Torre's dedication.

[23] The articles' full titles are: "Problemas teóricos y estética experimental del nuevo lirismo: 'La poesía de hoy,' por el teorizante Epstein" and "El cinema y la novísima literatura: sus conexiones."

In two letters dated September 20 and October 10, 1921, Epstein praises the exactitude of Torre's understanding of his work and expresses his gratitude.

Ortega and Epstein were both important to Torre for their "antirealismo artístico," which he traces back to the critique of mimesis in Plato and Aristotle (*Literaturas europeas* 304-305):

> Pues, como es sabido, para Platón el arte era solamente una 'mimesis' y su objeto la fidelidad a la apariencia. Implícitamente pronunciaba una condenación contra el hombre, declarándole inepto para producir belleza. Y Aristóteles hacía consistir la esencia de la poesía en una imitación bella e inmaterial de la naturaleza . . . . (305)

Torre's imperative for the avant-garde is to divide "la realidad efectiva y atmosférica de la naturaleza" from "'la realidad artística'" that has gained autonomy from the natural world: "De ahí el concepto de las dos realidades, porque de hora en adelante, al determinar la verosimilitud de una obra–poemática, novelesca–, lo haremos no tomando la realidad objetiva externa como tipo de confrontación comparativa, sino la realidad interior de la obra, su organismo puramente artístico"[24] (305). He argues that the main problem of aesthetics facing the avant-garde relates to the need to abandon mimetic representation for *creación* ("Problemas teóricos" 588-89). His vocabulary here, credited to its source in *Creacionismo*, comes from the organization of diverse types of art into a tripartite hierarchy, which Huidobro outlines in the 1921 essay "La création pure." According to Huidobro, mimetic art, or "Arte inferior al medio (Arte reproductivo)," occupies the lowest position in the hierarchy, followed by "Arte en armonía con el medio (Arte de adaptación)," and then "Arte superior al medio (Arte creativo)" at the top due to its origin in artistic inspiration instead of the natural world (Huidobro, "La creación pura" 656). Ortega and Epstein share with *Creacionismo* a privileging of the creativity and inventiveness associated with *poiesis* over *mimesis*.

---

[24] Torre acknowledges his borrowing of the term "la realidad artística" from Ramón Pérez de Ayala's *Las máscaras* in a footnote on page 305 of *Literaturas europeas de vanguardia*.

The non-mimetic *creación* and *invención* that Torre espouses necessarily involve what Ortega called *deshumanización:*[25]

> La teoría de la 'deshumanización' del arte enlaza fraternalmente con las teorías creacionistas–por antonomasia–, propulsadas comúnmente por los lucíferos de vanguardia, pertenecientes a diversas fracciones. El anhelo deshumanizador, pictóricamente, se halla conseguido en numerosos cuadros cubistas y de un modo más o menos explícito se encuentra también en varias poematizaciones modernas. (*Literaturas europeas* 309)

In *La deshumanización del arte*, Ortega explains abstraction, with special reference to Cubism, in terms of its objective and distanced perspective on the subject represented. The term "deshumanización" does not imply the elimination of the human as might be expected, but rather a bracketing of emotional enmeshment in the creation and interpretation of art works.

In the section of *La deshumanización del arte* entitled "Unas gotas de fenomenología," Ortega describes different sorts of perspectives, arranging each on a scale from extreme subjectivism to complete objectivism. So as to categorize the various points of view that he delineates, he invents the story of an illustrious man on his deathbed, attended by his grieving wife. There are several other people in the room, and Ortega makes clear that they are each motivated by distinct attitudes, which in turn determine their particular perspective. Because the dying man's wife remains closest emotionally to the situation, her standpoint is the most subjective of all. More towards the objective end of the spectrum is the viewpoint of the doctor supervising the health of his patient, but as Ortega

---

[25] In Huidobro's manifesto, "Non serviam," he declares poetry's independence from Nature: "*Non serviam. No he de ser tu esclavo, madre Natura; seré tu amo. Te servirás de mí; está bien. No quiero y no puedo evitarlo; pero yo también me serviré de ti. Yo tendré mis árboles que no serán como los tuyos, tendré mis montañas, tendré mis ríos y mis mares, tendré mi cielo y mis estrellas*" (653). "Non serviam" comes from Huidobro's 1914 lecture at Santiago de Chile's *Ateneo*, in which he outlines the basic principles of *Creacionismo*. Estrella Busto Ogden explains how Huidobro derived his conception of a non-mimetic poetry from the Cubist painters and Guillaume Apollinaire. Braulio Arenas's recollection of Huidobro's poetic theory, as articulated by the Chilean poet in Buenos Aires's *Ateneo* in 1916, and again in his 1925 manifestos (*Manifestes*), reminds us of its essential message: poetry should have its own internal reality, unrelated to that of the external world ("Vicente Huidobro" 179). Torre's anti-mimetic stance is similar to Huidobro's.

demonstrates, the doctor's professional engagement colors the occurrences with a dose of the subjective–"su oficio le obliga a interesarse seriamente en lo que ocurre: lleva en ello alguna responsabilidad y acaso peligra su prestigio" (*Deshumanización* 22). Ortega places the reporter who simply observes the events as they happen further towards the objective on his scale. Since, unlike the doctor, the reporter does not feel ethically obliged to intervene in the scene, he at first only takes in the actions and sentiments of the principal actors. However, when he subsequently becomes called upon to recount the dying man's tale–to represent it–his perspective shifts from neutral contemplation to emotional implication:

> No participa sentimentalmente en lo que allí acaece, se halla espiritualmente exento y fuera del suceso; no lo vive, sino que lo contempla. Sin embargo, lo contempla con la preocupación de tener que referirlo luego a sus lectores. Quisiera interesar a éstos, conmoverlos, y, si fuese posible, conseguir que todos los suscriptores derramen lágrimas, como si fuesen transitorios parientes del moribundo. (22-23)

The sympathetic entanglement of those who ultimately read the reporter's tale depends on how the episode is recounted; his responsibilities shape the emotional tenor and tone of his writing just as the doctor's affect his attending to the sick man. Ortega means us to see the relationship between the reporter's perspective and the form of the newspaper story. As he writes, "el periodista procura fingir emoción para alimentar con ella su literatura" (23).

Ortega's use of the verb *fingir* suggests Plato's idea of mimetic representation as false and the poet's work as suspect. We may apply it as well to the avant-garde's refashioning of classical critiques of mimesis. Located at the objective end of the range, the painter embodies a posture of objective contemplation untainted by sentiment. He occupies himself not with the viewer's reaction, but rather with aesthetic form: "Su actitud es puramente contemplativa y aun cabe decir que no lo contempla en su integridad; el doloroso sentido interno del hecho queda fuera de su percepción" (23). The painter's entirely artistic response–the stylization of an emotionally charged situation–fits with the aesthetic of Ortega's *arte joven*–the "young art" of the avant-garde.

Although abstraction *per se* is not Epstein's focus as it is Ortega's, for Epstein like Ortega, the abstract, or extreme stylization, goes hand in hand with the new aesthetic. Abstraction, in Epstein's work, is what results when the authorial psyche becomes liberated and its creative potential maximized. In *La poésie d'aujourd'hui, un nouvel état d'intelligence. Lettre de Blaise Cendrars* (1921; hereafter *La poésie d'aujourd'hui*), he explains the parallel that he draws between the abstract form of modern literature and modernity's effects on the psyche. Epstein holds that modern literature's apparent chaos, and feeling of simultaneity and rapidity comes from the nature of experience in modernity. He conceptualizes the structured character of non-modern and stylistically traditional literatures as stemming from the imposition of rules on the authorial subject's subconscious thoughts, and the psyche's consequential need to defend itself from destructive controls (67-68). In Epstein's appraisal, it is for this reason that logical as opposed to spontaneous thinking must be avoided, as well as why modern literature has to suppress grammar and rhetoric (*La poésie* 95-98).

In his writing on cinema, the concern for the authorial psyche in Epstein turns into an exploration of perception. The term *photogénie*, a coinage of the director, screen writer, and critic Louis Delluc (1890-1924) that in the 1920s became the main principle of Epstein's cinematic theory, describes the representation of time, space, and spatio-temporal perception in film. Delluc regarded the real as "the basis of film representation and signification," while emphasizing that cinema transformed this reality through the camera and screen, rendering it wholly novel. The metamorphosis of the external world in "framing, lighting, and mise-en-scène relations within the frame," with the effect of making the viewer see in unprecedented ways, came to be known as *photogénie* (Abel 110). From Epstein's perspective, *photogénie* alters and hones perception by showing objects in a hitherto unforeseen light; it constitutes a "new leavening," a "dividend, divisor, and quotient," the indefinable something that is to truly see ("Senses" 243). Since the purpose of filmic reproduction is to reveal the "mobile aspects of the world, of things and souls" hitherto invisible to the naked eye, a key characteristic of *photogénie* is the capturing of mobility in space and time ("Certain Characteristics" 315).[26] In *Esprit de cinéma*

---

[26] In "On Certain Characteristics of *Photogénie*," Epstein adds a pantheistic dimension to his idea of *photogénie*. He writes, "I would even go so far as to say that the cinema is polytheistic and theogonic. Those lives it creates, by summoning

(1955), Epstein typifies *photogénie* as movement–the complex inter-action of space and time (9-12). The image projected on the screen appears in the fourth dimension, or the space-time of the universe. The heightened visual powers of the camera add time to the three spatial dimensions, which the human perceptual apparatus cannot do because, under normal circumstances, it distorts the temporal, failing to reconcile it properly with space: "Le cinématographe est actuellement le seul instrument qui enregistre l'événement dans un système à quatre références. En cela, il s'avère supérieur à l'esprit humain, qui ne semble pas organisé pour saisir facilement l'ensem-ble d'une continuité à quatre dimensions" (10).

Whereas Epstein's conceptualization of literature remains grounded in the corporeal process of perception, his idea of *pho-togénie* is linked with the mechanical camera lens. This "machine aesthetic" as he calls it–"the click of a shutter"–creates *photogénie's* boundless vision (Epstein, "Senses" 244). Indeed the cinematic camera functions prosthetically, expanding vision's natural capabili-ty and taking it to unprecedented levels. *Photogénie* generates ab-stract form by representing an object or series of objects in space and time and, under the camera's tutelage, the eye learns to per-ceive all of their features.

Epstein provides Torre with a model for augmenting and ener-gizing perception, which *Ultraísmo's* leader then uses to free the subject from spatial and temporal constraints. In "Problemas teóri-cos y estética experimental del nuevo lirismo," Torre discusses Ep-stein's *La poésie d'aujourd'hui*, describing the book as filling an ur-gent need for "algún libro teórico que exponga sintéticamente" the most significant "principios estéticos generales" of avant-garde poet-ics (585). He writes that *La poésie d'aujourd'hui* "es el primer ensayo de codificación de los caracteres psicológicos que enlazan las nuevas tendencias, y una exposición originalísima de ese 'nuevo estado de inteligencia' que Epstein fija en la 'fatiga intelectual,' considerada como una 'salud'" ("Problemas teóricos" 586). For Epstein, since abandoning logic removes unproductive constraints on thought and

---

objects out of the shadows of indifference into the light of dramatic concern, have little in common with human life. These lives are like the life in charms and amulets, the ominous, tabooed objects of certain primitive religions. If we wish to understand how an animal, a plant, or a stone can inspire respect, fear, or horror, those three most sacred sentiments, I think we must watch them on the screen, liv-ing their mysterious, silent lives, alien to the human sensibility" (317).

its representation, the modern author does best to revert to internal existence at its most basic. What he terms "la vie végétative," or "léthargie d'origine digestive ou tabagique ou reconnaissant une cause quelconque (intoxication, maladie, fatigue)," becomes the perfect creative state of mind because the return to an almost animal existence supposed by this condition unshackles the psyche from the tyranny of regulation from outside the self (*La poésie* 68, 75). Epstein compares the "attitude intellectuelle des auteurs modernes" to that of a boxer who approaches the world from the physiological instinct of musculature (68-69). In the creative psyche, the mental–because physical–agility metaphorically represented by the boxer turns into a "spontanéité" that "nous apparaît grâce au débit haché, rapide, souvent incorrect autant qu'une conversation, décousu, illogique comme un rêve, brusque, violent, ici enfantin et deux lignes plus loin sénile, ivre par moments, et, pour tout dire, dénué et de grammaire et d'ordre" (69-70). The most desirable attitude for the modern author, therefore, is one of "rêverie" and "distraction," which lets "les sens libres d'enregistrer ou non les mouvements du monde extérieur" (74).[27]

Unfettered by the logic of intellect, the psyche generates spontaneous connections among the impressions that it produces:

> l'homme est poète avec son tube digestif. Puisqu'il y a des moments où le fonctionnement de ce tube digestif inhibe plus ou moins certaines formes d'activité cérébrale, il est naturel qu'on retrouve des correspondances à ces moments dans la littérature. (Epstein, *La poésie* 75)

The dream-like distraction that comes from this "vie végétative" causes a situation in which "tout est cœnesthésie" (153; 82). Synaesthesia, which Epstein defines as the synthesis of input from the different senses becomes, in his view, paradigmatic of the modern artist's psychological experience and, therefore, of the new art and literature:

---

[27] We can compare Epstein's boxer to Walter Benjamin's Baudelaire. In "On Some Motifs in Baudelaire" (1939), Benjamin makes a parallel between a fencer and Baudelaire, arguing that the poet's distractibility constitutes a defense mechanism against the multitude of stimuli with which he is continually bombarded. According to Benjamin, "Baudelaire made it his business to parry the shocks" of the psychic trauma that comes from living in the city (163). This shielding mechanism becomes the structure of the new poetry just as the simultaneous perception associated with modern urban existence.

La cœnesthésie étant le visage physiologique du subconscient, on voit comment l'égotiste se rapproche de ce subconscient. Plus la cœnesthésie devient vive, et plus l'individu a de facilités à s'observer lui-même, puis à s'exagérer, par pythiatisme, ses propres sensations. Or, la cœnesthésies s'accroît dans la mesure où les organes fonctionnent avec davantage d'instabilité, d'accrocs, de phases successives de mieux et de pis. Sans parler de maladie aigüe, ni même de chronicité, il est clair qu'une physiologie imparfaite accroît la cœnesthésie qui accroît la sensibilité de l'individu et par conséquent ses dispositions artistiques. (*La poésie* 83)

So as to arrive at the desired abstract form, there must be a transition from "la pensée-phrase"–logical thought–to "la pensée-association"–the random aggregation of impressions. Epstein contrasts *la pensée-phrase*, related to the ordering functions of syntax and grammar, with *la pensée-association*, the semiconscious stream of images that he elsewhere terms "cœnesthésie" (100):

L'enchaînement des idées, si on peut appeler cela des idées, se fait selon des associations partielles et absolument illogiques. La mémoire reste le seul guide, tantôt attentif au son et à la couleur, tantôt à l'anecdote du souvenir. Qu'on se rappelle un quelconque de ses rêves. Si j'ai appelé ce mode de pensée, pensée-association, c'est à cause de la façon dont les idées s'y enchaînent par association, par contiguïté de souvenirs, d'images, de sons et de couleurs. (*La poésie* 102)

In "Problemas teóricos y estética experimental del nuevo lirismo," Torre seizes on the binary that Epstein creates between *la pensée-association* and *la pensée-phrase*. He examines the way in which *la pensée-association* can be employed as a standard for abstract form and the representation of perception in poetry. Torre applies Epstein's principle of association to poetic figure, above all, to the "metáfora noviestructural," which he characterizes as "en unión de la imagen múltiple, el elemento esencial del nuevo complexo lírico" ("Problemas teóricos" 600).[28] In *La poésie d'aujourd'hui*, Epstein notes that "La métaphore est un mode de compréhension, de com-

---

[28] Torre discusses Diego's concept of the *imagen múltiple*, which Diego elucidates in his 1919 article, "Posibilidades creacionistas." He quotes this important and influential article on pages 330-31 of *Literaturas europeas de vanguardia*. I delineate Diego's points in Chapter 4.

préhension brusque, de compréhension en mouvement" (131). Metaphor clears away the temporal and spatial barriers between impressions, thereby bringing them together in innovative ways and increasing their expressivity: "La métaphore est le pivot de l'induction. Elle est un théorème où de l'hypothèse on saute à la conclusion sans intermédiaire. Les termes moyens de la déduction ont été échoppés. L'analogie enjambe les distances et les espèces" (135).[29] Torre's *metáfora noviestructural*, modeled on the notion of metaphor articulated in *La poésie d'aujourd'hui*, likewise underscores this sense of immediacy–the overcoming of time and space as obstacles to cognition–in poetic form. Torre reiterates the assertion of metaphor's mutability that we find in Epstein. He elucidates the figure of metaphor, quoting Epstein in his own Spanish translation, as "la relación entre dos ideas, que tan pronto se atraen como se repelen, se juntan o se disocian" ("Imagen" 219).

Torre explains how the movement of film links images in a similar way to the new metaphor, comparing these "metáforas de aproximación por exceso, que poseen un atractivo relieve visual instantáneo y deslumbrante" with the "desfile cinemático de paisajes simultáneos" in cinema ("Problemas teóricos" 601). He makes an analogy between the structure of avant-garde poetry and the cutting of a film, pointing out that there is "una irrefragable similitud entre algunos *films* norteamericanos que a su proyección rápida simulan segmentar y superponer sus cuadros espaciales, y el poema novimorfo que por la multiplicidad de sus imágenes–único nexo del tema–produce una sensación simultaneísta en la fusión y actualización de planos espaciales y temporales" ("El cinema" 100).

Torre, like Epstein, emphasizes the surmounting of temporal and spatial divides to produce images of great expressive potential (106). Association and juxtaposition–the core principles of metaphor–help create the complex textual landscapes of Torre's poetry. Permeating his discussion of metaphor we find a language that relates psychic freedom and the maximization of perception with an expansion of the space bounding experience:

> La metáforas de suprema audacia son aquellas que barajan arbitraria y divinamente los elementos cósmicos y geográficos, dán-

---

[29] Torre quotes (in Spanish) these comments that Epstein makes about the nature of metaphor in *Literaturas europeas de vanguardia* (333).

donos una nueva y sorprendente visión de la tierra: De ahí la
gran lluvia de estrellas, líneas meridianas, soles, trópicos y
cordilleras que tejen caprichosos contrastes en los nuevos poe-
mas. ("Imagen" 224)[30]

The "gran revolución" that reconfigures metaphor, becomes, in
Torre, a "nuevo sistema de interpretación objetiva" (abstraction)
and a "nuevo credo de comunión cósmica" (224).

In a way comparable to metaphor, the adjectives, neologisms, ty-
pography, and rhythm of the poetic text become engines of change
with regard to perception. According to Torre, in *Literaturas euro-
peas de vanguardia*, the adjective, apart from its primary, descriptive
function of giving the poem its own peculiar stamp, "en ocasiones
puede tener un valor creador, semejante al de la imagen, o ser su efi-
caz colaborador"; such creative adjectives, which include those that
incorporate antithesis and oxymoron, work like metaphors in their
capacity for synthesizing multiple ideas and conveying them to the
reader simultaneously, thereby interrupting and altering predictable
thought-patterns (356). Neologisms and barbarisms promote the
creation of a new poetic language, which is Torre's precondition for
the cosmopolitan transformation that he envisions: "Lo innegable es
que la pureza lingüística tiene cada día menos adeptos. Sufre un es-
pejismo nacionalista quien la acepte a cierraojos. ¡La fuerte tromba
actual del cosmopolitismo se los hará abrir meridianamente!" (*Lite-
raturas europeas* 364). Likewise, the jettisoning of rhyme, the use of
rhythm to reflect the dynamism of modern urban experience (to
which the frequency of proparoxytones in *Hélices* contributes), and
the new typography and calligrammatic structure of poetic lines, in
renovating the text, open the way towards the revolution in percep-
tion that Torre regards as essential to the extension of Spain's hori-
zons towards the rest of Europe.

Torre molds *Hélices* in accordance with Epstein's concepts of
accélération vitale and *fatigue mentale*, both of which he envisions
as features of the vigorous mind: for him, in spite of the shocked
state that results from modern existence's bombardment of the
senses, the creative psyche nevertheless increases its cognitive abili-
ty. The "Ondulación discontinua de la trayectoria impresional" in
Hélices is analogous to the dominance of "distraction, c'est-à-dire

---

[30] The 1923 article was reprinted in a 1924 volume of the journal *Alfar*.

d'occupation, pour laisser les sens libres" over an "attitude de rêverie" in Epstein (Torre, "Diagrama mental," *Hélices* 2/85; Epstein, *La poésie* 74). Torre's turn from contemplation to "el espejismo accional" of the city-dweller's perception uproots the subject from the space of the collective past: "No existe la belleza eternal / Oh maravillas un instante aprehensibles de la fugacidad / Se desvanece todo lo históricamente mayestático" ("Diagrama mental," *Hélices* 8, 26-28/85). The play of associations in his poetry situate the subject in the haptic and optic experience of a cosmopolitan urban modernity, thus redefining experience.

In a group of five poems in *Hélices*, entitled "Poemas fotogénicos," Torre exemplifies the liberating potential for subjectivity of film's transformation of perception, as according to Epstein.[31] Each of these poems–"Color," "Fotogenia," "En el cinema," "Charlot" and "En el 7° episodio"–exhibit some of *photogénie's* properties.[32] "Color" depicts the opening of a lens to the play of light:[33]

> Luz
> Desde el Zenit se abre el diafragma del objetivo fotográfico
> sobre las perspectivas frondosas dinámicas y coloreadas
> que multiplican sus reflejos tornátiles–
> Se destríen las fibras luminosas de la Vida
> Irradiaciones concéntricas del violeta al rojo
>
> Arco Iris de los acordes fotogénicos
> El sol
> crisol de los colores
> Fruto abierto en sazón
> Aureo surtidor
> Pulpa omnicromática–
>
> Mis ojos radiografían el sexo del espectro solar
> Y mis dientes apresan segmentos del gran disco frutal pendiente
>   del árbol celeste
> Ante el reflector de Helios se proyecta la metáfora del color en la
>   pantalla de mi horizonte
> Cinematografía pictórica
> Alquimia y electrolisis colorista–(1-17/101)

---

[31] The "Poemas fotogénicos" were first published in the journal *Cosmópolis* in 1922.

[32] Torre prefaces the "Poemas fotogénicos" with an epigraph from Epstein's *Cinéma* (1921): "Photogénie, photogénie pure, mobilité scandée..." (100).

[33] "Color" is dedicated to Barradas.

The eye acquires mechanical capabilities–"Mis ojos radiografían el sexo del espectro solar"–acquiring the strength required to generate ever more complex metaphorical expressions. Expansion of the eye's focus joins impressions into metaphors in a similar way as film links images. A lens-like eye catalyzes "las fibras luminosas de la Vida" in an "Alquimia y electrolisis colorista," which it then projects in the form of the multi-layered *metáfora noviestructural*: "Formación de la rosa del color / Nueva floración integral pluricromática / Jubilosa totalidad de la síntesis rósea prevista en la reminiscencia de un amanecer cósmico" (18-20/101). The empowered eye, which Torre compares in an extended metaphor to the capabilities of a film camera and to the sun, causes his garden of images to flower and bloom. A series of metaphors unfolds under the life-giving sun like a "Fruto abierto en sazón," producing an extreme kind of synaesthesia: "Aureo surtidor / Pulpa omnicromática"– // Mis ojos radiografían el sexo del espectro solar / Y mis dientes apresan segmentos del gran disco frutal pendiente del árbol celeste" (10-14/101).

Heightening the perceptual activity of the eye-as-camera enlarges the objects that Torre depicts–as if the text were a screen. The poet imitates the mutual approximation of eye and image in the cinematic close-up:

> Rostros
> Muecas
> Visajes
> Acordes faciales
> de la emoción iluminada
> Gestos dardeantes
> Rostros tendidos   como arcos tensionales
> clavan la flecha fotogénica
> en la pantalla cinemática
>
> En el taller   ante los focos voltaicos
> los músculos se distienden
> con avidez expresional
> Los cuerpos sufren corrientes de alta frecuencia
> El arqueamiento ciliar de los ojos
> pespuntea las emociones
> Todo el cuerpo posee aletas
> y nada meridianamente   en el estanque de luz
> Los cineactores son dinamómetros emocionales
> Gira el conmutador de los nervios

El logaritmo de la movilidad
en el relieve táctil del primer plano
Oh elocuencia plástica de Hayakawa!
Claridades
Dinamismos
Fotogenia (Torre, "Fotogenia," *Hélices* 1-25/102)[34]

Dedicated to Epstein, "Fotogenia" recalls the French theorist and cinéaste's formulations about the close-up which, in his essay "Magnification," he calls the "soul of the cinema" (236). Epstein imagines close-up shots as drawing the viewing subject and image together, magnifying vision: "I will never find the way to say how much I love American close-ups. Point blank. A head suddenly appears on screen and drama, now face to face, seems to address me personally and swells with an extraordinary intensity. I am hypnotized" (235). The enormous size of the close-up, projected onto the big screen, augments vision, captivating and channeling it–nearly swallowing it whole (Turvey 28). Keeping in mind that movement remains the key quality of *photogénie*, it is the spectator's response to the close-up's motion that increases the eye's capacity to perceive.[35] The peculiar motion of the close-up demonstrates the way in which the "photogenic is conjugated in the future and in the imperative," moving the cinematic image and the gaze that follows it forward towards the next frame, and thereby giving the viewing subject the ability to see in the fourth dimension–in space-time (Epstein, "Magnification" 236).

Yet at the same time, *photogénie* involves a latency whose intensification of perception equals that of its tendency towards speed. In all of the "Poemas fotogénicos," Torre depicts the dual temporal character of *photogénie*–a strong motive force and retarder of time. He cuts and splices images so that they seem to speed up, while also saturating and transfixing the gaze. His repeated use of juxtaposi-

---

[34] The cinema actor Sessue Hayakawa's (1889-1973) career bridged silent films and "talkies." A Japanese immigrant to the United States, he found stardom in Europe and America.

[35] "Even more beautiful than a laugh is the face preparing for it," Epstein confesses, "I love the mouth which is about to speak and holds back, the gesture which hesitates between right and left, the recoil before the leap, and the moment before landing, the becoming, the hesitation, the taut spring, the prelude, and even more than all these, the piano being tuned before the overture" ("Magnification" 236).

tion in "Fotogenia," for instance, creates the semblance of high velocity, which contrasts with the sustained vision demanded by the "close-ups" of the "Rostros / Muecas / Visajes / Acordes faciales" (1-4/102):

> Una estación trepidante   vaivenes sincopados
> Un puerto   balcón a lontananzas
> Hangars   nidos de hélices
> Las calles revolotean
> entre las gentes embriagadas
> En el kilómetro 247 la sierpe

> ---
> **Peligro de muerte**
> **Aminorad la velocidad**
> ---

> Las carreteras saltan los obstáculos
> El tiralíneas de la avenida subraya la ciudad
> Los mecánicos domadores
> sacan chispas con el látigo de la electricidad
> sobre la piel de los inductores
> Luchas   boxeo de las esquinas
> Actuación del lirismo muscular

> Trayectorias insondables
> La Vida
> recorta sus perfiles fotogénicos
> Biología psíquica ante el acelerador
> Vida de la hiperrealidad sensibilizada
> que descubre el rayo del Cinema
> y perfora una nueva dimensión plástica
> Fragante pintura animada (38-60/103)

To take another example, in "En el cinema" the synthesis of image and eye occurs with split-second timing. As the fictive body of spectators regards "la pantalla desbordada," their mode of perceiving is changed by the "cut" of Torre's filmic text. "El impulso la astucia la celeridad" unleashes a storm of images–"Constelaciones de aviones / Sierpes de automóviles / Ramilletes de hélices / Encajes de humaredas"–whose sheer velocity "forja las diplopias / y arma el mecanismo / de la expectación" ("En el cinema," *Hélices* 18, 22, 25-28, 45-47/105). In a similar way as in Epstein, the force of Torre's images derives from their capability to shape the viewer's expectations of what will be seen–not just what can be discerned during the present moment. As a consequence, the experience of seeing these images orients the perceiving subject towards the future, strengthening and educating the eye for forthcoming encounters.

Torre's dynamizing of perception causes the subject's thought-patterns to change, shifting from a meditative contemplation conducive to logic and remembrance to an association of perceptions that happens haphazardly and in the present tense. In "Diagrama mental," part of the "Kaleidoscopio" section of *Hélices*, the "anti-intelectualismo cenestésico de la nueva lírica" works in a way analogous to the fatigued yet hyper-productive psyche described by Epstein (Torre, "Problemas teóricos" 594):

> *Todo es ritmo contraste y simultaneidad*
> *Ondulación discontinua de la trayectoria impresional*
> *Taquicardía*
> *El motor de mi inquietud acuerda sus latidos al síncope contrapuntístico de los jazz-band*
> *Saltan los nervios en la hipertensión lírica*
> *Avidez noviespacial*
> *Miradas roentgénicas*[36]
> *No basta el espejismo accional*
> *Hay que multiplicarse en los horizontes vitales*
> *Y rehuir la insolación del cafard*
> *Aunque Epstein formule la ley de nuestra fatiga intelectual*
> *Conmoción sísmica de estéticas e ideologías*
> *Pero la vida nos clava aún sus aristas hostiles*
> *En las curvas peligrosas hay que enfundar la sensibilidad*
> (Torre, "Diagrama mental" 1-14/85)

The discontinuous waves of impressions delineated in the poem evoke the same distracted free-association that predominates in Epstein. Perception's acceleration–"la fuerza estimulante y motriz de la velocidad, en el desarrollo que acelera nuestro ritmo cardíaco ante la expectación de lo imprevisto"–happens at the expense of remembering–dislocating the subject from the past ("El cinema" 105). Liberating perception through rapid cinematic cuts brings about the end of contemplation: the remembering *vita contemplati-*

---

[36] After Wilhelm Conrad Röntgen (1845-1923), the German physicist and discoverer of x-rays. He was the first recipient of the Nobel Prize for Physics in 1901.

va that Henri Bergson contrasts with the *vita activa* of consciousness (Benjamin, "Some Motifs" 157).[37] The focusing of vision by the camera lens and the projector stops the meditative movement of the psyche necessary for engaging in recollection. In drawing on "el espejismo accional" of cinema, Torre suspends any possibility of comparing the present with anterior moments in time. He privileges perceptual associations that occur in the instantaneous click of the camera shutter or between frames of film, thus situating the eye and the subject in the now instead of a circumscribed and eternal Castile of memory ("Diagrama mental" 8/85).

Torre mixes Epstein's transformation of perception with Ortega's concern for perspective. His view, which he articulates in *Literaturas europeas de vanguardia*, is that Epstein's subjective vision and Ortega's idea of abstraction are complementary. Torre seeks to temper what he perceives to be the excessive coldness of abstract art in Ortega, noting that "la desrealización, por regla general, no implica fatalmente deshumanización" (310). His intention is to reclaim the human and the subjective: "El artista podrá metamorfosear los elementos orgánicos, estilizar las almas y los paisajes, dar una proyección inesperada a sus sentimientos, situando el todo en un marco irreal, pero nunca podrá prescindir de lo específicamente humano, es decir de lo que es por esencia sensibilidad e inteligencia" (310). At the same time, however, he takes exception to the turn inward that Epstein's work represents:

---

[37] Torre shares with Walter Benjamin the overwhelming sense that the historical moment of contemplation has passed. However, whereas this passing is a source of deep pain and ambivalence for Benjamin (who nonetheless holds out hope for memory's recovery in perception), it is not in Torre. Benjamin situates the camera in a long line of modern inventions that have the effect of mechanizing the senses. For him, the experience of time after these inventions becomes akin to the conveyor-belt: "The camera gave the moment a posthumous shock, as it were. Haptic experiences of this kind were joined by optic ones such as are supplied by the advertising pages of a newspaper or the traffic of a big city. Moving through this traffic involves the individual in a series of shocks and collisions." He further holds that, "technology has subjected the human sensorium to a complex sort of training. There came a day when a new and urgent need for stimuli was met by the film. In a film, perception in the form of shocks was established as a formal principle. That which determines the rhythm of production on a conveyor belt is the basis of the rhythm of reception in the film" (Benjamin, "Some Motifs" 175). Siegfried Kracauer makes the similar argument that the film spectator perceives with intense rapidity in response to the speed with which cinematic images succeed each other, so that "there is no room left between them for even the slightest contemplation" (326).

[P]ues no es exactamente cierto que los poetas nuevos prescindan de la vida exterior. Al contrario–según en ocasiones anteriores hemos insinuado–reaccionando contra la monotonía de un ahogado subjetivismo sentimental, del afán de registrar y apresar hasta los últimos matices del yo–que inician los románticos y llevan al summum los simbolistas–, estos nuevos líricos se asoman al exterior de sí mismos y hacen cara a los frondosos panoramas vitales, no captándolos en su escueta aprehensión objetiva, sino en una interesante proyección y transformación intraobjetiva. (*Literaturas europeas* 312)

The "subjetivación intraobjetiva" to which Torre refers turns out to be one of the most significant features of his perceptual cosmopolitanism, and it has three basic characteristics. First, *subjetivación intraobjetiva* bridges the gap between the interior of the psyche and the exterior world. Second, it combines abstract representation with the subjective viewpoint of the psyche. Third, it becomes a means toward synthesizing subjective and objective perspectives:

En los poetas de ciclos precedentes el sujeto del poema, originariamente contenido en una objetividad material, pasaba a ser el *subjectum*, o sea, se imbibía en la trama espiritual del poeta. Y el sujeto fue así–como dice Drieu La Rochelle–un pretexto merced al cual se reveló la facultad poética. Por el contrario, en la nueva lírica cubista y ultraísta se efectúa la trayectoria opuesta: la inquietud subjetiva, no debiendo presentarse escuetamente por sí misma, irradia hacia las materiales concreciones, las transforma y vivifica y, al penetrarlas, les insufla un espíritu nuevo, reformando sus aspectos y, en definitiva, recreándoles estéticamente. (*Literaturas europeas* 312-13)

Unlike the *paysage d'âme*, which is produced through the objectification of the poet's sentiments, the avant-garde textual landscape is filtered by an objective perspective, which gives it form.

In Torre's poem "Al volante," the subject and the outside world are brought together in perception:

Al volante
todas las carreteras se encabritan
En el juego de velocidades
los pedales

barajan un kaleidoscopio
de perspectivas tornátiles
El coche es un arco combado
que dispara
trayectorias insaciables (*Hélices* 1-9/45)

Normally a boundary between subject and object, the car here functions as an instrumental aid to vision, just as a "kaleidoscopio de perspectivas tornátiles."[38] The subject's eye melds with the windshield in motion, taking on its power to view different aspects of the landscape simultaneously: "El parabrisas multiplica nuestros ojos / que cosen los panoramas evasivos / Y el viento liquefacciona los sonidos" (24-26/45). Contributing to the indeterminacy surrounding subjectivity in the poem is the emergence of the second-person plural:

Trepanamos aldeas naufragadas
y campiñas que galopan
. . . .
Cogidos de las manos
paralelamente
avanzamos con los cables y los ríos
que permutan sus cauces (11-12, 16-19/45)

The referent of the unidentified *nosotros* could be a couple on their travels, the reader and the subject, or the subject and the car. Torre's blurring of the boundaries between subjects, as well as between perceiver and perceived, parallels the mutual approximation of subject and object in *subjetivación intraobjetiva*. The lack of differentiation among the automobile, road, landscape, and perceiving subject shows that Torre has tossed the conventional categories of "interior"–subject–and "exterior"–the object of perception–out the window. Perceptual hyperactivity, the symptoms of which fashion the poem's images, is cause and effect of Torre's synthesis of subject, perceptual instrument, and external world: "Saltos entre las mallas de itinerarios / Trepidaciones / El motor padece taquiarrit-

---

[38] For a discussion of Torre's "Al volante" from the perspective of the representation of perception, consult Maria Pao, "The View from the Wheel: De Torre, Salinas, and Hinojosa."

mia" (20-22/45). This crossing constitutes the principal formal and structural condition of perceptual cosmopolitanism.

In "El subjetivismo intraobjetivo: La 'Einfühlung,'" a section of the theoretical Part 2 of *Literaturas de vanguardia*, Torre gives a brief philosophical history of the relationship between subject and object in perception, in connection with the development of Ultra poetics.[39] "Se efectúa así, en las novísimas poematizaciones," he argues, "una lírica electrolisis que descompone los elementos objetivos: un metabolismo de subjetivación intraobjetiva, un subjetivismo genuinamente personal, objetivado sobre elementos de la realidad viviente. Prevalece así el mundo exterior, visto con los lentes del mundo interior" (*Literaturas europeas* 313). He envisions the avant-garde poem as a chemical reaction between the subject and the external world, catalyzed by perception. The divides between subject and object, and subjective and objective perspective melt away, forging a poetic text whose true subject of representation is the interaction among perception, the impressions in the psyche, and the external world.

In order to explain *subjetivación intraobjetiva* as the engine of the interchange between subject and object, Torre compares it with the nineteenth-century German philosophical concept of "Einfühlung." He investigates the roots of the idea of *Einfühlung* (or empathy) in the theories of Theodor Lipps (1851-1914) and Wilhelm Worringer (1881-1965).[40] In *Abstraction and Empathy*, Worringer expounds his aesthetic theory, centering on the problem of abstraction in modern art (Kramer vii-ix).[41] He critiques the notion, articulated by Lipps, that posits *Einfühlung* and abstraction as two opposite human urges (Worringer 4-5). Instead, as Worringer believes, abstraction stems from two impulses that he categorizes as acts of aesthetic creativity, or "artistic volition," both of which derive from

---

[39] While Torre does not directly mention Ortega in this section of the book, it is logical to attribute his knowledge of neo-Kantianism and the *Einfühlung* at least somewhat to the author of *La deshumanización del arte*, given Ortega's philosophical orientation and the two men's relationship.

[40] Torre traces the *Einfühlung* to Victor Basch's (1863-1944) "simpatía simbólica," James Mark Baldwin's (1861-1934) "empatía," Francesco de Sanctis's (1817-1883) "intropatía," and the Swiss psychologist Édouard Claparède (1873-1940) (*Literaturas europeas* 313). See Mildred Galland-Szymkowiak's article, "Le 'symbolisme sympathique' dans l'esthétique de Victor Basch."

[41] *Abstraction and Empathy* (*Abstraktion und Einfühlung*; 1908), originally Worringer's doctoral thesis, was based on Lipps's philosophy.

human attitudes towards the external world: one, the desire to identify with the non-"I," and two, the need to escape from the self (9-11, 14-25).

Torre aims to reimagine the text, via *subjetivación intraobjetiva*, as a space of exchange among the subject ("I"), the outside world (non-"I") and, by extension, other subjects. He holds that "sólo hoy en rigor" does the *Einfühlung* of Lipps and Worringer "con el subjetivismo intraobjetivo de la nueva lírica alcanza su verdadera expresión" (*Literaturas europeas* 313). For him, it is only with the adoption of *subjetivación intraobjetiva* that poetry can finally and rightly shift its emphasis from subjectivism and the *paysage d'âme* to the productive combination of subject and object. Indeed *subjetivismo intraobjetivo* works against a sentimental subjectivism which registers every nuance of the "I." By proposing a model of equal exchange between subject and object, rather than one in which the self is projected onto the outside world, Torre also implies a cosmopolitan pattern for intersubjectivity.

The interchange between subject and object in *subjetivación intraobjetiva* runs counter to the way in which they combine in the *paysage d'âme*:

> Liminarmente, ¿qué medios ópticos utilizaremos, qué trayectoria visual debemos seguir para hallar la sensación fragante de la Naturaleza desnuda en el paisaje campestre? Y después, ¿tiene existencia independiente, autonomía emocional y repercusión sensitiva el paisaje exterior, o es sólo un reflejo amplificado y complementario de nuestra panorámica psiquis intimal?
> ¡Arduas interrogaciones, abocadoras al Vértice Sugeridor! (83)

The free exchange of subject and object in *subjetivación intraobjetiva* goes against Machado's firm situation of the subject in the landscape:

> ¿Cómo penetró en mí la inquietud vívida del paisaje, y el anhelo introspectivo de captar sus inmaculadas perspectivas y su itinerario noviespacial? Castilla, antes de su exacta vislumbranza y a través de pictóricas visiones literaturizacas [sic], era para mí la topificación pétrea del paisaje cardinalmente español y la síntesis de los más enraizados tropismos iberos, en cuyo páramo osificado se aventaban las últimas alegolías (sic) [alegorías] marchitas...: Sombras de siglos. Tradiciones heroicas. Soledades cóncavas. Y al

fondo, la silueta dementizada de Don Quijote visionario... Mas una de mis emotivas pesquisas a través del paisaje me ha descubierto algunas facetas insospechadas de Castilla ubérrima y potencial y otras sugerencias frondosas en su misma escueta arborescencia. Y en la dilección comprensiva, mis miradas fluyeron proyectadas inicialmente hacia el dintorno característico de la realidad paisajista castellana, tan sutilmente estilizada en las primorosas interpretaciones azorinianas.

Urge ratificarlo, jóvenes amigos. (Torre, "Itinerario" 82)

Torre dampens the glow of the eternal and authentic *pueblo* by targeting the way in which the subject becomes located in the space of the collective, rupturing the representational norms governing the landscape's mapping: "Así, pues, salgamos de Castilla, aunque en su dintorno espacial situemos las características del paisaje límpido y abstracto, henchido de perspectivas estéticas y sugerencias meditativas" ("Itinerario" 83).

Torre beats a path out of Castile by breaking the spell of the gaze that conjures it into being. He replaces Machado's contemplative vision with the hyperbolic perception of *subjetivación intraobjetiva*: "En definitiva: la ruta visual del paisaje no es contemplación extática de ruralistas encantos, sino captación e ineterpemetración (sic) [ineterpenetración][42] dinámica de los elementos panorámicos con la sensibilidad automovilística" (84-85). The exchange that occurs between the eye of the subject and the terrain, or object, that it beholds becomes as fast as a racing automobile:

Así es muy distinta la aprehensión paisajista del caminante nostálgico que va lentamente surcando la gleba, a la del motorista ubérrimo que rasga velozmente en un 80 HP. las carreteras serpeantes, fijando en su retina y en su mente la sensación simultánea, en la apoteosis del vértigo, de los horizontes vibracionistas... (84)

The rapid trajectory of the eye leaves the collective past in the dust of its antiquated landscape. It revs up the perceptual engines that enable Torre's "80 HP" to gather speed:[43]

---

[42] "Ineterpemetración" should read "ineterpenetración"; there is a typographical error in the text. *Ineterpenetración* is a neologism, by which Torre means *in-éterpenetración*, or *penetración en el éter* (penetration in the ether).

[43] Torre's discussion of the car's speed ("80 HP") in relation to the landscape recalls Pedro Salinas's poem "Navacerrada, abril" from *Seguro azar*.

> El más bello y perfecto paisaje rústico o cosmopolita, estático o móvil, unilateral o tornátil, será aquel que armonice en su dintorno la calidad ofrendorosa de sus rasgos exornadores, fundidos con las proyecciones o emanaciones psíquicas de los viajeros que surcan su latitud, en una telúrica asunción emocional. ("Itinerario" 86-87)

The perceptual simultaneity that is bound up in *subjetivación intraobjetiva* provides the subject with the necessary tools to navigate cosmopolitan terrain.

Torre further jolts Arcadia's peaceful countryside into the age of electricity in the "Frisos" section of *Hélices*. He dismantles, in the poems "Guiñol de natura" and "Friso primaveral," the pastoral tradition's construction of vision, which arranges the landscape into a harmonious idyll:

> Los nuevos brazos de los árboles florecen las yemas de sus dedos
> y arrojan verdes especímenes de Arcadia
> Eros humorista lanza cardiogramas cifrados a los ingenuos espíritus románticos
> que caen en el lazo sexual y naufragan caricaturescamente en el
> espejo cóncavo del sentimentalismo morganático (Torre, "Friso primaveral," *Hélices* 14-17/113)

Mixed with the sentimental and lyrical language of the poem are terms from modern science and medicine–"verdes especímenes" and "cardiogramas cifrados"–suggesting a sensibility that is anything but calm. Torre's energized language interrupts the pastoral's meditation on natural beauty and sexualizes its evocation of romance. His diction catalyzes the Arcadian landscape, and substitutes pastoral's meditative and centered vision for the immediate hyperactivity of the electrocardiograph. Similar to Torre's language, the electrocardiograph and the other mechanical devices depicted by the poet assume a prosthetic function, the power of which ultimately destabilizes vision and causes the textual landscape (the visual and sensorial order of the text) to mirror the jumbled-up psychic experience of the city's cosmopolitan subject: "En el paisaje cósmico extrarradial todas las perspectivas / amplifican sus radios: Simultáneamente se desprenden de / sus facies yuxtapuestas y ofrecen sus más inesperadas super- / ficies inéditas: Con la imprecisión fragante de células recién nacidas" (1-5/111).

Dynamizing the subject's perception in this way renders the language in the text hyperbolic, producing a rapid transition between tropes and metaphors:

> . . . –Sobre el poliedro de la realidad los panoramas liberados tallan caras intactas de alma recreacionista perfil acrobático y ritmo acelerado: Paralelamente en el torbellino espacial simultáneo los sentidos permutan sus virtudes propiciando insólitas percepciones taumatúrgicas: Y desde su atalaya oculta el prestímano lírico baraja las visiones poliédricas y mueve los hilos del guiñol de Natura. . .
> (Torre, "Guiñol de natura," *Hélices* 5-11/111)

From the height of the "atalaya oculta," the eye of "el prestímano lírico" shuffles the terrain below–"baraja las visiones polié- / dricas y mueve los hilos del guiñol de Natura." Torre figures this conjurer of lyrics as possessing an augmented capacity for perceptual simultaneity. "El prestímano lírico" becomes the puppet-master of "Guiñol de natura," who expertly stages and manipulates the poem's wild contrapositions:

> Montañosas pirámides lavan los senos erectos de sus desmelenados picachos en el mar cerúleo de las nubes aviónicas
> Otras avanzan sus gibas azules hacia las bocas calcinadas de soles remotos
> La colina serpeada por el torrente extiende sus belfos obscuros con una avidez abismal
> Las nubes nostálgicas evolucionan planeando sobre la terraza de los vésperos
> El cielo monocorde como el hastío nos muestra su frente tatuada por los velívolos caligráficos (12-16/111)

Torre–"el prestímano lírico" of *Ultraísmo*–marks his textual landscapes with the signs of modern life–the "velívolos caligráficos" that ensue from perceptual simultaneity. Perception becomes as an instrument, negotiating the complex exchanges among the subject, the object, and the senses:

> Atención: Los carteles cerúleos del horizonte nos anuncian la inauguración plenisolar
> Aparición ritual: La Primavera desnuda repliega los últimos toldos brumosos y rasga los ventanales meridianos

Incitantes senos ácueos de las mujeres coritas que desfilan
riegan nuestros ojos ávidos y multiplican las irisaciones del pa-
norama renaciente
Bajo la aspersión floreal
los paisajes móviles barajan sus reflejos como en un kaleidosco-
pio tornátil
(Torre, "Friso primaveral," *Hélices* 1-7/113)

The dynamized perception advertised in "El primer número de *La Primavera*" changes and is changed by the new psychic order of which it is a part: "Y en los jardines y cinemas todas las neuróticas sin novio / inyectan en su endocardio morfina primaveral" (30-31/113).

In "Carteles," time and space are organized in reaction to the dictates of the market–"los carteles cuadriculan nuestras horas"–altering the situation of the subject with regard to its surroundings. Torre's personification of the city speaks of this transformation in the relationship between subjectivity and place: "Todo el flúido cómico-industrial de la ciudad / fluye en las arterias carteleras" ("Carteles," *Hélices* 13, 17-18/41). The arteries of this strangely human city interconnect a diverse body of subjects, thus re-envisioning commonality as a heterogeneous network. Torre has the plural subject of "Carteles" slip in and out of urban space–"Saltemos entre la pauta de los 'affiches'"–rather than containing subjectivity within an *a priori* image of the collective (14/41). So as to highlight his conception of cosmopolitan liberty, he humorously converts the poem's urban jungle into a giant garden bursting with perceptual fecundity:

En el jardín de la mañana
                    urbana
        hay un florecimiento panorámico
            de franjas hiperfoliadas
                y multícromas
            sobre todas las fachadas

    La rosa polipétala del cartel
        abre sus verticilos
            con letras que gesticulan espectáculos
        Bebamos el rocío
                    de este friso hiperbólico y falaz
        Jovialidad   Jovialidad ("Carteles" 1-12/41)[44]

---

[44] There are some holdovers in Torre's diction from Symbolism and *modernismo*–for example the garden and flowers.

"Espectador / elige tus rutas / y cómprate un postizo ojo ubicuo": purchasing the prosthetic eye hawked by Torre means learning to employ perceptual simultaneity to gain access to all the goods that the city has to offer ("Carteles" 19-21/41).

The perspectival and perceptual construction of Torre's work bears out the complexity of his project for *Ultraísmo*: creating a textual model for cosmopolitanism; opening Spain's borders to the other; and integrating the first avant-garde into Europe.[45] These constructive moves—what I have called perceptual cosmopolitanism—constitutes a major change from Machado's *Campos de Castilla*, in which the relationship among perspective and perception, on the one hand, and memory, on the other hand, positions the subject in collective space. In making his own Ortega's idea of abstraction, Epstein's perceptual simultaneity, and the *Einfühlung* (*subjetivación intraobjetiva*), Torre relocates the subject to an infinitely mutable present. From its lofty perch atop his "Torre Eiffel," Torre's expansive subject takes on a protean multiplicity appropriate to an international and urban existence. Yet at the same time, the consequences of perceptual cosmopolitanism should be understood as double-edged: simultaneity can lead to psychic fragmentation and a loss of bearings with respect to identity, just as abstraction may have the effect of diminishing subjectivity's expressiveness. It is finally the simultaneousness of perception on which the delicate balance between freedom and disorientation hangs. Perceptual simultaneity, as Torre's textual paradigm, can lock the subject into a solipsistic cycle, or anchor it firmly in its own sensory experience, thus conserving identity while opening the psyche to the outside world.

---

[45] See my "Questioning the Territory of Modernism: *Ultraísmo* and the Aesthetic of the First Spanish Avant-Garde."

CHAPTER 3

PERCEPTUAL SIMULTANEITY AND *ULTRAÍSMO*:
THE IMPACT OF *SIMULTANEISME*

WORLD War I brought the artists Robert Delaunay and Sonia
Delaunay-Terk to Spain as if in answer to the questions that
Torre posed from *Ultraísmo's* inception: How can we break with
the past and begin anew? What might be an innovative form for the
new poetry? How might it be possible to collaborate with the
avant-garde in the rest of Europe?[1] And perhaps most importantly:
In which ways could poetic form reflect cosmopolitanism? The De-
launays' arrival in Madrid and their subsequent friendship with
Torre brought the leader of *Ultraísmo* into close contact with *Simul-
taneisme*, the Parisian avant-garde movement in the visual arts and
poetry that was founded by the Delaunays, Blaise Cendrars, and
Guillaume Apollinaire. "Destruction-construction," the paradigm
that Delaunay conceived for the representation of visual percep-
tion, in which vision is broken down and restructured in abstract
pictorial form, offered a response to all of these essential queries
(Delaunay, *Projets de couverts*). The idea of deconstruction fit with
the rebellious attitude characteristic of the avant-garde, as well as
Torre's desire to leave *castizo* Spain behind. Delaunay's dissolution
of vision into relationships of color and light, and his transforma-
tion of perspective became models for Torre's rupture of the
boundaries that would confine and define Spain's collective identi-

---

[1] Robert Delaunay (1885-1941) and Sonia Delaunay-Terk (1885-1979), the
Parisian painters and founders (with Blaise Cendrars and Guillaume Apollinaire) of
the Paris-based *Simultaneisme* movement, were married in 1910.

ty. Learning from the Delaunays, Torre discovered his peculiar way of deconstructing and reconstructing perspective and perception in poetic form. In his work, these changes took on the additional significance of cosmopolitanism. Altering the rules governing the representation of perspective and perception was analogous to reconfiguring the reader's viewpoint: if the subject could be uprooted from a fixed position in time and space–allowing it to "see" or "perceive" beyond former limits–then Torre's readers could likewise become so liberated. Through my formulation, "deconstruction-(re)construction," I interpret the significance of Delaunay's French-language phrasing, "destruction-construction," and Torre's rendition of it in Spanish as "destrucción, reconstrucción." Although the literal translation of the French "destruction" and the Spanish "destrucción" into English would be "destruction," this is not the meaning that the word had to either Delaunay or Torre. Instead, both men had in mind the idea of "deconstruction," since *Simultaneisme* as well as Torre's *Simultaneisme*-influenced *Ultraísmo* was not about destroying, but rather breaking down perception to its most elemental parts, and then using these components to construct new artistic and literary forms which would reflect the experience of perceptual simultaneity.

Whereas Torre made *Simultaneisme's* deconstruction-construction paradigm the formal foundation of his poetry, his fellow members of the Spanish avant-garde paid more attention to the cosmopolitan sophistication of the Delaunays themselves.[2] Their popularity can be attributed to the typical view of them as artists of rupture, internationalism, and experimental interdisciplinarity (Rousseau, "El arte nuevo" 66). While Torre certainly made a play at cosmopolitanism by association, he also seriously engaged *Simultaneisme*. Since he frequented the Delaunays' Madrid studio, he

---

[2] In homage to the Parisian painters, two authors active in the *Ultraísmo* movement, Isaac Vando-Villar and Luis Mosquera, penned their comic play *Rompecabezas*, in which the character of "Nancy" bears an uncanny resemblance to Delaunay-Terk (Martín i Ros 75, 81). Vando-Villar, editor of the Ultra journal *Grecia* during its early years headquartered in Seville, reproduced Delaunay's *Fenêtre simultanée* as a visually striking cover for the same 1920 issue which contained his poem "Sonia Delaunay" (Rousseau, "El arte nuevo" 66; Wheelen 428). "Sonia Delaunay" was published in issue number 48 of *Grecia* in September, 1920. In Rafael Cansinos-Assens's semi-fictional account of the first Spanish avant-garde, *El movimiento V.P.*, Delaunay-Terk comes to life in the humorous figure "Sofía Modernuska"–a caricature of the international high-fashion designer that she became.

would have seen first-hand the Iberian-period paintings in which the artists continued the work that they had begun in Paris of developing an abstract pictorial language to represent visual perception. In contrast with Ramón Gómez de la Serna, one of the deans of the Spanish avant-garde, Torre comprehended *Simultaneisme* in terms of visual perception made form, as well as the possibilities that this conception of form offered for the renovation of Spain's art and literature. While Gómez de la Serna admired the Delaunays and praised their artistic innovations, he argued dismissively that "*simultanismo* es una bella palabra indiscreta, aunque bella. No podía ser una cosa duradera, congregante, y en ese principio de decadencia estaba su indiscreción" (*Sagrada cripta* 427).

Torre authored two monographs on the Delaunays, *Destrucción, reconstrucción: la pintura de Robert Delaunay* (1920) and *El arte decorativo de Sonia Delaunay-Terk* (1921), and one study of Cendrars, titled simply *Blaise Cendrars* (n.d.). While *Destrucción, reconstrucción* and *Blaise Cendrars* never reached publication, *El arte decorativo de Sonia Delaunay-Terk* eventually took on a slightly different and shorter form in a 1925 article, which appeared under the same title in the journal *Alfar*.[3] *Destrucción, reconstrucción* is illustrative of the way in which Torre adapts *Simultaneisme* and how the *destruction/construction* paradigm shapes his work. He relates Delaunay's simultaneous representation of the Eiffel Tower to the international emission of the Parisian avant-garde's innovations—and their reception in Madrid.

In *Destrucción, reconstrucción*, Torre quotes a series of poems about the Eiffel Tower by those connected with the Paris vanguard and, in doing so in the context of his analyzing Delaunay, he compares himself to the painter and inscribes his work in an expanded history of the European avant-garde.[4] Torre's citation of these

---

[3] *El arte decorativo de Sonia Delaunay-Terk* is an exception to this rule. It was published–in different form–as an article in a 1925 issue of the journal *Alfar*. See Guillermo de Torre, "El arte decorativo de Sonia Delaunay-Terk." Although the manuscript *Blaise Cendrars* remains undated, as I note in Chapter 2, we can be reasonably certain that it is from between 1918 and 1925. Handwriting as well as Torre's interests and friendships at the time would point in this general direction. In parenthetical references, I use *Arte decorativo* to mean the unpublished text and "Arte decorativo" to indicate the published article.

[4] Torre accords Delaunay primacy with respect to the tendency of using the Eiffel Tower to represent cosmopolitanism and avant-garde aesthetics. In *Destrucción, reconstrucción: La pintura de Robert Delaunay*, he writes: "¡Máximo acierto

134   MAPPING THE LANDSCAPE, REMAPPING THE TEXT

avant-garde representations of the Tower is suggestive of the parallels that he consistently makes among "vertical" perspective, perceptual simultaneity, and cosmopolitanism:

> La Torre Eiffel ha sido exaltada líricamente por todos los poetas vanguardistas que han erigido y simbolizado en la cúspide de esta esbelta torre la antena vibrátil de sus inquietudes y de sus polarizaciones líricas intermundiales. Y alcanzan desde la plataforma más alta una perspectiva total . . . .

Torre reproduces (in Spanish translation) a portion of Apollinaire's poem "Tour," which is dedicated to Delaunay: "Tú te inclinas, graciosa palmera!–Eres tú quien en la época legendaria del pueblo hebreo–confundiste la lengua de los hombres–oh Babel!–Tú resplandeces con toda la magnificencia de la aurora boreal de tu telegrafía sin hilos."[5] He does the same with Cendrars's poem of the same title (*Destrucción, reconstrucción*).[6] In the lines that Torre selects from Cendrars's "Tour," Babel represents the breakdown of a single language into disparate variants. Torre turns this Babel into an allegory of *destruction/construction*, as well as the way in which the paradigm becomes prototypical of the transformation and renewal of poetic language in *Ultraísmo*.[7] To this end, he includes lines from his own "Torre Eiffel," giving emphasis to the links that he envisions among aerial perspective, perceptual simultaneity, and international communication.[8]

---

pictórico. . . alcanzado por Robert Delaunay con su cuadro 'La Tour Eiffel'! Esta Torre rebasa su significación recordatoria y adquiere la alta categoría de un símbolo de nueva estética, a partir del cuadro de Delaunay."

[5] Apollinaire's "Tour" reads: "Au Nord au Sud / Zénith Nadir / Et les grands cris de l'Est / L'Océan se gonfle à l'Ouest / La Tour à la Roue / S'adresse" (*Œuvres poétiques* 1-6/200).

[6] Cendrars's "Tour" is from *Dix-Neuf poèmes élastiques* (1919). In French: "Tu te penches, gracieux Palmier! / C'est toi qui à l'époque légendaire du peuple hébreu / Confondis la langue des hommes / O Babel! / Et quelques mille ans plus tard, c'est toi qui retombais en langues de feu sur les Apôtres / rassemblés dans ton église / En pleine mer tu es un mât / Et au Pôle-Nord / Tu resplendis avec toute la magnificence de l'aurore boréale de ta télégraphie sans fil" (Complete Poems 260). The Spanish translations are presumably Torre's.

[7] Torre also incorporates the French Nicolas Beauduin's poetic evocation of the Tower, which makes reference to the monument as symbol of victory in World War I: "'Tú que alzas al cielo vencido tu Torre de hierro–como un símbolo de victoria... Oh! En lo alto de tu plataforma metálica,–oh gran Torre, oh simbólica–yo oigo voces nuevas–que se elevan y gritan hacia mí" (*Deconstrucción, reconstrucción*).

[8] The text is as follows: "Torre: Hélice del tiempo–gimnasta del espacio–cohete señal–de las intenciones verticales–Bandera de júbilo al viento–Reflector solar de las

Fittingly, Torre dedicates "Torre Eiffel" to Delaunay and "Arco iris" to Delaunay-Terk–the two poems were conceived as companion pieces–and places an epigraph from Cendrars's *Le Panama* at the beginning of the "Trayectorias" section of *Hélices*.[9] Torre's homage to Cendrars, and the dedications of "Torre Eiffel" and "Arco iris" to Robert and Sonia Delaunay respectively indicate how important it was to him to introduce *Simultaneisme* to the Spanish avant-garde. In "Torre Eiffel," his punning on the meaning of the Spanish word *"torre"* and his surname, and moving of the Eiffel Tower from Paris to Madrid–"Yo la Torre de Madrid / sobre el campanario de Santa Cruz"–highlights his adaptation of *Simultaneisme* (lines 5-6/33). Torre's "Torre de Madrid," now situated above the bell-tower of Madrid's Santa Cruz Church, is regrounded in *Ultraísmo's* milieu; such a positioning has strategic importance for his remapping of the Spanish avant-garde relative to Europe (6/33). "Escuchad el ritmo aviónico / del motor de mi Verbo": by this high-flying rhythm Torre not only means his "speech" as poet of *Ultraísmo*, but also his activity as the movement's spearhead and "tower" of communication with Paris ("Torre Eiffel," *Hélices* 9-10/33).

The representation of perspective and perception in *Hélices* derives from *Simultaneisme*: "Rayos–luminarias–relámpagos / Eclosión de los paisajes simultáneos / Los puentes saltan a la comba / sobre el Sena" ("Torre Eiffel" 20-24/33). In "Torre Eiffel," the dizzying perspective from the top of the tower explodes perception, dissolving the view into fragmented images:

---

proyecciones inéditas–sus ojos cartografían el cuerpo de Paris"; "Torre del occidente–Brújula de las orientaciones estéticas–Línea del meridiano lírico"; "Torre, flecha perpendicular–directriz del nuevo espíritu–pararrayos de la belleza" (*Destrucción, reconstrucción*). It is reasonable to assume that Torre had already written "Torre Eiffel" or that he was actively working on it during the writing of *Destrucción, reconstrucción*. The title page of *Hélices* would confirm that the poem was written between 1919 and 1920, although there remains the possibility that Torre changed the dating to fit with the aims and trajectory of the volume. In the *Hélices* version, the passages quoted in *Destrucción, reconstrucción* are: "Torre / Hélice del tiempo / Gimnasta del espacio / Cohete-señal / de las intenciones ascensionales // Bandera de triunfo al viento / Reflector solar / de films inéditos"; "Torre del Occidente / Brújula de los vientos estéticos / Línea del meridiano lírico / Espectro del arco iris / Espectáculo de la novedad perpetua" (Torre, "Torre Eiffel," *Hélices* 53-60, 68-72/34-35).

 9 The epigraph from Cendrars's *Le Panama* reads, "La poésie date d'aujourd'hui / La voie lactée autour du cou / Les deux hémisphères sur les yeux / A toute vitesse." There is an additional epigraph from Arthur Rimbaud's (1854-1891) *Le bateau ivre* (1871): "'...J'ai vu des archipels sidereaux et des îles / Dont les cieux délirants sont ouvertes au vogueur...'" (Torre, *Hélices* 18).

APOTEOSIS DINÁMICA
Puzzle vibracionista
de la Torre volcánica
sobre las calles móviles
las casas contorsionadas
y las gentes ébrias (sic)
==como en el cuadro-kaleidoscopio
del destructor Delaunay== (27-34/34)[10]

By means of simile, Torre compares his breakdown of perception–the subject scales the Eiffel Tower and experiences the defamiliarizing perspective that its height affords–to the "destructor Delaunay" and his "cuadro-kaleidoscopio"–a reference to Delaunay's *Tour* series. Torre patterns his splintering of perception–resulting in the juxtaposition of "las calles móviles," "las casas contorsionadas," and "las gentes ébrias (sic)"–on these Eiffel Tower paintings in which Delaunay breaks up the picture plane, detaching the gaze so that it sees all the Tower's facets simultaneously. "Ya estoy arriba": by imitating the perspective of Delaunay's *Tour* paintings, he renders "Torre Eiffel" an "apoteosis dinámica" of the deconstructive vision that he would then resolve into a new, "reconstructed" poetic form.

In her memoir *Nous irons jusqu'au soleil*, Delaunay-Terk remarks upon the groundbreaking effect of "la luminosité violente de ce pays"–by which she meant Spain and Portugal–when combined with the scientific study of vision that the Delaunays made while still living in France:

> Les lois, scientifiquement découvertes par Chevreul et vérifiées par lui sur l'expérience de couleurs pratiques, furent observées par Robert et moi dans la nature, en Espagne et au Portugal où l'irradiation de la lumière est plus pure, moins brumeuse qu'en France. La qualité même de cette lumière nous permit d'aller plus loin que Chevreul et de trouver, en plus des accords fondés sur des contrastes, des dissonances, c'est-à-dire des vibrations rapides qui provoquent une exaltation plus grande de la couleur par le voisinage de certaines couleurs chaudes et froides. (71, 75-76)

---

[10] Through the phrase "Puzzle vibracionista," Torre makes reference to *Vibracionismo*, a term that the Uruguayan painter Rafael Barradas invented to indicate a phase of his work that had much in common with Italian Futurism and Cubism, specifically spatio-temporal simultaneity, the representation of motion, and the exaltation of modern urban life.

"[L']animation de la rue" in Spain and Portugal reminded Sonia of "la Russie de mon enfance, les fêtes, les marchés, les chants, les danses populaires" (Delaunay, *Nous irons* 71). Yet while the folkloric ambience of Spain and Portugal informs the subject matter of the Delaunays' major Iberian canvases, the principal significance of these works comes from their substantive development of Simultaneist form. By 1912-1913, Robert had already pared the representation of visual perception down to circular shapes. These concentric "circular forms" evoke light sources such as the sun, moon, and electric bulbs; they also suggest the shape of the human eye and the color wheel which, in Michel Eugène Chevreul's theory of vision, explains perception in terms of interactions among hues of the spectrum (*Principles of Harmony*).[11]

In Delaunay's *Formes circulaires* (1912-1914), the process of perceiving and reproducing color contrasts in the retina becomes paradigmatic of painted form: the relationship among the various concentric circles structurally encodes the interaction between eye and external world; the rhythmic pulse generated by the color contrasts replicates the synthesis that occurs in visual perception. In a similar way as for the French Impressionist Georges Seurat, for Delaunay the central problem of painting consists in the invention of techniques that could be made to reduplicate the experience of seeing (Roque 53-64). Delaunay and Fernand Léger recreate the experience of visual perception in abstract form. Both painters, influenced by the Impressionists and Paul Cézanne, "believed that profound experience could be found through perception, and that pure painting could so deeply involve the spectator in its physical being that it could give him an intense consciousness of the essence of life, of its movement, energy, and dynamism" (Spate 160-61). Virginia Spate calls this conjoining of form and vision "perceptual Orphism," modifying Apollinaire's original terms "orphisme" and "cubisme orphique," which he employed to describe the type of pure abstraction that developed in the painting of Delaunay, Léger, Frances Picabia, and Marcel Duchamp (Apollinaire, *Méditations esthétiques* 22-23).[12] Sherry Buckberrough notes that Apollinaire used the label

---

[11] Michel Eugène Chevreul based his color theory on the observations that he made of the Gobelin tapestry works' dye processes. These findings shaped his treatise, *De la Loi du contraste simultané des couleurs.*

[12] See Virginia Spate's *Orphism: The Evolution of Non-Figurative Painting in Paris, 1910-1914*, particularly Chapter 2, "Perceptual Orphism: Robert Delaunay:

"Orphic Cubism" to differentiate Delaunay, Léger, Picabia, and Duchamp from the other Cubists, and specifies, in agreement with Spate, that the poet and critic started to equate "simultaneity" with Orphism after the publication of "Réalité, peinture pure" in 1912 (217). In an article on the 1913 *Salon des Indépendants* (Paris) for *L'Intransigeant*, Apollinaire speaks of *Orphisme* as a new tenden-cy–"On a déjà beaucoup parlé de l'Orphisme. C'est la première fois que cette tendance se manifeste"–and posits Delaunay as the maxi-mum exponent of *Orphisme's* simultaneous form–"*L'Équipe de Cardiff, troisième représentation*, de Delaunay, est une toile très mod-erne. Rien de successif dans cette peinture; chaque ton appelle et laisse s'illuminer toutes les autres couleurs du prisme. C'est la simul-tanéité" (qtd. in "Opinions" 39-40).

Throughout the Iberian period, which stretched from 1914 to 1920, Robert and Sonia used the color contrasts of the *Formes circu-laires* as basic vocabulary and method for the at once figurative and abstract *Verseuses, Portugais au potiron, Femme nue lisant, Portugais-es, Jouets portugais* and *Chanteurs flamencos*.[13] The intense sun of

---

Fernand Léger." Spate distinguishes "perceptual Orphism," which in her view is based on abstract form, from what she calls the "mystical Orphism" of František (Frank) Kupka, and the "psychological Orphism" of Francis Picabia and Marcel Duchamp. Apollinaire invented the terms "orphisme" and "cubisme orphique" to describe the work of Delaunay, Léger, Picabia, and Duchamp. While it is possible that he conceived Frank Kupka, the Czech painter, as an additional member of the group, he chose not to include Kupka in his discussion of "cubisme orphique" in *Les peintres cubistes* (1913). It should be noted that not all the artists included in Apollinaire's list necessarily agreed with his characterizations. For an overview of Orphism, see Spate's Introduction and Chapter 1. Also consult Apollinaire, *Médita-tions esthétiques: les peintres cubistes*.

[13] With the outbreak of World War I began what Sonia rather drolly called the Delaunays' "grandes vacances." Until the 1917 Russian Revolution, Robert, Sonia, and their young son Charles enjoyed financial independence due to income from her estate–her inheritance from her family (Delaunay, *Nous irons* 71-81). After Robert was exempted from French military service on medical grounds, the couple decided to wait out the conflict and try their luck in Spain and Portugal. The Delaunays' pleasant exile ended in 1920, when circumstances again permitted them to return home to Paris. A letter to Robert and Sonia from Mexican painter Diego Rivera from early 1915 situates them in the heart of Madrid, installed on the central *calle Goya*. Although they were successful there, the Delaunays decided to relocate to Portugal as a result of the ill-effects of the Madrid heat (Rousseau, "El arte nuevo" 43). Once settled in Oporto, the couple ingratiated themselves with the Portuguese Futurists, Amado de Souza-Cardoso, Eduardo Vianna, José Pacheco, and José de Almada Ne-greiros (Rousseau, "El arte nuevo" 44, 48; Wheelen 424-27). (See also Paulo Fer-reira, *Correspondance de quatre artistes portugais: Almada-Negreiros, José Pacheco, Souza-Cardoso, Eduardo Vianna avec Robert et Sonia Delaunay*.)

Spain and Portugal provided ideal conditions for examining the movement and gradations of light and color, and the Delaunays blended the knowledge gained there with developments from the *Formes circulaires* period. During a 1914 stay in the Spanish seaside town of Fuenterrabía, the Mexican painter Ángel Zárraga taught them methods of painting with wax, the adoption of which intensified the colors of their palette.[14] They further developed the wax technique during their first Madrid residence (Rousseau, "El arte nuevo" 41-42; Wheelen 423). Combining the new wax techniques with the circular forms simulated the vibration of the midday sun and the quotidian rhythms of Portuguese street life: "Au Portugal, plus qu'ailleurs, il nous était donné de partir du réel pour aboutir naturellement à l'abstrait, aux éléments essentiels, aux formes circulaires dont la ligne ne brise pas le rythme de la couleur" (Delaunay, *Nous irons* 76). In the Portuguese paintings, a brilliant white light shines down on disk-shaped objects as if they were illuminated by the noonday sun, effectively stressing the color contrasts and reproducing them much as in actual visual experience. In Robert's *Nature morte portugaise ou symphonie colorée* (1915-1917), the still life of flowers, Portuguese ceramics, and market fruits metamorphoses into a vibrating play of concentric disks. The viewer immediately recalls his breakthrough *Formes circulaires* series and the riot of colored circles in the related *Hommage à Blériot* (1914). Likewise, the interplay of color contrasts in the many concentric circles of *La grande portugaise* recapitulates vision while still forming part of a group of figurative images–a large female body, furnishings, and decorative objects. Sonia's work of a comparable moment–the *Étude pour 'Le marché au Minho'* (1915), *Fillette aux pastèques* (*Étude pour 'Le marché au Minho'*) (1915), and the flamenco singers of 1916–brings together figuration with the abstract portrayal of visual perception.[15]

---

[14] Fuenterrabía, or Hondarribia in the local *Euskera* or Basque language, is located in the *País Vasco*, near the French border.

[15] As a compositional technique, the circular forms were so successful at signing the movement of color and light that despite the good order of Robert's military papers, officials in France and Portugal grew suspicious of the motivation for the Delaunays' Lusitanian residence. So as to escape rumors that the vibrating disks in their paintings functioned as signals to German submarines on the coast, Robert made arrangements to transfer their workshop to Vigo, in the northwest Spanish region of Galicia. However, discovery of the Delaunays' contact with the German *Der Blaue Reiter* group complicated the situation. Robert and Sonia had extensive contact with the painters Franz Marc, August Macke, and Paul Klee, which they

Torre and the Delaunays developed their relationship in Madrid in 1918, where Robert and Sonia were then living, although it is possible that they met earlier.[16] The rapidly deepening friendship among the three brought *Simultaneisme* to Torre's critical vocabulary, as well as leading to several proposed collective projects. These undertakings were discussed in the extensive correspondence between Torre and the Delaunays, which began in 1920 and ended in 1937 (Torre, *Lettres*). Torre promoted Delaunay-Terk's art work in Spain, including her 1920 exhibition in Madrid; the monograph and article version of *El arte decorativo de Sonia Delaunay-Terk* formed part of his publicity efforts on her behalf.[17] In the prefatory pages of the

---

maintained while they were in Portugal (Rousseau, "El arte nuevo" 46; Ferreira 53). The subsequent accusation of espionage against the Delaunays turned out to have its causes in the personal affairs of the secretary of the French consulate, and was eventually resolved through intervention on the part of friends. (Wheelen 425).

[16] The Delaunays' second residence in Madrid occurred in 1918. See also Torre, "Juan Gris y Robert Delaunay: Reminiscencias personales." To combat their economic reversal of fortune, Sonia began work as a designer of clothes and *bibelots*. The Delaunays initiated contacts in the world of the fine arts in Barcelona, befriending the gallery owner and major supporter of the avant-garde, Josep Dalmau (1867-1937), with whom they would maintain correspondence during their 1914-1915 Madrid residence. The Delaunays earned enough recognition for Catalan painter and critic Joan Sachs to publish "El simultanisme del senyor i la senyora Delaunay" in the influential journal *Vell i Nou* (Bonet 215). In the December 15, 1917 issue of this same journal appeared another piece by Sachs which included Robert's letters about his painting, in addition to a version of Apollinaire's article "Les réformateurs du costume," retitled "Els Delaunay i la moda del vestir" (Martín i Ros 72). Joan Sachs is a pseudonym for Feliu Elias (1878-1948)–painter, critic, caricaturist, and founder of the satirical review *Papitu*. He wrote extensively on Cubism in *Vell i Nou* and in his book *La pintura francesa moderna fins al cubisme* (Bonet 215, 544). Apollinaire's article, "Les reformations du costume" appeared in the journal *Mercure de France* in 1914. It describes Delaunay-Terk's innovations in fashion design, including a number of articles of clothing worn by Robert and Sonia.

[17] Despite the Delaunays' considerable Barcelona connections, they nevertheless elected to launch Sonia's designs in Madrid. Their decision was driven by the greater presence of potential aristocratic patrons in the capital city, and the increase in the population of international exiles there during World War I. The Marquis de Valdeiglesias's letters to Delaunay-Terk are conserved in the Fond Delaunay, Bibliothèque Nationale de France. They are labeled "4 minutes de lettres. 1919-1920 with corrections by RD [Robert Delaunay]." During Christmas 1915, after the Delaunays' relocation to the socially prestigious address of Bárbara de Braganza, 14, Madrid honored Sonia with an exhibition of her *bibelots*–thus launching her design career. During this period, Delaunay occasionally took on a more active role in the promotion of his wife's designs. With this document are a pair of sketches–probably for a corresponding poster. There is also a fragment, in Delaunay's handwriting: "Sonia Delaunay-Terk Exposition Madrid–12-20" (Delaunay, Projets de couverts).

original edition of *Hélices*, Torre includes a short catalogue of forth-coming works, assumedly for the purposes of drawing attention to his work and to *Ultraísmo*. Mention of "Destrucción & Construcción: El arte de Delaunay," which assuredly corresponds to *Destrucción, reconstrucción*, comes towards the middle of the list:[18]

GUILLERMO DE TORRE

HA PUBLICADO:
Manifiesto Ultraísta: Vertical.–Madrid, 1920.
Hélices: Poemas (1918-1922).–Editorial Mundo Latino. Madrid, 1923.

PUBLICARÁ:
Las novísimas direcciones literarias y estéticas. (Críticas.) Editorial Mundo Latino, 1923.   (*En prensa*.)
Prólogo y traducción de El Cubilete de Dados, por Max Jacob. Editorial América, 1923.   (*En prensa*.)
Antología crítica de la poesía francesa de vanguardia.
Destrucción & Construcción: El arte de Delaunay.
El Lucífero: Prosas politemáticas.
Film vibracionista.
El meridiano adolescente. (Novela.) (*Hélices*, n. pag.)

Inclusion of the monograph shows that *Simultaneisme* played a meaningful role in the development of *Ultraísmo*.

Delaunay drew up a series of sketches that bear the inscription *Destruction/Construction*, which is roughly equivalent to the title that Torre would give his projected monograph on Robert's theo-

---

In another key professional development, Robert and Sonia renewed the friendship that they had begun previously in Barcelona with Sergei Diaghilev, impresario and founder of the *Ballets Russes*. Diaghilev introduced Sonia to the daughter of Eduardo Dato, the Marquis de Valdeiglesias and the current President of the Spanish government. Sonia's acquaintanceship with the Valdeiglesias family opened the door to noble patronage, as well as the Madrid press, through Dato's directorship of the newspaper *La Época*. From 1918 on, approving reviews and analyses of the Delaunays' art works began to appear regularly in Spanish periodicals (Martín i Ros 72-73). In 1919, Sonia became successful enough to consolidate her business ventures in *Casa Sonia*, a design firm located on Madrid's *calle Columela*. Revenues from *Casa Sonia*, in combination with Robert's commission to design the interior of the music hall *Petit Casino*, allowed the Delaunays sufficient resources to exhibit at the esteemed *Asociación de Artistas Vascos* in Bilbao (Demase, *Sonia Delaunay* 83; Martín i Ros 74-75; Wheelen 428).

[18] Most of the works advertised by Torre remain unknown or unpublished. The list was reprinted in the 2001 facsimile edition.

ries. Delaunay's drawings, designed for the cover of the book, most likely date from sometime between 1915 and 1920, the year marked on the manuscript copy of *Destruction/Construction* (Delaunay, *Projets de couverts*).[19] In one of the sketches, Delaunay juxtaposes the words "destruction" and "construction" in the form of a "T," while on another of the six pages in the set of drawings, he foregrounds Torre's authorship: "Destruction Construction Delaunay par de Torre." A separate document, marked with the dates 1918-1919 and inscribed with notes indicating that it was to be sent to Torre, outlines the content of the proposed project:

1. Perspective à R.D.
2. Réalité-Peinture-Pure.
3. Réalité peinture pure-autre manuscrit.
4. Quelques dates-de Cendrars.
5. Simultaneisme de l'art moderne Français.
6. Représentation et métier.
7. Lumière et construction R.D.
8. La lumière de R.D. (Letter to Torre, *Lettres*, 1918-1919).

The vocabulary and intellectual concerns reveal the brief summary to be Delaunay's brainchild.

Torre's "Esquisse–Índice de capítulos" of the 1920 *Destrucción-Reconstrucción* is oriented differently, according to his interests:

I. El carácter constructivo de nuestra época: la plenitud de R. Delaunay. – Su arte constructivo. Su conexión con los neo-impresionistas.

II. Retrospección de sus etapas. Delaunay cubista puro. – Su paso al 'orfismo.' – Su ascensión al 'simultaneismo.' Su teoría del 'color-forma.'–

III. Examen de los cuadros de su primera época: Las Tours-Saint-Séverin.

---

[19] It should be noted that one of the originals is inscribed, in what looks to be Delaunay's handwriting, with the date "1915," which lends some small credence to the idea that Torre and the Delaunays became acquainted in that year. However, Torre would have been only fifteen years old at the time and, although his career as a writer began early, a full collaboration with an established artist of Delaunay's stature would have been unlikely, even for the precocious youth. It is far more probable that Delaunay conceived the project before meeting Torre, and that Torre's work was shaped by the French painter.

IV. Transcripción de opiniones y teorías sobre el simultaneismo. –Apollinaire, Smirnoff, Vromant, Huntington-Wright.
V. Etapa constructiva: El simultaneísmo literario de Barzun, el 1er color simultaneísta de Cendrars y Sonia Terk.–
VI. Teorizaciones de Delaunay mismo, referentes a sus cuadros.
VII. Teorizaciones de Vromant: la pintura 'pura' de Delaunay.
VIII. La conexión con los futuristas italianos y su influencia sobre los simultaneístas ingleses.
IX. Su enlace con el moderno expresionismo alemán.
X. Síntesis y exaltación. (*Destrucción, reconstrucción*)[20]

Delaunay's goal becomes streamlining *métier*–which he defines as both form and technique–so that it becomes the constructive equivalent of vision in his painting–the color and light contrasts. As a result, his outline of the Destruction/Construction project primarily reflects a concern with visual perception and the taking shape of vision in form. Contrastingly, Torre's schema parlays Delaunay's *métier* into a model for the main avant-garde literary currents of the day, including *Ultraísmo*.

Torre conceives *Destrucción, reconstrucción* as a definitive handbook to *Simultaneisme* for the Spanish vanguard. In a letter of June 23, 1921 to Robert Delaunay, he expresses a wish to become familiar with Cendrars's contribution–in order to make his project even more comprehensive. He inquires about a "manifeste simultanéiste" that he believes Cendrars to have published in 1914–apparently depending on information from Delaunay–which would be of "grand intérêt maintenant pour compléter l'histoire du Simultaneisme dans 'Destruction.'" *Destrucción, reconstrucción* stayed unpublished in spite of the efforts of the Delaunays and Torre, and the substantial critical content of the monograph. In a 1921 letter to Robert, Torre proposes Paul Dermée as a potential publisher for the monographic study: "j'ai écrit à mon ami Mr. Paul Dermée avec l'objet de lui proposer la publication d'un extrait de notre 'Destruction & Construction,' avant de faire l'édition. Je suis en attendant sa réponse, ainsi que le no. 4, où je pense á été publié mon chronique sur l'art de Sonia" (Letter to Robert Delaunay, February 5, 1921). The difficulty of getting the two monographs published, particularly the work on

[20] Laetitia Branciard has discussed *Destrucción, reconstrucción* in relation to the friendship between Delaunay and Torre in her article "Guillermo de Torre et l'œuvre de Robert Delaunay."

Robert, became a source of increasing frustration for Torre between 1920 and 1923–showing his attachment to the project.[21] In a different part of his June 23, 1921 letter to Robert, he asks, "Faisiez-moi un cadre de sa situation actuelle dans les meilleurs d'avant-garde. Et plus particulièrement, disiez-moi le résultat de votre gestion de Povolozky et autres éditeurs pour éditer notre livre."

During the same period in which Torre worked on disseminating the Delaunays' art in Spain, he sent Robert and Sonia copies of the poems "Torre Eiffel" and "Arco iris," which would appear in *Hélices* in 1923. In a letter to Robert of December 13, 1920, Torre writes, "Aujourd'hui je vous donne la petite surprise de vous envoyer ces deux poèmes 'Arco iris' dédié a Sonia, et 'Tour' pour vous." Torre remarks that "Arco iris" "pourrait être une bonne affiche verticale–pour une prochaine exposition de Sonia." He envisions "Torre Eiffel" as the precursor to a second simultaneous poem-painting, along the lines of Cendrars's and Delaunay-Terk's collaboration, *La Prose du Transsibérien et de la petite Jeanne de France* (1913): "vous pouvez essayer avec lui le premier poème-tableau, dont nous avons parlé." Torre's tone grows urgent as he talks of placing the poems in Spanish journals; "Tour Eiffel" and "Arco iris" would ultimately be printed in *Cosmópolis* in 1921, accompanied by a brief essay by Torre on *Simultaneisme* (Postal Card to Robert Delaunay, October 24, 1921).[22] His quest to make the Delaunays' work known drives him to unveil, in a letter to Robert of March, 1922, an ambitious proposal for creating an international council on avant-garde art and literature:

> Je propose au 'Congrès de Paris' la formation d'un COMITÉ MONDIALE DE LA JEUNESSE D'AVANT-GARDE centralisée a Paris et avec des succursales dans les principaux villes du monde européen et américain: là où il peut se trouver une groupe de jeunes gens atteints aux vibrations de la conscience littéraire et artistique. Ce Comité au dehors de grouper les esprits les plus jeunes et vivants pourra constituer a la manière d'une commission technique spéciale pour contrôler et registrer les apports et les découverts de tout genre dans le domaine esthétique, parues dans le monde entier.

---

[21] In a communication of July 24, 1921, Torre painstakingly explains to Delaunay that the manuscript has been rejected by "Mr. Mercereau"–quoting at length from Mercereau's letter. (Torre means the socialist writer Alexandre Mercereau.)

[22] In the postal card, Torre writes, "Mon cher ami: COSMOPOLIS est sorti avec 'Tour' et 'Arco Iris.' Je vous enverrai un exemplaire."

His motive for the creation of the committee and the regularization of avant-garde aesthetics stems from his negative assessment of the situation in Spain: "Ainsi réalisera une fonction utile envers la détermination des nouveaux valeurs et personnalités et fera impossible le chaos et le malentendu qui règnent actuellement dans les ambiances sans contrôle–tel le cas de l'Espagne." (Letter to Robert Delaunay, March, 1922)

For his part, Robert writes to Torre in 1923–the year of *Hélices's* publication–about an interdisciplinary and cross-cultural project of considerable scope. In his letter, he describes the creation of a Franco-Spanish publication that would represent the best of the European avant-garde in the visual and verbal arts.[23] Robert goes on to imagine the journal juxtaposing his engravings and lithographs of Paris with poetic representations of the same views. He envisions an "album de gravures et lithos des *Paysages de Paris*," paired with cityscapes by "les meilleurs poètes modernes," which would serve as a retrospective of *Simultaneisme* and a history of its formal language's creation. The anticipated journal, the Destruction/Construction project, and the other works discussed by Torre and Delaunay share a pedagogical attitude, as well as a commitment to bringing new concepts across borders.[24]

---

[23] Delaunay suggests including a "collection des poètes"–namely Philippe Soupault, Tristan Tzara, Ilia Zdanevich, André Breton, Nicolas Beauduin, Ivan Goll, and Vladimir Mayakovsky–and Sonia's decorative art. The look of the manuscript letter recalls the experimental typographical layout of many of the poems which were to be incorporated into the project:

Ça reprise de manège électrique =1905=
les vues de Paris – la Seine

la concorde
arc de triomphe
la cité =
les grands magasins –
Cirque   les courses, les fêtes!!!
(Letter to Torre, October 18, 1923)

[24] In an October 18, 1923 letter to Torre, Delaunay describes his current painting and the planned Franco-Spanish journal through a metaphor of altitude. Here he highlights his interest in painting the Eiffel Tower, which at its most intense, lasted from the early 1910s until the 1920s. Delaunay's phrasing underlines the monumentality of his ideas, and the importance of synthesizing visual perception and performative form in Simultaneist painting:

Je [suis] venu faire les esquisses cette année de mon très grand tableau (un des plus grands du monde) que je vive depuis 1920. La Tour Simultanée: Toute une vision du monde–un grouillement de rythmes

Torre seized upon *Simultaneisme* because he saw in Delaunay's transformation of simultaneous perception into form and reconfiguration of perspective the potential to create a new language for *Ultraísmo*. Yet beyond linguistic and poetic innovation, perceptual simultaneity became paradigmatic with respect to Torre's perceptual cosmopolitanism. For him, as we have seen, it meant the possibility of freeing the eye and "I" from temporal and spatial bounds. By using perceptual simultaneity to uproot the subject, Torre jettisons the past and confining conceptions of collective identity.

Delaunay's construction of perspective in his pre-*Formes Circulaires* paintings constitutes his initial step towards melding perception and form–a step that Torre imitated with his aerial views. In his *Ville* and *Tour* series–Delaunay's renderings of the spire of Notre-Dame (1909-1915), Saint-Séverin (1909-1910), *Les tours de Laon* (1912), and the Eiffel Tower–the architecture of Paris at once forms and frames the subject of representation. As a consequence, Delaunay suspends the gaze of the fictive observer, letting it hover rather than grounding the "I"/eye in a particular area. This is a major reason for his obsession with architecture and the development of his painting towards abstract and monumental forms (Dorival). According to Pascal Rousseau, "La mayoría de los motivos predilectos de Delaunay son 'objetos-espectáculo,'" a category of constructions that are "al mismo tiempo instrumentos y sujetos de observación." In Rousseau's estimation, "Tanto si se trata de la Torre Eiffel como del Arco de Triunfo o de la Noria Gigante, son siempre lugares de observación que permiten arrojar sobre la realidad una mirada inédita, cuyos denominadores comunes son la distancia aérea, la gestión circular de la mirada y la extensión panorámica del campo visual" ("Vértigo" 35).

In his *Saint-Séverin no. 3* (1909-1910), Delaunay takes Renaissance perspective to an extreme: he situates the disembodied eye of the fictive observer at the point of optical convergence, making it float between the neo-gothic arches of the church. Delaunay applies the free-form vision that characterizes *Saint-Séverin no. 3* to his subsequent evocations of the Eiffel Tower. He structures the composition of *Tour Eiffel aux arbres* (1910) and *La Tour aux rideaux* (1910-

infinis–un journal planétaire transplanétaire, une vision multiforme et mouvement multicolore des vibrations de toutes nos connaissances de toute modernité. (Letter to Torre, October 18, 1923)

1911) so that that the trees and curtains, located at top, bottom, left, and right, reduplicate the picture frame. The recapitulation of the frame emphasizes that the eye is its ultimate source, as well as affirming the subjective character of vision. Yet the frame's function here is the opposite of the usual one: instead of restricting the movement of the gaze and determining the subject's identification with that which is being represented, it actually frees the "I"/eye from all such attachments and restraints. Delaunay's redoubled framing in *Saint-Séverin no. 3* and *Tour aux rideaux* reminds us not only that we are seeing, but also that we are seeing as modern subjects, uprooted from all external contexts and bounded only by our perceptual apparatus. It must be remembered, however, that Delaunay was more interested in discovering the scientific laws of vision, and inventing a formal language to articulate them in painting than in exploring the character of visual perception in modernity. Nonetheless, his playing with the conventions of the frame, dissociating vision, and liberating the subject from perspectival and perceptual restrictions, means a loosening of bonds with the established culture and the hierarchies of representation that it seeks to impose (Llorens, Personal interview).[25]

As Delaunay writes in *Du cubisme a l'art abstrait*, the translation of visual perception into a formal paradigm constitutes "Ce grand procès mystérieux des temps modernes: de la *destruction à la construction,* où la refonte d'une Europe nouvelle à touts les points de vue est, en ce qui concerne le côté conscience universelle, le côté le plus captivant actuel, et le plus nécessaire."[26] Delaunay refers not to any European geopolitical or cultural reorganization, but to "un crise fondamentale" in modern art, which comes from its reevaluation of the conceptualization and means of representation (*Cubisme* 55). Gilles de la Tourette divides Delaunay's early career into deconstructive and constructive periods, drawing on the painter's argument that the evolution of modern painting proceeds from *destruction* to *construction* (*Robert Delaunay*). According to La Tourette, the deconstruction of vision in the *Saint-Séverin* and *Tour* series becomes the reconstruction of visual perception in the simultaneous forms of the *Fenêtres* and *Formes circulaires*.[27]

---

[25] Tomàs Llorens directed the 2002-2003 exhibition of the Delaunays' painting at the Museo Thyssen-Bornemisza, Madrid, Spain.

[26] Delaunay's remarks appear in the "Constructionnisme et néo-classicisme" section (c. 1924) of *Du cubisme à l'art abstrait*.

[27] Gilles de la Tourette classifies the *Tower* and *City* series as "deconstruction," and the *Fenêtres* and *Formes circulaires* as "construction." According to la Tourette's

Simultaneisme, whose life as a movement began the same year as Delaunay's seminal essay "La lumière" (1912), treats the natural behavior of light as the basis for representation and representation's constructive language:

> Sans la sensibilité visuelle aucune lumière, aucun mouvement. La lumière dans la Nature crée le mouvement des couleurs. Le mouvement est donné par les rapports *des mesures impaires*, des contrastes des couleurs entre elles qui constitue *la Réalité*. Cette réalité est douée de la *Profondeur* (nous voyons jusqu'aux étoiles), et devient alors la *Simultanéité rythmique*. ("La lumière" 146; emphasis in the original)

During the time period in which Delaunay worked on the *Fenêtres* (1912-1913), he began to employ the phrase "contrastes simultanés" to describe his *métier*. Delaunay situates *Simultaneisme's* terminology in the philosophy and science of visual perception: "J'employais le mot scientifique de Chevreul: les *contrastes simultanés*. Je jouais avec les couleurs comme on pourrait s'exprimer en musique par la fugue des phrases colorées, fuguées. Certaines formats de toiles étaient très larges par rapport à la hauteur–Je les appelais les

---

logic, the *Fenêtres* and *Formes circulaires* can be considered more "constructive" than the *Towers* series due to the representational techniques that their creation establishes. At the same time, it must be recognized that Delaunay never applied the binary "deconstruction-construction" to his artistic trajectory.

Delaunay broke with Cubism and the Cubist-style fragmentation of perspective after the *Tour* series. From the period of the *Fenêtres* on, he could no longer be considered a member of the Cubist *Section D'Or*, but rather fully a Simultaneist painter. At the same time, the development of *Simultaneisme* resulted from the delayed rapprochement between the *Section D'Or* and the neo-Impressionists at the 1912 *Salon D'Automne*. *Simultaneisme* and the *Section D'Or* imitated the parallel made by Impressionism between the representation of light and the workings of vision. With the *Fenêtres* and *Formes circulaires*, Delaunay inaugurated the use of color-light contrasts as a constructive language; this formal vocabulary replaced Cubism's broken perspectives. As Apollinaire notes, Delaunay credited his predecessor Seurat with inventing the contrast of colors in light as technique, while at the same time critiquing the limitations of his Impressionist painting: "Seurat fut le premier théoricien de la lumière. . . . Sa création reste le contraste des couleurs complémentaires. (Le mélange optique par points, employé par lui et ses amis, n'était que technique et n'avait pas encore l'importance des contrastes comme moyens de construction pour l'expression pure)" ("Réalité, peinture pure" 346). "Réalité, peinture pure" was translated from the German language of its original source–the December, 1912 issue of the journal *Der Sturm*.

Fenêtres" (Molinari 58).[28] In a short article of 1919, Cendrars adopts this vocabulary, privileging *métier* in a similar way to Delaunay:

> L'art d'aujourd'hui est l'art de la profondeur.
> Le mot '*simultané*' est un terme de métier, comme *béton armé* en bâtiment, comme *sublimé* en médicine. Delaunay l'emploie quand il travaille avec tour, port, maison, homme, femme, joujou, œil, fenêtre, livre; quand il est à Paris, New-York, Moscou; au lit ou dans les airs. Le simultané est une technique. La technique travaille la matière première, matière universelle, le monde. . . . Le contraste simultané est le perfectionnement le plus nouveau de ce métier, de cette technique. Le contraste simultané est de la profondeur vue. Réalité. Forme. Construction. Représentation.
> La profondeur est l'inspiration nouvelle. Tout ce que l'on voit est vu dans la profondeur. On vit dans la profondeur. On voyage dans la profondeur. J'y suis. Les sens y sont. Et l'esprit. ("Delaunay: Le contraste simultané" 204; emphasis in the original)

In the *Fenêtres* and *Formes circulaires*, it is the play of light and color that sets the retina's perceptual mechanisms in motion. Delaunay's great breakthrough in the *Fenêtres* series lies in his use of color contrasts not for decorative or figurative purposes, but instead to performatively represent vision. Whereas in Impressionism the juxtaposition of contrasting colors simply imitates the play of light on objects, with the *contrastes simultanés*, Delaunay takes Impressionism's simulation of light's movement further, making form reduplicate the experience of visual perception. In "La lumière," Delaunay assigns light a constructive role with respect to form:

> Si de même il représente *les relations visuelles* d'un objet ou *des objets entre eux* sans que la *lumière joue le rôle d'ordonnance de la représentation*, il est conventionnel, il n'arrive pas à la *pureté plastique*, c'est une infirmité, il est la négation de la vie, *la sublimité de l'art de la peinture*.
> Pour que l'Art atteigne la limite de sublimité, il faut qu'il se rapproche de notre *vision harmonique: la clarté*. La clarté sera couleur, proportion. ("La lumière" 147; emphasis in the original)

---

[28] Danielle Molinari traces Delaunay's *Simultaneisme* back to Chevreul's "*le contrastes simultanés.*" She relies on Guy Habasque's art-historical scholarship, as well as his editing and compilation of Delaunay's unpublished papers (81).

Several of the most crucial writings related to *Simultaneisme* came out of the 1912 *Der Sturm* exposition of Delaunay's work (in which the *Fenêtres* were featured), including "La lumière," and three significant texts by Apollinaire–the poems "Tour" and "Les fenêtres," and "Réalité, peinture pure." Apollinaire wrote "Les fenêtres" while temporarily living and working with the Delaunays in their studio, and conceiving the poem was part of their collective quest for a simultaneous *métier*. He evokes the way in which Delaunay's painting dissolves vision into fragmentary perceptions, which are then reconstructed in the *contrastes simultanés*:[29]

> Du rouge au vert tout le jaune se meurt
> Quand chantent les aras dans les forêts natales
> . . . .
> Tu soulèveras le rideau
> Et maintenant voilà que s'ouvre la fenêtre
> Araignées quand les mains tissaient la lumière
> Beauté pâleur insondables violets
> Nous tenterons en vain de prendre du repos
> On commencera à minuit
> Quand on a le temps on a la liberté
> Bigorneaux Lotte multiples Soleils et l'Oursin du couchant
> Une vieille paire de chaussures jaunes devant la fenêtre
>   (Apollinaire, "Les fenêtres," *Œuvres poétiques* 1-18/168-69)

Both Apollinaire's visual metaphors and Delaunay's color contrasts depend on the apposition of different elements. In *Fenêtre sur la ville* (1914), for instance, the tension between opposite colors on the spectrum–the contrasts created by placing blues and orange-yellows, and reds, purples, and greens next to each other–becomes the formal basis of the painting. Also productive of its form are the subtle gradations between colors of the same family: purples, blues, and

---

[29] The *Der Sturm* gallery accorded Delaunay the honor of a one-man show in 1913. He and Apollinaire traveled together to Berlin for the occasion. Delaunay's first contact with the *Der Sturm* group was through Wassily Kandinsky, whom he met in Paris in 1911 through the painter Elizabeth Epstein (Hoog, *Robert Delaunay* 69). Regarding the French painter's German connections, see the section of the Galerie Gmurzynska's exhibition catalogue entitled "Robert Delaunay und die deutschsprachigen Länder: Arbeiten und Projekte von 1919 bis 1931" / "Robert Delaunay et les pays de langue allemande: réalisations et projets 1919-1931" (Rubinger 34-65).

reds blend into each another to suggest shadow; darker oranges alongside yellows indicate variations in brightness. The contraposition of visual impressions and images is Apollinaire's answer to Delaunay's *contrastes simultanés.* In "Les fenêtres," Apollinaire pulls back the curtain of representation to reveal the relationship between (visual) perception and form; his "window," like Delaunay's, becomes a meta-artistic analogy between simultaneity as *métier.*

Part and parcel of Delaunay's streamlining of form is his selection of an eye shape for the 1912 *Fenêtres ouvertes simultanément 1ère partie, 3e motif* (see fig. 3.1, p. 263). Such a choice reflects his objective of making visual perception and form synonymous, and of returning this perception to the viewer. In a way analogous to Impressionism, the visual perception that is the form as well as the subject of representation ultimately comes from the observer, whose eye is needed to produce the color contrasts. Delaunay's language in "La lumière" underscores the way in which actual vision is essential to his conception of form:

> L'Art vient de la fonction la plus parfaite de l'homme
> l'Œil. Les yeux sont les fenêtres de notre âme.
> Il peut devenir l'harmonie vivante de la Nature
> et c'est alors un élément fondamental de notre jugement vers
> la pureté. Voir devient la compréhension [du] bien.
> . . . .
> Notre compréhension est donc adéquate à notre vue. Il faut
> chercher à voir.
> Une perception auditive ne suffit pas à notre jugement
> pour connaître l'univers, puisqu'elle ne reste pas dans la durée.
> (148-49)

Delaunay's use of Bergson's term "durée" is attached to two essential principles of his art: one, perception and representation must flow into each other seamlessly, in a similar way as do sensation and memory in Bergsonian phenomenology; and two, the subjectivity inherent in both representation and perception should be made manifest.[30] As Bergson holds, perceptions are stored in the psyche in suc-

---

[30] What Bergson terms quantity is really the manifestation of quality, which is necessarily subjective. The subjectivity of time and duration means that the "I" experiences sensation as simultaneity. Spatial simultaneity, therefore, can be understood as the outward sign of intensely felt sensation. See Bergson, *Time and Free Will:*

cessive fashion, while memory stays temporally fluid, rendering the separation of impressions from diverse moments in time impossible. A certain "continuity" or duration, "a memory within change itself," he argues, "prolongs the before into the after, keeping them from being mere snapshots and appearing and disappearing in a present ceaselessly reborn" (*Duration and Simultaneity* 30). The theory of the *durée* connects perception and memory, while also joining memory's recording of sensory impressions with representation. Delaunay's reference to the *durée* in "La lumière" is suggestive of his combining of perception with representation–that which is remembered or re-presented–in his simultaneous color contrasts.

With the *Formes circulaires* series, Delaunay's stress shifts from the exploration of light and color to the movement, or rhythm, generated by the color contrasts. All traces of the figurative are gone now, leaving the color wheels of Chevreul, Goethe, and Ogden Rood[31]–and the scientific laws of vision that they explain–in their pure state. According to Chevreul, the juxtaposition of opposite colors on the spectrum produces a shining light. In Claude Monet's *Impression, Soleil levant*, which can perhaps be considered the first artistic experiment based on Chevreul's *De la loi du contraste simultané des couleurs* (1839), the contrast between the orange disk and sky-blue background creates a luminous landscape.[32] The effect on the retina is akin to the sensation produced by the sun's brightness, and the eye's impulse–analyzed extensively by Goethe in his *Zur Farbenlehre* (*Theory of Colors*)–is to complete the color wheel and imagine complementary shades where, at times, none may exist (Le Rider; Rousseau, "L'œil solaire" 123-29). In *Formes circulaires, Soleil no. 1* (1912-1913), contrasting hues in four separate color

---

An Essay on the Immediate Data of Consciousness. Delaunay would almost certainly have read Bergson since the philosopher was popular among Paris artists and writers in the 1910s; the notion of simultaneity is reflected in the pervasive Bergsonism of Delaunay's milieu. Spate confirms the Bergsonian character of Delaunay's ideas: "The fact that Delaunay tried to fuse images connected with the past with others which clearly refer to the dynamism of the present, suggests that he may have been influenced by Bergson's considerations about the way the past is transformed into present consciousness by memory, particularly since such notions preoccupied the poets with whom Delaunay was acquainted" (185).

[31] I refer to Ogden Rood's *Modern Chromatics* (1879).

[32] The complete title of Chevreul's treatise is: *De la loi du contraste simultané des couleurs et de l'assortiment des objets colorés* (*The Principles of Harmony and Contrast of Colors and their Applications to the Arts*). It was first published in English in 1854.

wheels cause the eye to perceive each individual wheel as spinning on a central axis (see fig. 3.2, p. 264). At top left, Delaunay presents the viewer with a complete wheel, in which the colors are turned up to maximum brightness. The intensity of the shades here attracts the eye–becoming the natural focal point of vision in the painting. Together, the three remaining wheels, each only partially depicted, form a reverse arc that extends from bottom left to top right. In contrast with the brightness and strength of the colors in the circle at top left, muted hues comprise the minor circular forms that create the inverted arc. Composed of contrasting but noticeably dimmer shades, these fractional circles resemble the afterimages generated in the eye by extremely vivid colors. *Formes circulaires, Soleil no. 1* is set up to approximate the eye's processing of the relationship between colors, depending on the play of light around them.

In *Formes circulaires, Soleil no. 2* (1912-1913), something other than light and color contrasts begins to take shape–movement (see fig. 3.3, p. 264). At the center of the depicted circle, the sketchy outline of a helix/propeller becomes visible. The viewer's eye, obeying the laws of color and light, makes this helix turn on its axis in a meta-artistic representation of the workings of form in *Simultaneisme*. When compared to the *Formes circulaires* series, the 1914 *Hommage à Blériot* can similarly be considered part of Delaunay's exploration of the eye's transformation of light into movement. André Salmon's observations on *Hommage à Blériot* at the time of its exhibition at the Paris *Salon XXX des Artistes Indépendants* center on the way in which Delaunay creates movement from the "light" that emanates from the color contrasts:

> M. Robert Delaunay broie et décompose la lumière avec l'hélice du triomphant vaisseau aérien; il tente de nous suggérer la notion du mouvement par excellence. Hors des zones lumineuses, nées de ce mouvement, la stérile immobilité de l'avion en vol plané; en le halo correspondant au rythme horizontal la fuite, plus lente d'être plus lointaine, d'un dirigeable. Enfin: immobilité absolue hors de toute matrice lumineuse: la tour Eiffel, si chère au cœur du peintre. ("Le salon" 22)

Delaunay turns the conversion to movement of color-light interactions into a rhythmic pattern, thereby creating a structured yet malleable visual language that is actualized by the viewer's perception.

Johanna Drucker terms the potential for performative enact-
ment in the visual ordering of poetry "visual performativity"–a no-
tion that can be extended to the Delaunays' brand of abstract paint-
ing. For her, the making present that is the expressive aim of the
poetic text–the phenomenalization of subjectivity, time, and
place–relies not on the enunciation of subjectivity but instead on
form and the perception of this form by the reader ("Visual Perfor-
mance" 131-32).[33] Correspondingly, Delaunay's *Formes circulaires*,
and the major paintings that Delaunay-Terk completed in Paris,
Madrid, and Portugal in the 1910s can be said to be about the de-
velopment of a performative form. In both Delaunay's and Delau-
nay-Terk's painting, the viewer's visual perception discharges that
which form holds in a state of potential–making it perform the
process that leads to its creation.

The rhythms of Delaunay-Terk's *Le Bal Bullier* (1913) and
Prismes électriques (1914) take inspiration from the modern city.[34] In
Nous irons jusqu'au soleil, she describes the impact of Paris's mod-
ernization on her representation of visual perception. She remem-
bers the way in which the halos of the street lamps "faisaient tourner
et vibrer autour de nous les couleurs et les ombres, comme si des
objets non identifiés nous tombaient du ciel, amicaux aux insensés,"
on her nightly promenades along *Le Boul'Mich* and the *Fontaine-
Saint-Michel* where, around 1912-1913, electric bulbs multiplied like
stars after the sunset (*Nous irons* 43). She might as well have been
outlining the contours of her *Le Bal Bullier* or *Prismes électriques*,

---

[33] Johanna Drucker introduces the concept of "visual performativity" in "Visual
Performance of the Poetic Text" and discusses the "materiality of signification" in
The Visible Word: Experimental Typography and Modern Art, 1909-1923 (109).

[34] Drawing a contrast between Robert and herself, Sonia reminisces:

> Robert avait gardé de l'enfance son amour de la nature. Il n'était pas
> un homme des villes, et s'il peignait des Tours, c'est parce qu'il était un
> apôtre de la modernité. Moi, j'étais plus excitée par la ville que par la
> campagne. J'aimais l'électricité. Les éclairages publics étaient une nou-
> veauté. La nuit, en nous promenant, nous entrions bras dessus, bras
> dessous dans l'ère de la lumière. (43)

The *Bal Bullier* was a dance hall known for its modern Parisian ambience. As
Delaunay-Terk recalls about the genesis of *La Prose du Transsibérien*, "Ce sont des
choses qui ne s'expliquent pas. Le *simultanéisme* était en nous; c'est pour cela que
l'exécution ne demanda que très peu de temps." She further asserts the spontaneity
of her artistic creation: "J'étais russe. Je venais de Saint-Pétersbourg. Cendrars y
avait été. Le sujet du poème relate un voyage sur la transsibérienne, et nous créions
dans la plus pure spontanéité" (qtd. in Sidoti 18).

and the radiating vibrations of the electric lights depicted in these canvases. In *Prismes électriques*, a series of concentric circles figuratively portray the light sources indicated in the painting's title, as well as producing a glow through *contrastes simultanés*. The color contrasts composing the lights generate an afterimage just as would looking at an electric bulb. In other words, the viewer's perception "turns on" the series of contrasts that make up the painting's formal structure. Play among the color contrasts highlights the jubilation of the dancing couples, but the real subject of representation is not the spectacle associated with the Left Bank, but rather the pulse of the city's activity made form.[35] *Le Bal Bullier's* performativity derives from the way in which its reiterated forms become self-sustaining: the rhythm of the dance is produced (and reproduced) by the perceptual loop that is built into the color contrasts.

Comparable to *Le Bal Bullier* and *Prismes électriques*, the form of the designs for *La Prose du Transsibérien*, which Delaunay-Terk created using the stenciling technique known as *pochoir*, performatively represents perception. The first and best-known version of *La Prose du Transsibérien*, a combination narrative poem by Cendrars and visual art work by Delaunay-Terk consists of a two-meter-long by 0.36-meter-wide vertical panel, folded in half lengthwise and then accordion-style into a parchment cover of ordinary book size, just as a road map or Baedeker guide collapses upon itself.[36] The right half of the top of the doubled-up book forms a long rectangle on a colorful background; the uppermost part of this area maps the geographical trajectory of the Trans-Siberian Railroad, on which travel Cendrars's protagonists, the young poet Blaise and the adolescent prostitute Jeanne. The poetic text, occupying the right half of the long panel, uses no less than twelve different type faces and

---

[35] In describing *La Prose du Transsibérien*, Stephen Kern centers on the contraction of time and space in travel as theme and metaphor of modernity: "Time is compressed and reversed to break down the divisiveness of sequence, and space is ignored to undo the divisiveness of distance and bring together separate places in a single vision of his [Cendrars's] train racing across Russia as his mind raced around the world" (74).

[36] "*Pochoir*" refers to the use of stencils to create visual images. The version of *La Prose du Transsibérien* described herein was exhibited in 2002-2003 at the Museo Thyssen-Bornemisza, in Madrid, Spain. It is composed of the following materials: gouache, oil, and type on paper, with *pochoir* on the cover. Collapsed into a book, the scroll measures 52.5 x 37.7 centimeters. For a reproduction of this particular example, see Robert and Sonia Delaunay 1905-1941.

several colors. Delaunay-Terk's designs spill over from the right to fill the blank spaces left by the typographical arrangement of the text on the left. As she noted years later in retrospect, the enhanced typography was designed to "'interpréter par les couleurs et leurs nuances les thèmes et les sentiments exprimés par le texte poétique'"–but not mimetically or symbolically (qtd. in Sidoti 28).[37] The eye's ordering of the different shapes, unconsciously following the scientific laws of color and vision, creates an illusion of movement that is at once independent and inseparable from the poetic text. Delaunay-Terk employs the rules governing the spectrum strategically, juxtaposing hues close to and distant from each other on the color wheel so as to make a legible map of the journey. The main stops on the Trans-Siberian Railroad are signaled through the placement of blocks of color at such significant points in the poem as the various refrains, ellipses, and line and stanza breaks, thereby causing the designs to assume the syntactic and grammatical functions normally accorded to text.

Delaunay-Terk's stencils unfold from top to bottom, descending from a single large arc into multiple intercalated arches, spirals, triangles, squares, and arabesques–leading the eye to sort the different areas of the poem-painting according to formal similarities and differences. On the one hand, related colors blend into each other harmoniously, giving the eye the same sensation of multiplicity and nuance that occurs when perceiving single bright shades. On the other hand, contrasting colors parallel the experience of viewing several hues at the same time, or of seeing an afterimage. Repetition of these colors, in brighter or paler tones, between strophes reiterates the feeling elicited by an afterimage–immersion in a time-window that corresponds to the Trans-Siberian trip and Blaise's recollection of it–as does the contrast among the colors of the *pochoir* and those of the printed text. Sharp divergences between opposite shades on the spectrum propel vision forward and intensify its trajectory: the mutually repelling contrapositions of red and green, and yellow and blue drive the eye down the scroll until it comes to rest, briefly, on the relative comfort of more closely related hues; the gaze then takes off again, attracted by the pull of another arresting visual opposition.

---

[37] The quoted material about the interpretive value of *La Prose du Transsibérien's* color typography comes from Antoine Sidoti's private conversations with Sonia Delaunay between September 3 and 8, 1971 (40).

Becoming accustomed to the flow of the illustrations teaches the viewer to perceive visual information in the process of transformation, as well as to understand how the different manifestations of the color contrasts are linked through the space-time of perception.

The text of *La Prose du Transsibérien*, in a way similar to Delaunay-Terk's designs, metapoetically represents the development of *métier* (the *contrastes simultanés*) and its role in *Simultaneisme*.[38] In the poem, Jeanne's presence reminds Blaise, a poet like his namesake creator, of his home in bohemian Montmartre; she becomes a foil for his impressions of the Russian countryside at the time of the 1905 Revolution and the Russo-Japanese War (1904-1905). The protagonist remembers his experience as a developing poet:

> En ce-temps-là j'étais en mon adolescence
> J'avais à peine seize ans et je ne me souvenais déjà plus mon
>   enfance
> J'étais à 16.000 lieues du lieu de ma naissance
> J'étais á Moscou, dans la ville des mille et trois clochers et des
>   sept gares
> Et je n'avais pas assez des sept gares et des mille et trois tours
> Car mon adolescence était alors si ardente et si folle
> Que mon cœur, tour à tour, brûlait comme le temple d'Ephèse
>   ou comme la Place Rouge de Moscou
> Quand le soleil se couche.
> Et mes yeux éclairaient des voies anciennes.
> Et j'étais déjà si mauvais poète
> Que je ne savais pas aller jusqu'au bout.
> (Cendrars, *La Prose du Transsibérien*, *Œuvres complètes* 1-11/16)

The last two lines of this strophe, in which Blaise refers to himself as a "mauvais poète," becomes one of several refrains in the poem.[39] His self-deprecating claim that he didn't yet know how to "take it all the way" can be ascribed to the typical modernist and

---

[38] See my "*La Prose du Transsibérien et de la petite Jehanne de France* (1913): Abstraction, Materiality, and an Alternative *Simultaneisme*."

[39] For example: "Pourtant, j'étais fort mauvais poète / Je ne savais pas aller jusqu'au bout" (24-25/17); "Moi, le mauvais poète qui ne voulais aller nulle parte, je pouvais / aller partout / Et aussi les marchands avaient encore assez d'argent / Pour aller tenter faire fortune" (50-52/18); "Autant d'images-associations que je ne pas développer dans mes vers / Car je suis encore fort mauvais poète / Car l'univers me déborde / Car j'ai négligé de m'assurer contre les accidents de chemin de fer / Car je ne sais pas aller jusqu'au bout / Et j'ai peur" (337-42/28).

avant-garde concern for starting afresh and creating anew, as well as to *Simultaneisme's* preoccupation with form.[40] Through the fictional Blaise, who attributes his inadequacy as a poet to the uncontrollable upsurge of associations and images in his psyche, Cendrars arrives at the solution to the problem of the relationship between perception and form. *Simultaneisme*, the mature style of the real Blaise (Cendrars) and of *La Prose du Transsibérien*, uses precisely this perception-generated profusion of sensory input. Form–the sonic and rhythmic structure of the text, the iterations of the refrain, and synaesthesia–is turned back into sensation by means of the reader's perception.

Blaise can be described as a split subject who exists in the interstices of the remembered past and the present moment. His artistic frustration, stemming from a burning desire to arrive at a form through which he might express himself, divides him between raging youth boiling over with perceptions that he cannot as yet articulate, and mature poet possessed of a form for organizing the impressions in his psyche. "Et tous les jours et tous les femmes dans les cafés et tous les verres / J'aurais voulu les boire et les casser": Blaise's recalled wish to smash the café's drinking glasses parallels the frayed state of his nerves during his travels on the Trans-Siberian Railroad (Cendrars, *Œuvres complètes* 27-28/17). However, it is his nervously fragmented perception–"Et pourtant, et pourtant / J'étais triste comme un enfant / Les rythmes du train / La 'moëlle chemin-de-fer' des psychiatres américains / Le bruit des portes des voix des essieux grinçant sur les rails congelés"–that eventually would have a transformative effect on his art (Cendrars, *Œuvres complètes* 85-89/19). In the course of his journey, he comes to distinguish the sound of the train's doors from the screeching noise made by its axles, which his poet's ear translates into the rhythmic repetitions, assonance, alliteration, and rhyme. Cendrars's dedication of *La Prose du Transsibérien* "aux musiciens"–an allusion to music's architectonic form–emphasizes the crucial part played by perception and the transposition of perception into his poetic language.[41]

---

[40] Cendrars's English-language translator, Ron Padgett, points out that the Swiss-French author was obsessed with writing and what it meant to be a poet throughout his life (Translator's Preface ix). The translation "take it all way" is Padgett's ("The Prose of the Trans-Siberian" 11/15).

[41] There are other references to music in *La Prose du Transsibérien*: "Mon browning le piano et les jurons des joueurs de cartes dans / le compartiment /

Related to the issues of simultaneous perception and the perfor-
mativity of form are the nearly identical titles that Torre and Delau-
nay give their respective works of 1923–the poetry volume *Hélices*
and the oil-on-canvas *Hélice*. The relationship between the two
meanings of *"hélice"* in Spanish and French, "helix" and "airplane
propeller," are analogous to the confluence, in their work, between
perceptual and formal simultaneity. In Delaunay's *Hélice*, the rain-
bow colors of the blade are at once part of the figurative represen-
tation of the airplane propeller and the formal equivalent of the
synthesis that constitutes visual perception–the blending of color
and light in the eye. In reproducing the propeller's sinuous curves
in the arches and semi-circles in the painting's background, Delau-
nay replicates the rhythm of this visual conjoining.[42] He develops a
comparable strategy in his earlier *Hommage à Blériot*, which cele-
brates the famous flight of Louis Blériot across the English Channel
on July 25, 1909. In a similar way to *Hélice*, the ludic spectacle of
Hommage à Blériot, as we have seen, is a meditation on the nature
of visual perception. Delaunay creates a series of visual analogies:
the arches that surround the propeller and the human figures (pre-
sumably spectators in motion) are repeated in the shapes floating in
the sky; the semi-circles, circles, and colored bands outlining the
airplane at upper right complement each other in terms of hue and
their role in the painting's composition.

---

d'à côté" (91/19); "La clarinette le piston une flûte aigre et un mauvais tambour /
Et voici mon berceau / Mon berceau / Il était toujours près du piano quand ma
mère comme Madame / Bovary jouait les sonates de Beethoven" (142-45/21); "Le
monde s'étire s'allonge et se retire comme un accordéon / Qu'une main sadique /
tourmente" (180/23); "Le diable est au piano / Ses doigts noueux excitent toutes
les femmes" (214-15/26); "Des couleurs étourdissantes comme des gongs"
(258/242); "C'est le pays des oiseaux / L'oiseau du paradis, l'oiseau-lyre" (261-
62/26); "Rien n'y fait, j'entends les cloches sonores/ Les gros bourdon de Notre-
Dame / La cloche aigrelette du Louvre qui sonna la Barthélemy / Les carillons
rouillés de Bruges-la-Morte / Les sonneries électriques de la bibliothèque de New-
York / Les campanes de Venise / Et les cloches de Moscou . . ." (300-306/27);
"l'hymne au / Tzar" (359/29); "Maintenant c'était moi qui avais pris place au piano
et j'avais mal aux dents . . . Moussorgsky / Et des lieder de Hugo Wolf . . . Moi j'é-
tais au piano et c'est tout ce que je vis" (389/30-31). Cendrars was a pianist and or-
ganist in his youth, before losing his right arm in World War I (Bochner, *Blaise Cen-
drars* 16; Bochner, Introduction, *Complete Poems* xvii). However, Sidoti notes that
the dedication "aux musiciens" was not included in the first edition, and adds that
Delaunay-Terk remained puzzled by its addition in subsequent versions (28).
    [42] Just as Jules Romains argues for the unity of energy, Delaunay conceives all
motion as one. See Romains, *La vie unanime: Poème 1904-1907*.

In Torre, the two meanings of *"hélice"* parallel the connections among perception, form, and modern urban life. The helix is synecdoche for airplane (itself a metonym of modernity and long-distance travel), meta-sign for the destruction and construction of vision in *Simultaneisme*, and the break-down and rebuilding of language in *Ultraísmo*. Torre uses Delaunay's critique of vision in the *Saint-Séverin* and *Tour* canvases to resituate the subject in an international geography. His portrayal of aerial views, inspired by Delaunay, changes the position of "I" and eye, freeing the subject. Once Torre has made "I" and eye transcend the ordinary limits of perspective, he turns to the second half of Delaunay's destruction-construction equation. Perceptual simultaneity becomes, just as in Delaunay and Delaunay-Terk, the formal backbone of his work, yet it also turns into something else: it is a paradigm for the subject's crossing of the borders that the representation of perspective and perception help police.

In *Destrucción, reconstrucción, El arte decorativo de Sonia Delaunay-Terk*, and *Blaise Cendrars*, Torre develops the concept of "subjetivación intraobjetiva," which he articulated in "Itinerario noviespacial del paisaje" (1920) as the formal foundation of Ultra poetry and the basis of perceptual cosmopolitanism. In using a variant of the term in his discussion of Delaunay's "pure art" in *Destrucción, reconstrucción*, he compares the new poetry and *Simultaneisme*:

> ¡Desposeída de todo argumento realizando así una pintura pura! Solo a través de una escrupulosa selección de medios que permitan hallar el equivalente plástico de los objetos y modelos, en planos, volúmenes o colores llegan a *subjetivizar intraobjetivamente* los primitivos elementos plásticos característicos de la pintura pura. Es aquí en este anhelo de purificación artística, mejor aún de reintegración pictórica, en que la pintura solo aspira a ser pintura, donde marca este arte tangencialidad que el lirismo novísimo que tiende hacia una idéntica finalidad. (Torre, *Destrucción, reconstrucción*)

The paradigmatic approximation between subject and object that Torre delineates in "Itinerario noviespacial del paisaje" is modeled on the representation of perceptual simultaneity in *Simultaneisme*. In the article, Torre asserts that the Cubist and Simultaneist poets–and those in Spain, like the *Ultraísmo* group, who have been influenced by their work–have come the closest thus far to *subjetivación intraobjetiva*:

> De ahí [subjetivación de lo objetivo, objetivación de lo subjetivo] que intentemos crear un paisaje espiritual dentro del paisaje objetivo. Por el momento, los líricos cubistas y simultaneístas–desde Cendrars a algún epígono ultraísta español–consiguen formar cuadros poemáticos donde el paisaje aparece manumitido de su aprehensión real, en estilizadas síntesis geométricas, o desdoblado en una serie de perspectivas cinemáticas. ("Itinerario" 86)[43]

At the same time, Torre reminds his readers that *subjetivación intraobjetiva* remains yet to be fully achieved in Spanish avant-garde poetry: "Mas la visión inmaculada y dehiscente del paisaje, sólo surgirá oprimiendo el resorte taumatúrgico de la imagen múltiple o noviestructural en el poema creacionista" (86). Torre's conception of *subjetivación intraobjetiva* turns on transforming perception into form and form into perception, much as in *Simultaneisme*: "Pues el paisaje, para emocionarnos o captarnos literariamente, ha de ser transformado–aunque no falseado–en la extravasación interpretativa de la realidad atmosférica, re-creada, al abocar, tras la trayectoria sensorial, en las vías líricas" ("Itinerario" 86). The exchange that occurs between subject and object parallels the workings of perceptual simultaneity: perception becomes form and form performatively recapitulates perception.

Torre's view of Cendrars is informed by the notion of *subjetivación intraobjetiva*, in which he posits the approximation between the poetic subject and object as occurring through perceptual simultaneity: "El autor de *Le Transsibérien*, como subraya Paul Neuhuys, tiene una perpetua sed de espacio. Se halla alucinado por los viajes, la transmutación de perspectivas, los desfiles cinemáticos y las sensaciones simultáneas" (*Literaturas europeas* 177). In *Blaise Cendrars*, Torre explains Cendrars's development of a poetic form that is capable of representing simultaneous perception: "En su desdén por la 'literatura' y su exaltad[o] amor creciente por los paisajes cósmicos, Cendrars ha llegado a una depuración, a una economía verbal suma." His argument centers on the way in which

---

[43] In *Destrucción, reconstrucción*, Torre refers to Cendrars's analysis of Delaunay's work in *Le Rose Rouge*, as well as Apollinaire's "Reality, Pure Painting."

Cendrars moves beyond the "literary"–the descriptive, the mimet-
ic–to create–like in the Delaunays' art–a performative model in
which form reduplicates perception and perception reduplicates
form. This pattern holds for the perception of a textual "subject" as
well as for the reader, whose apprehension of poetic form makes
this form recapitulate the same perceptual experience that created
it. In a news-release (*prière d'insérer*) analysis of his own *La Prose
du Transsibérien*, Cendrars centers on the rhythm produced by re-
peating the cycle of perception becoming form and form becoming
perception, which he sees as an antidote to the mimetic representa-
tion that the avant-garde rejects:

> Le simultanisme de ce livre est dans sa représentation simultanée
> et non illustrative. Les contrastes simultanés des couleurs et le
> texte forment des profondeurs et des mouvements qui sont l'in-
> spiration nouvelle. (qtd. in Bochner, *Blaise Cendrars* 98)[44]

The notion of *subjetivación intraobjetiva*, in terms of the perfor-
mance of perception in form permeates *El arte decorativo de Sonia
Delaunay-Terk*. Torre notes that the form of Delaunay-Terk's deco-
rative art work parallels that of *Simultaneisme*, the development of
which he rightly credits to her as well as to Delaunay:

> Ayant débuté comme peintre simultaneïste de la première
> époque du cubisme orphique–du même que son mari R. Delau-
> nay–elle s'est adornée à la décoration d'ensembles, d'intérieurs et
> d'objets artistiques, en continuant, sans ce chemin, son évolution
> artistique vers la construction nouvelle. (*Arte decorativo*)

In his view, Delaunay-Terk melds the decorative with *Simultane-
isme's* pure abstraction and non-mimetic pictorial language:

> C'est de ses premières recherches picturales, datés de 1909, comme
> nous l'avons dit, et des lois de l'art cubiste, que Sonia est parti pour
> arriver a des singulières constructions décoratives actuelles. Elle á

---

[44] Cendrars's remarks appeared as a *prière d'insérer* (news release) in the Octo-
ber 17, 1913 edition of the *Paris-Journal*. Bochner notes that the crucial word 'non'
was omitted in Delaunay's quotation of the passage on page 114 of *Du Cubisme a
l'art abstrait* (*Blaise Cendrars* 256n11). With regard to the text that he includes in
Blaise Cendrars, Bochner credits Michel Hoog (Hoog, "Quelques précurseurs" 165-
66; Bochner, *Blaise Cendrars* 256).

commencé, tout spiritualement (sic), pour transformer les objets que l'entouraient et qu'elle aimant, pour les infiltrer d'une nouvelle expression. Ainsi furent reliés, dans des couvertures extraordinaires, les livres de ses poètes et écrivains préférés. (*Arte decorativo*)

Torre's description of the rhythmic patterns in Delaunay-Terk's interior and clothing designs recalls his discussion of form's performativity in Delaunay and Cendrars: "Movimiento subversivo simultáneamente centrífugo y centrípeto: desde el material turriebúrneo del espíritu íntimo del artista hacia el exterior, y una vez en él, devuelto fuertemente como una pelota en el frontón"[45] ("Arte decorativo"). He suggests that the liberation of color from the confines of line and shape in her design work has the same rhythmic effect as the color contrasts in *Le Bal Bullier*, *Prismes électriques*, and *La Prose du Transsibérien*:

> El color ya no vive aprisionado entre los cuatro barrotes de un cuadro, sino que desciende al suelo, se mete en nuestros bolsillos sentimentales, se adhiere a nuestros trajes, baila en las paredes, ríe bajo las pantallas y nos mira descaradamente desde el techo. El color está en libertad . . . . ("Arte decorativo")

Torre finds that Delaunay-Terk's decorative art brings together the movement generated by Simultaneist form (the color contrasts) and the rhythm of modern urban life: "Ses moyens d'expressions étant dérivés de l'Orient flamboyant, Sonia nous offre un orient occidentalisée au contact de la vie moderne, pleine de rythmes nouveaux et débordant de couleurs inédites" (*Arte decorativo*). In the *Alfar* article on the artist, he takes this argument further, remarking that her "Fusión de ambos ritmos o interpenetración de cualidades nacionales" becomes "Arte cosmopolita" ("Arte decorativo").

It is Delaunay's *destruction-construction* paradigm, however, that turns out to be the clearest parallel to *subjetivación intraobjetiva*. In *Destrucción, reconstrucción*, Torre describes the painter's "deconstructive" phase, in which vision is dissolved into simultaneous form. He goes on to delineate how the painter's idea of "construc-

---

[45] In Spain, a sport similar to racquetball is referred to colloquially as "frontón." The word *frontón* can also signify either the court or the wall off of which the ball bounces in *frontón*/racquetball. Another meaning of *frontón* is the place where the game of *Jai-alai* is played.

tion" makes this fragmented form set in motion its own reconstitution in visual perception. Torre's conceptualization of *subjetivación intraobjetiva* just as deconstruction-(re)construction involves two significant points: first, the breakdown of perception and its reconstitution in form creates the necessary conditions for the mutual approximation of subject and object (or external world); and second, the performativity of this form changes the representation and experience of perspective and perception. Both of these aspects model the psychic freedom that, in Torre's work, becomes equivalent to cosmopolitanism.

Torre's description of *Ultraísmo* as "un movimiento simultáneamente derrocador y constructor" stems from the stress that he, in a similar way to Delaunay, places on each phase of deconstruction-(re)construction (*Literaturas europeas* 73). In *Destrucción, reconstrucción*, Torre's understanding of the connection between "destruction" and Delaunay's *Tour* series leads him to correctly situate the painter's "primera etapa destructora" between 1909 and 1913. According to him, with respect to *Tour Eiffel, no. 10*: "Aparecen explícitos y realizados magistralmente en su dintorno los postulados teóricos basamentales del cubismo: no representación directa, simultaneidad de planos e interpretación; destrucción de perspectivas, multiplicación cinemática de las dimensiones y perforación del cuarto espacio." He continues: "La yuxtaposición planista armoniza perfectamente con la profundidad de los volúmenes espaciales y el ritmo del color voltificante que favorece la sugestión giratoria de la torre" (Torre, *Destrucción, reconstrucción*). Torre exemplifies the process through which the fragmented visual perceptions represented in the *Tour* paintings eventually become the building blocks of Delaunay's *Fenêtres* series. His discussion of the *Fenêtres* in the section entitled "Orígenes del simultaneísmo" is a demonstration of the value of the deconstruction-(re)construction paradigm for Ultra poetry. Torre judiciously accords the color contrasts developed in the *Fenêtres* the status of a constructive language:

> Mas la realización del color-forma exigía el empleo de medios totalmente nuevos, que no hubiesen sido utilizados antes y lleva al máximum de realización los efectos siguientes: la acción de la luz sobre los objetos; el color en su máximo desarrollo de elasticidad expresiva por medio de sus contrastes simultáneos y la visualización de sus acordes complementarios. Así se llega a obtener la

forma creada por el movimiento de los colores en la profundidad lumínica. Su descomposición prismática y su polarización roënt-génica. (*Destrucción, reconstrucción*)

Torre argues that Delaunay inaugurates his constructive form with the *Fenêtres*, and points out that Apollinaire's poem "Fenêtres," and *La Prose du Transsibérien* by Cendrars and Delaunay-Terk were related to these developments. He also cites Apollinaire's analysis of Delaunay for the *Der Sturm* exhibition–demonstrating a consider-able knowledge of the history of *Simultaneisme*–and traces the roots of the color contrasts back to the Impressionism of Seurat and Cézanne (*Destrucción, reconstrucción*).

Torre uses the idea of the shift from deconstruction to (re)-con-struction that is so central to *Simultaneisme* and Delaunay's art to describe the trajectory of *Ultraísmo* and the direction of the first Spanish avant-garde: "Desde nuestro ángulo visual percibimos có-mo todas las vanguardias han cerrado, o se disponen a cerrar, su preliminar etapa de análisis y destrucción, entrando en un período de síntesis o constructivo" (*Literaturas europeas* 35). Throughout his discussion of Delaunay in *Destrucción, reconstrucción*, he returns to the phrases "arte noviestructural" and "colorismo noviestructu-ral" several times, referring to Delaunay's color-light theory as "nor-mas tetradimensionales" (*Destrucción, reconstrucción*). In "Itine-rario noviespacial del paisaje," Torre speaks of the turning of simultaneous perception into form, and form into simultaneous perception, as "nuestra avidez noviespacial," by which he means the adoption of this fundamental Simultaneist principle by *Ultraís-mo* (85). The repeated cycles of breaking down and rebuilding per-ception in form becomes the basis for *subjetivación intraobjetiva*, which translates into a means of transforming the meaning of place and belonging. Changing the way in which perception is represent-ed affects how it is used to position the subject, thus rewriting the rules of the game that determines with which spaces and collectivi-ties this subject may identify.

It should be noted that the newfound liberty of the subject in *Ultraísmo* not only comes from the deconstruction-(re)construction paradigm of *Simultaneisme*, but also from Bergson's conception of perception and memory–the turning of sensations into impressions across time and space in the psyche. For Torre, "Es el mismo Berg-son, como es sabido, quien en sus *Essais sur les données immédiates de la conscience* identifica la 'creación' con la 'duración real' la continuidad indivisa"[46] (*Literaturas europeas* 136). He puts the subjective character of time in Bergson together with the creative powers accorded to the subject–particularly the authorial subject–in *Creacionismo*–another major influence on *Ultraísmo*. In fact, Torre understands *Creacionismo* through the Bergsonian concept of spatiotemporal synthesis in memory: "Involuntaria o deliberadamente Huidobro, cuyas son estas precisiones, se olvida de citar a Bergson cuando el autor de *L'Evolution créatrice* es quien, en rigor y con más justicia, podría asumir el título de inductor teórico creacionista" (*Literaturas europeas* 136). Torre regards the way in which these impressions bring together different points in the time-space continuum as having an analogous effect on poetic language as the simultaneity of perception in form in *Simultaneisme*. The creation of impressions in Bergson–"simultaneous" in the sense of how present-moment perceptions interact with and change previously stored memories–becomes the mother of *invención*–the power to create anew. And *invención* offers a means of avoiding the mimetic representation that Torre, like Huidobro and Delaunay, views as static and *passé*:

> Bergson llega aún más lejos–recordémoslo–y sostiene que 'la vida es invención, como es la actividad consciente, y que como ella es creación incesante.' Así pues, la idea de movilidad, de variación que va aneja al creacionismo tiene una clara estirpe bergsoniana. Incluso–si hemos de creer manifestaciones verbales de Huidobro–este nombre de poesía creacionista fue pronunciado, por vez primera, por Bergson al leer algunos specimens primiciales de la nueva modalidad. (*Literaturas europeas* 136-37)

In the section of *Destrucción, reconstrucción* entitled "El arte de creación=La pintura pura: El color-forma de Delaunay," Torre connects Delaunay's color contrasts with *creación*, a term that in *Creacionismo* is bound up with *invención*: "Pues así como el creacionismo lírico extrae solo del conjunto literario el elemento primordial de la imagen, destacando temas y sentimentalismos y forjando un conjunto lírico puro de creación, así la pintura simultaneísta concede su exaltación al colorismo puro, disco solar o arte del color-

---

[46] *La réel durée* stands for "real duration," or undivided continuity.

forma."[47] His discussion of the *Fenêtres* series in particular draws heavily on the anti-mimetic attitude characteristic of *Creacionismo*–"No es definitiva otra cosa sino la resultante de la nueva pintura de concepción–por encima de la antigua manera imitativa."[48] He gestures towards Huidobro's exclusion of imitation from poetic creation: "'Inventar . . . es hacer que dos cosas paralelas en el espacio se encuentren en el tiempo, o vice-versa, presentando así, en su conjunción, un hecho nuevo. El conjunto de los diversos hechos nuevos, unidos por un mismo espíritu, es lo que constituye la obra creada'" (*Literaturas europeas* 137). Torre renames the rhythmic movement of color and light in Delaunay's painting "forma creada" in order to give additional heft to his comparison of *Simultaneisme* and the non-mimetic *creación* in Huidobro (*Destrucción, reconstrucción*). For Torre, the color-forms of the "lienzos derivados del 'disque-solaire-simultané,' y el 'purisme-électrique': La serie de les 'fenêtres'" manifest the features of this combined *invención-creación* (*Destrucción, reconstrucción*). *Creación* becomes the equivalent of Delaunay's *destruction-construction* and Torre's *subjetivación intraobjetiva* in that the goal of each is to invent a new language for the avant-garde.

The title of the poem "Arco iris" (*Hélices*) is symbolic of the renewal that Torre intends to bring about through formal innovation, as well as a visual metaphor for the perceptual simultaneity that he finds crucial to this renascence. Dedicated to Delaunay-Terk, the juxtapositions and elaborate metaphors in the text obey a rhythmic logic that pushes the lines forward in a way comparable to *La Prose du Transsibérien*. Such a motive force distinguishes the sections of *Hélices* that are directly influenced by *Simultaneisme* and lends them a formal elasticity that goes beyond Apollinaire's *calligrammes* and the Huidobro of the 1910s and early 1920s. "Arco iris" brings to mind Delaunay-Terk's unique art: "Oh la vibrátil perspectiva

---

[47] Torre makes an analogous comparison between *Creacionismo* and Delaunay's *métier* in *Literaturas europeas de vanguardia*. In his view, the "intención constructiva" characteristic of Huidobro's poetry shows itself in two ways. Torre relates the first of these with the formal construction of the text, including techniques such as the suppression of punctuation, and the production of multi-layered images and metaphors, which create "un ritmo cinemático." He links the second to internationalism (Torre, *Literaturas europeas* 126-27, 86).

[48] Torre also refers to *Hommage à Blériot*, and the Spanish- and Portuguese-themed canvases.

pluricromática / Juego polirrítmico de los colores" (1-2/36). He alludes to the worldly image created around her–for example in Apollinaire's novel *La femme assise* (1920)–the successful decorative artist and fashion designer of the "primer vestido simultaneísta," and the abstract painter of *Le Bal Bullier*:[49]

(Evocación de Sonia fantasista
con su primer vestido simultaneísta
retratada en 'La femme assise'
por el jovial Apollinaire:
1912: Baile Bullier: Sonia Terck:
Sobre el 'tailleur' violeta
una banda verde pradial
y sobre el busto un 'corsage' pluricolor
fragmentado en trozos de colores vivos
–azul eléctrico, escarlata violento–
que dibujan un arco iris sensual) ("Arco iris," *Hélices* 32-45/37)

The poem describes and recapitulates the way in which form works in *Simultaneisme*:

Florescencia de los colores simultáneos
que avanzan en la profundidad

Fluye un lírico espasmo visual
de pictórica afirmación

Las brisas policromadas
barnizan el panorama
novidimensional (10-16/36)

Torre's diction, notably the adjectives "cromática" and "rítmico," and the prefixes "pluri-" and "poli-" evoke the simultaneity of form in Delaunay-Terk's (and Delaunay's) work. He translates the vocabulary of *Simultaneisme* into his peculiar poetic language, demonstrating his grasp of simultaneous form's performativity:

---

[49] Torre gestures towards Cendrars' analysis of *Simultaneisme* according to Delaunay. The lines "'Le profondeur de la couleur simultanée / est l'inspiration nouvelle'" refer to Cendrars's formulation, "le contraste simultané": "Le contraste simultané est le perfectionnement le plus nouveau de ce métier, de cette technique. Le contraste simultané est de la profondeur vue. Réalité. Forme. Construction. Représentation" (Cendrars, "Delaunay: le contraste simultané").

Ante el arte exultante de Sonia
todo gira canta y gesticula
en la rueda helicoidal

    Fragancia fulgurante
    Subversión planista
    Profundidad espacial
        Arcos   }
        Acordes   }   del color inaugural
        Contrastes }   (51-59/37)

In Sonia's art, Torre suggests, "todo gira canta y gesticula" to the rhythm of the constant cycling between the deconstruction of perception and its reconstruction in form–and the setting in motion of this circuit by the eye of the viewer–"Contrastes simultáneos / del color-forma jubiloso / ante el foco plenisolar" (17-19/36). The brackets function like the color contrasts to which he refers; they direct the reader to synthesize the "arcos," "acordes," and "contrastes . . . del color inaugural," thereby giving shape to the text and producing a coherent meaning from form.

Just as the *contrastes simultanés* guide the viewer's gaze, Torre's visual metaphors and organization of the text on the page establish rules for reading the poem:

    Al romper las suturas pluviosas
        la boca plegada del horizonte
        insinúa una sonrisa heptacromista
    exhibiendo
    s i e t e   d i e n t e s   l u m i n o s o s

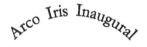

                          (4-9/36)

The typography and the arrangement of the poetic lines, including the calligrammatic drawing of the "arco iris inaugural" in the arc shape of a rainbow, can be compared with the verbal-visual doubling in *La Prose du Transsibérien*. Torre's crossing of the verbal and visual, as both source and expression of perceptual simultaneity, strengthens the foundation of the text until it becomes a "lírico espasmo visual / de pictórica afirmación" (12-13/36). If Delaunay-Terk's color contrasts can be said to take on the grammatical and syntactic roles of language, Torre's formal "contrasts" do just the opposite, making poetic language represent simultaneous visual perception:

> Contrastes simultáneos
> del color forma jubiloso
> ante el foco plenisolar
>
> En las superficies plásticas
> incide un rayo transmutador
> Y las estrictas franjas primitivas
> azul
> índigo
> amarillo
> violado
>
> cernidas en el horizonte
> destríen sus fibras hialinas
> en una prolongación sideral
> Sonia irradia un haz inédito
> que crea la forma-color (17-31/36-37)

Each constructive layer of the text acts as a "rayo transmutador," setting the shifting between form and simultaneous perception in motion. The quasi-synaesthesia involved in the phrases "Fluye un lírico espasmo visual / de pictórica afirmación" and "Las brisas policromadas / barnizan el panorama / novidimensional" parallels the contrasts among "azul / índigo / amarillo / violado" in Delaunay-Terk, and the way in which they "destríen sus fibras hialinas / en una prolongación sideral," creating the fiber or form through which simultaneity is at once generated and represented visually (12-16/36). This perceptual simultaneity endows Torre's poetry with a high degree of performativity. Just as the viewer's eye initiates the reduplication of perception in form in Delaunay-Terk's art, the reader makes Torre's combined visual-verbal language work as the representation of perceptual simultaneity–a representation that can be experienced only through perceiving the text.

The representation and performance of simultaneous perception becomes the central problem of "Trayectorias," the second section of *Hélices*. In "Circuito," Torre makes the subject assume the perspective of the Zodiac's axis, and he describes the way in which, from this lofty viewpoint, "los paisajes múltiples" of the Earth down below "se desenrollaban . . . con un ritmo cinemático" (18-20/19). The penetrating gaze of the perceptually empowered subject operates like a super-charged kaleidoscope: "Mis ojos tejen kaleidoscópicos / la red arácnida de los circuitos / A través de mi prisma / se descomponen las edades líricas" (Torre, "Circuito," *Hélices* 23-26/19). In response to the rapid movement of the strengthened eyes of the *yo*, the poem's textual topography shifts from side to side on the page, forming small strophic continents of text.

Not only does the subject's perception spark the performance of form in a way similar to *Simultaneisme*, but also the consequence of this perception resembles that which results from *subjetivación intraobjetiva*–diminished distance between subject and object. Torre's revved-up poetic language serves as a prosthesis for the human perceptual apparatus–"todos los oídos humanos en los auriculares"–in order to draw together subject and object in accordance with the concept of *subjetivación intraobjetiva*–"Nuestro planeta ambulante / se espasma en un grito jubiloso / de interpenetración espiritual" ("Auriculares," *Hélices* 30/26; 20-22/25). In acquiring the capacity for simultaneous perception associated with *subjetivación intraobjetiva*, the subject penetrates conventional shells of meaning, making language signify in different and productive ways:

> Oídos errantes
>   Nervios de las palabras
>   Corazones del sonido
>   Las palabras que vuelan
>   se despojan de sus cáscaras ("Auriculares" 5-9/25)

Amplifying perception through simultaneous form becomes a means of maximizing the potential for *creación* and *invención*:

> Sobre las cumbres
>   todos los oídos humanos en los auriculares
> Se oyen múltiples resonancias
>   Desde las melodías astrales
>   y los ruidos dinámicos de hoy
>   hasta los vientos sincrónicos
>   de nuestro ritmo porvenirista
>   ("Auriculares" 29-35/26)

Measuring devices frequently appear in the poems of the "Trayectorias" section of *Hélices*–from the kaleidoscope of "Circuito" to the "brújula" of "Ariadna" (39/28) and the "voltámetro" (sic) of "Atmósfera" (7/29).[50] Gauging thus becomes one of the primary purposes of perceiving: "En los descotes de las sombras / triangulicé el área de los besos" ("Circuito" 55-56/21); "En los laboratorios marcianos / los endocrinólogos / cultivan la pertenogénesis (sic) [partenogénesis] astral" ("Circuito" 72-74/21); "Con la brújula del sol en mi mano / descubro trayectorias inmaculadas" ("Atmósfera" 17-18/29). Torre's diction mirrors the performative work of this instrumentalized perception. His vocabulary of interpenetration, such as the verbs "tejer," "perforar," and "recortar," recalls the way in which form and the viewer's perception mutually transform each other in *Simultaneisme*, as well as the approximation of subject and object in *subjetivación intraobjetiva*:

> Mis manos luminosas
>   barajan las trayectorias increadas
>
> Mis rayos de lucífero
>   perforan los países nocturnos
>
> Soy el jinete de los meridianos
>
> . . . .
>
>   Entre mis piernas
>   permutan su cauce los ríos
>
>   Y en las antenas de mis oídos
>   vibra el Zodíaco
>
> Mis pupilas radiográficas
>   perforan los senos lunarios
>   y auscultan las palpitaciones selenitas
>
>   Sobre el tapete de las ciudades
>   manejo los edificios transeuntes
>
> He ahí mi circuito ("Circuito," *Hélices* 27-44/20)

---

50 I point out also the image of the compass in "Atmósfera," which appears in other poems of *Hélices*. Torre employs the odd "voltámetro" instead of the common word "voltímetro," or voltmeter.

The hyperactive eye generates images and impressions that go beyond ordinary experience: "Sobre las terrazas colgantes / multísonas orquestas negras / frivolizan el tango de los instantes"; "Y los paisajes new-yorkinos / vibran orquestados / en ritmos maquinísticos" (52-54, 64-66/21).

Torre links performativity, simultaneous perception made form, and the redoubling of the subject's perceptual capacity in "Auriculares" in a manner comparable to "Circuito." In "Auriculares," the *yo* creates circuit-like connections among perceptions: "A través del mundo / yo persigo / la trayectoria estelar / de los hilos telegráficos" (1-4/25). The "antena" of its "cráneo" attracts and emits "vibraciones auriculares," and regulates "los latidos emocionales" of sensation (10, 12-13/25). Its telegraphic system accumulates information until "En la apoteosis / desfilan las ciudades redivivas / bajo una lluvia de aviogramas"; Torre's diction reflects the relationship among perceptual simultaneity, empowered perception, and the creation of new linguistic forms ("Auriculares" 26-28/25). "Su mímica cosmopolita / traducía los colores del faro" (7-8/19): the Zodiac's "cosmopolitan" (in the sense of "mobile" or "synthetic") axis "translates" perceptual simultaneity into Torre's poetic language. A series of tropes in "Circuito" represents the conversion of this simultaneous perception into performative form:

> En el boscaje microfónico
>   nidifican los óvulos
>   del Verbo Nuevo
>
> . . . .
>
> Balando entre el brumario
>   espíritus aurorales
>   solicitan de los intérpretes
>   el reino de la cuarta dimensión
>
> Los ríos eróticos
>   se desangran en espumas cardíacas
>
> Como solloza entre las olas
>   la sirena de cabellera sinfónica
>
> Una amada candorosa
>   rima mis sístoles emotivas ("Circuito" 69-88/21-22)

Torre's references to interpretation and translation, the fourth dimension, and the symphonic are united by ideas of synthesis, transformation, multiplicity, and the architectonic–all of which act upon perception and form in order to maximize poetic invention.

In "Semáforo," Torre metamorphoses language by experimenting with the organization of the lines of poetry on the page. They spiral down like a staircase–or as if following the trajectory of an eye trained in simultaneous perception:

> En mi cráneo se barajan
>   los colores de una geografía inédita
>   Mis meningies circunvolutorias
>   son redes de itinerarios
>   El verticilo cósmico
>   se destríe en pétalos intactos
> A los acordes maquinísticos
>   se rasgan los paisajes ambulantes
>   Sobre mis ojos giratorios
>   el cielo sacude sus ramas
>   ("Semáforo," *Hélices* 1-10/23)

Here *subjetivación intraobjetiva*–Torre's answer to the perceptual simultaneity of *Simultaneisme*–brings about the approximation of subject and object, which causes the *yo* to temporarily lose consciousness of its own boundaries: "En mi cráneo se barajan / los colores de una geografía inédita"; "Mis meningies circunvolutorias / son redes de itinerarios." In subsequent lines, the subject drops out of the picture–"El verticilo cósmico / se destríe en pétalos intactos / A los acordes maquinísticos / se rasgan los paisajes ambulantes"–but then reappears, energized by the multiplicity of perceptions elicited by the external world. A series of complex visual metaphors, given additional weight and meaning by the calligrammatic arrangement of the poetic lines, emerges from this meeting between the subject's psyche and that which lies outside its parameters:

> En todas las ventanas
> manos de doncellas   bordan como recuerdos
>   los signos radiotelegráficos
>   los dientes luminosos
> En las lejanías me sonreían
>   de todas las bahías (15-20/23)

"Y al despedirme / un semáforo tornátil / me arroja los discos del iris": it becomes difficult to tell from which "iris" "los discos" come from–the eye of the perceiving subject or that of the "semáforo tornátil" (33-35/24). The deliberate confusion among perceptions, subject, and external world turns into a powerful textual paradigm for Torre's cosmopolitanism. This blurring of boundaries becomes a model for breaking down the borders created by other modes of representing perception, as well as analogy for the opening of frontiers separating *Ultraísmo* from the rest of the avant-garde.

"Friso primaveral" is Torre's missive to his fellow members of the Spanish vanguard as well as the avant-gardes outside the country regarding his innovations:

> ATENCIÓN: Los carteles cerúleos del horizonte nos anuncian la inauguración plenisolar.
> Aparición ritual: la Primavera desnuda repliega los últimos toldos brumosos y rasga los ventanales meridianos.
> Incitantes senos ácueos de las mujeres coristas que desfilan riegan nuestros ojos ávidos y multiplican las irisaciones del panorama renaciente.
> Bajo la aspersión floreal
> los paisajes móviles barajan sus reflejos como en un kaleidoscopio tornátil.
> Quién exprime los lagrimales de las nubes ancladas? (*Hélices* 1-8/113)

The urban scene unfolds from a "vertical" perspective–"Sobre la pantalla impoluta del nuevo horizonte montado por escenógrafos célicos / se proyecta el film floreal en 21 episodios"–which results in the contraposition of diverse views–"Bajo la aspersión floreal / los paisajes móviles barajan sus reflejos como en un kaleidoscopio tornátil" (22-23, 6-7/113). The poem's formal simultaneity reproduces the noise and bustle of the fast-moving city:

> Las ciudades resurrectas se abren al barnizaje inaugural de las lluvias leticias.
> Y en las avenidas los tranvías de uniforme nuevo
> disparan con su (sic) trolleys a los muequeantes carteles eléctricos.
> El klaxon estridente es la zampoña con que el pastor de motores saluda el alba dinámica (9-13/113)[51]

---

[51] "Muequeantes" is derived from the verb *muequear* ("hacer muecas," or "make faces") ("Muequear").

Torre's dynamic because simultaneous representation of the city constitutes the proclamation of a new poetic language, textual construction, and psychic disposition for reciprocity, notice of which is spread through "El primer número de *La Primavera*":

> En la bandeja del crepúsculo
> desde las últimas bambalinas diurnas
> caen pomas aurirrosadas y colores joviales
> Y acuchillando las esquinas todas las voces del ocaso nos gritan
> ¡El primer número de *La Primavera*! ¡Acaba de salir! (32-36/114)

His transformation of media, genre, form, and style makes news in the fictive broadsheet. Torre advertises novelties like film and Ramón Gómez de la Serna's "greguerías," or haiku-inspired prose poems ("Greguería multiédrica en las calles desbordantes" [25/113]).

The news broadcast from Torre's "torre" and circulated in "La Primavera" spreads the word of perceptual freedom and poetic invention to the members of *Ultraísmo*. Torre recreates the vanguard forms that his sources gather in order to achieve a simultaneity that structurally encodes the idea of cosmopolitan exchange into the poetic text. Inspired by Delaunay's *Tour* series, the condition of antenna-like "verticality," expressed through aerial or otherwise removed perspectives, boosts both a formal and an international kind of simultaneousness. The multi-faceted simultaneity of Torre's poetic texts alternatingly takes the form of synaesthesia, juxtaposition, the conflation of the verbal and visual, and typographical complexity–evincing a Bergsonian (and Huidobrian) emphasis on synthesis, fluidity, and flexibility. For just as in Bergson and Huidobro, as well as *Simultaneisme*, in Torre, simultaneity consists of the mixing of time, space, and perception in the psyche. This combination becomes paradigmatic of a liberated subjectivity capable of creating avant-garde poetic form, as well as standing for the border-crossing mobility that Torre envisions for *Ultraísmo*. In a way comparable to the work of the Delaunays and Cendrars, the form of Torre's poetry performs its simultaneity, bringing itself into being through the perceptual participation of the reader-viewer. The performative thrust of *Hélices* at once serves to teach his audience to use perceptual simultaneity and understand its implications for remapping subjectivity, identity, and the Spanish avant-garde.

CHAPTER 4

GERARDO DIEGO'S MUSICAL ARCHITECTURE:
IMAGEN AND *MANUAL DE ESPUMAS*

Estribillo   Estribillo   Estribillo
El canto más perfecto es el canto del grillo.

Gerardo Diego, "Estética," *Imagen*

"LA defensa que en tu carta me haces de tu *heterocronismo* no
llega a convencerme," protests Spanish poet Juan Larrea in
a letter of June 22, 1919 to his intimate friend and collaborator Ge-
rardo Diego (1896-1987), in a demonstration of intense frustration
with Diego's apparent inability to jettison the past and fully commit
himself to the avant-garde poetics of *Creacionismo* (93).[1] At the ti-
me of Larrea's letter to Diego, both maintained close ties with the
Chilean Vicente Huidobro, self-styled inventor and leader of the
Creacionismo movement. Larrea (1895-1980), an iconoclastic au-
thor rather like Diego, began his career as an avant-garde poet and
supporter of Huidobro, although he later permanently abandoned
poetry for prose in 1932. The neologism *heterocronismo* refers to
Diego's propensity for mixing poetic styles from different periods
in literary history–a tendency that would have been an anathema to
the "advance-wing" of the avant-garde. The skepticism that Larrea
shows regarding Diego's *heterocronismo* (literally meaning "multi-ti-
me-ism") implies that for him, temporal multiplicity is deeply sus-
pect. Larrea's further comments in his June 1919 letter demonstrate

---

[1] See also José Luis Bernal, "Gerardo Diego: Heterocronismo y visión del mun-
do."

just this position: "Lo que a ti te sucede, me parece, es que aún no ves la manera de desfogar tu emoción en moldes nuevos, y por eso lo haces en los antiguos. Pero se puede, créeme que se puede. Inténtalo si no. Y espero cosas muy hermosas" (94). The aesthetic range circumscribed by Larrea would limit Diego's heterodox aesthetic to the absolutely new; Larrea's posturing is in keeping with the general spirit of rebellion that characterizes avant-garde movements, as well as the specificity of the first Spanish avant-garde's bid to be taken seriously around the world.

Recollection and temporal multiplicity govern the shape of Diego's literary career as well as the structure of the early avant-garde poetry volumes, *Imagen* (1922) and *Manual de espumas* (1924). Diego cycles between the experimental and the traditional even during his initial vanguard period. His volume *Soria. Galería de estampas y efusiones*, released in 1923 between *Imagen* and *Manual de espumas*, is marked by fidelity to the conventions of the modern lyric and landscape poetry. The volume plays with the Spanish *fin-de-siècle* tradition of locating collective culture in the landscape, in the manner of Antonio Machado's *Campos de Castilla* (1912, 1917).[2] Conversely, the neoclassicism of Diego's *Versos humanos* (1925), reflected in the volume's affirmation that "es grato renovar el aula / polvorienta de la retórica," does not preclude a swing back to an experimental sensibility in 1932, with the appearance of *Poemas adrede* and *Fábula de Equis y Zeda* ("Poesía de circunstancia," *Versos humanos* lines 11-12/127). The different strains heard in the music of his poetry have the effect of Marcel's *madeleine* in Proust's *A la recherche du temps perdu*–to take the reader back and forth in time. This constant movement of prolepsis weaves a fabric of time and memory unusual for the avant-garde.

The series of anthologies and "biographies" produced by Diego–particularly the 1932 *Poesía española contemporánea*—are suggestive for their commitment to cultural continuity and stylistic heterogeneity. *Poesía española contemporánea*, which enjoyed a lasting influence in cultural circles and academic institutions, inscribes

---

[2] One of the most well-known and affecting poems from Antonio Machado's *Campos de Castilla* is entitled "Campos de Soria." Diego's evocation of Soria can be understood as a reference to Machado's affinity with the Castilian city, as well as his peculiar mix of symbolism and *modernismo* with the thematic concerns of the Generation of 98. In 1920, Gerardo Diego obtained, by state examination, the chair of Language and Literature in the high school in Soria; Machado held the chair of French before Diego.

avant-garde poetry in the register of Spanish literary history. Juan Larrea, who figures in the anthology, is without question "avant-garde." However, Diego includes the masters Juan Ramón Jiménez, Miguel de Unamuno, and Antonio Machado, the ten poets who would later go on to become the "Generation of 1927," and José Moreno Villa and Fernando Villalón.[3] Many poets of the first Spanish avant-garde are left out—notably the entire group from *Ultraísmo*—although Diego and Larrea are present as representatives of *Creacionismo*. In spite of its omissions, Diego's volume was extremely important in inscribing certain avant-garde poets in Spanish literary history. Diego likewise conceives retrospective accounts of his own work: he follows the *Primera antología de sus versos (1918-1940)* of 1941 with the 1967 *Segunda antología de sus versos (1941-1967).*[4] Diego's anthologizing activities are more than a bit paradoxical because the avant-garde tends to reject anterior influences of any kind.

Imagen and *Manual de espumas* are in their own way biographical, since they take shape around Diego's most consequential literary relationships of the years 1918-1924. *Creacionismo* and Huidobro in particular exert considerable influence on the direction of both volumes and on the development of his poetic. It is probable that Diego became familiar with Huidobro's work around 1918, when Huidobro introduced his poetic works, from *Horizon carré* (1917) to *Poemas árticos* (1918), in Madrid (Bernal, Introduction 37). An extensive correspondence between the two men dates from, at the latest, 1920; Huidobro's letter to Diego from April 28 of that year graciously accepts what the Chilean poet describes as Diego's attempts to make his acquaintance and seek his advice. In consequence, Diego makes a point of marking *Imagen* with the sign of *Creacionismo*,

---

[3] Regarding the history and membership of "Generation of 1927," see Andrew A. Anderson, *El veintisiete en tela de juicio: examen de la historiografía generacional y replanteamiento de la vanguardia histórica española.*

[4] Other auto-anthologies include the *Biografía incompleta* (1953), *Antología. Primer cuaderno (1918-1940)* (1958), *Antología poética (1918-1969)* (1969), and *Versos escogidos* (1970), as well as the *Poemas mayores (antología)* and *Poemas menores (antología)* of 1980. The compilation *Poesía de creación* (1974), Diego's reconsideration of his peculiar *Creacionismo*, consists of the avant-garde volumes *Imagen, Manual de espumas, Fábula de Equis y Zeda,* and *Poemas adrede,* in addition to the collections *Biografía incompleta* and *Biografía continuada.* Note that the expanded second edition of Diego's *Biografía incompleta* was published in 1967. A 1970 edition of the *Antología. Primer cuaderno (1918-1940)* reproduced the text of the original version. The reprint edition of *Poesía de creación* came out in 1980. José Luis Bernal's introduction to *Imagen* contains a useful bibliography of Diego's poetic works.

dedicating the "Imagen múltiple" section and its *ars poetica*, "Gesta," to Huidobro, and inscribing this key part of the volume with an epigraph from Huidobro's poem "Horizonte" (*Poemas árticos*): "Eras tan hermosa / que no pudiste hablar" (143). Diego devotes the whole of *Imagen* "Al poeta Juan Larrea, que ha explorado conmigo las rutas de este libro," along with its first section, "Evasión," which he prefaces with an epigraph from Larrea's poem "Cosmopolitano" (97, 101).[5] He dedicates "San Juan" ("Evasión") to Larrea and "Reflejos" ("Estribillo") to Pedro Garfías (1901-1967), his chief Spanish companions in the *Creacionismo* movement.

For his part, Huidobro is full of praise for *Manual de espumas*, which he calls "un hermoso libro con el cual hay muchas cosas de gran artista y en el cual se advierte al poeta verdadero" (Letter to Diego, July 3, 1922), and enthusiastically returns Diego's esteem:

> Yo pienso que Ud. debería formar un pequeño grupo de verdaderos poetas para hacer algo interesante y serio en España. No conozco bien a los jóvenes de allá pero acaso un joven Garfías, Eugenio Montes y quizás algunos otros podrían Uds. ayudarse mutuamente y ser los representantes en España para colaborar y enviarme notas a la Revista. (Letter to Diego, August 16, 1920)[6]

The correspondence between Huidobro and Diego also shows the enthusiastic and decisive role played by the Chilean with respect to Diego's 1922 journey to Paris, organized for the purposes of polishing his education and increasing his familiarity with Cubism and *Creacionismo.*[7] In a letter of July 3, 1922, Huidobro pledges, "Pronto le pien-

---

[5] Larrea's "Cosmopolitano" was published in the journal *Cervantes* in November, 1919. The epigraph to the "Evasión" part of *Imagen*, from "Cosmopolitano," reads: "'Mis versos ya plumados / aprendieron a volar por los tejados / y uno solo que fue más atrevido / una tarde no volvió a su nido" (101).

[6] The "Revista" to which Huidobro refers in his letter to Diego is the bilingual *Creación/Création*, published in Madrid and Paris between 1921 and 1924 (Bonet 179).

[7] In the July 3, 1922 letter, Huidobro encourages Diego to come to Paris: "No se imagina que gran bien le hará un viaje a París. Ánimo y viva el globtroterismo. No se olvide que hay que ser un poco aventurero y no tener miedo. ¡A París!" (Letter to Diego). He sends the following enthusiastic response to what must have been Diego's announcement, in a letter dated August 15, 1922, of his impending voyage to France: "En este mismo instante acabo de recibir su carta y estoy encantado con la idea de que haya resuelto su viaje." He then continues making plans: "Además de la carta debe ponerme un telegrama el día antes de partir diciéndome *llego a París a tal hora tal día.* Al recibir su carta me vengo a París, vengo casi día por medio, y aquí espero su telegrama" (Letter to Diego).

so escribir una carta crítica sobre su hermoso libro," adding that "No se necesita ser profeta para anunciar que será Ud. el gran poeta de esa lengua. . .."; we can surmise from the date and context of the letter that he refers to the as yet unpublished *Manual de espumas*. In December 2, 1922, Huidobro offers the criticism of the volume promised in his July 3 communication, although his comments might not have been what Diego expected or desired. He singles out the poem "Canción fluvial" as an example of Diego's *heterocronismo*, his ear having detected an overly Romantic tone that he found outmoded.

Similar to pictorial Cubism, the architectonic abstraction that typifies Huidobro's early work would restrict the temporal multiplicity of Diego's approach, which augments the expression of subjectivity in the poetic text. The Huidobro of the 1910s and 1920s draws upon Cubist innovations and, just as in Cubism, his poetry volumes, painted poems, and collages of this period create parallels between the multileveled architecture of the representational space and the workings of perception. Although the architectonics of Cubism and *Creacionismo* can be considered in this sense performative–with all of performativity's associations with subjectivity, movement, and change over time–an aspect of tautology remains present in the doubling between images, or image and text.[8] It is necessary to remember, however, that the typographical arrangement characteristic of Huidobro's later volumes, such as *Altazor* and *Temblor de cielo* (1931), actually generates the sensation of motion in time; at this point, the question of modern subjectivity takes on a much greater significance than in his first books of poetry. Yet even earlier than Huidobro, Diego returns subjectivity to modern poetry and the avant-garde by building a complex sense of time into his textual architecture. He brings the temporal–*heterocronismo*–back to the poetic text by reintroducing the rhythm of lyric's music and, in so doing, breaks through the potentially tautological structures of Cubism and *Creacionismo*. Diego restores subjectivity through lyric time, which is at once constructive and affective.

---

[8] Rosa Sarabia cites Waldemar George's criticism of Huidobro's *poemas pintados* as pleonasm in *Vicente Huidobro y las artes plásticas*, the catalogue of the 2001 Museo Nacional Centro de Arte Reina Sofía's (MNCARS, Madrid) exhibition on the Chilean poet. She also argues, contrastingly, that the semantic originality of, for example, Huidobro's *Tour Eiffel* breaks through any tautology: "el pleonasmo muere con la lectura de los versos." She continues, "Se trata de metáforas plásticas que surgen al llevar a cabo la percepción y recepción de la composición en su totalidad" (59–60).

While Diego shares Huidobro's desire to "make it new," he remains averse to dispensing with the tools of the trade that *heterocronismo* makes available. In his "Arte poética" (*El espejo de agua*), Huidobro makes *tabula rasa* creation, rather than the synthesis of past and present, the foundational principle of *Creacionismo*, drawing a parallel between the movement's poetics and the divine genesis of the earth:

> Por qué cantáis la rosa, ¡oh Poetas!
> Hacedla florecer en el poema;
>
> Sólo para nosotros
> Viven todas las cosas bajo el Sol.
>
> El poeta es un pequeño Dios. (*Obras completas* 14-18/255)

In Huidobro's allegory, the avant-garde poet is like the biblical Adam, rebellious and envious of the authorial status of his Creator.[9] His declaration of independence against Nature results in his generating a new world proper to poetry instead of that which is external to it: "*Non serviam.* No he de ser tu esclavo, madre Natura; seré tu amo" ("Non serviam" 653). Huidobro's newfound liberty is the freedom to create afresh, without being constrained by the exigencies of mimetic representation. Diego's "Creacionismo" follows Huidobro's "Arte poética," enjoining the movement's poets to defy the dictates of tradition and eschew mimesis:[10]

> ¿No os parece, hermanos,
> que hemos vivido muchos años en el sábado?
> Descansábamos
> porque Dios nos lo daba todo hecho.
> Y no hacíamos nada, porque el mundo
> mejor que Dios lo hizo...
> Hermanos, superemos la pereza.
> Modelemos, creemos nuestro lunes,
> nuestro martes y miércoles,
> nuestro jueves y viernes

---

[9] This is a theme in Huidobro's 1916 volume, *Adán.* For instance, in the poem "Adán ante los árboles," the passages in Genesis about the Tree of Knowledge become allegory for the empowerment of the *creacionista* poet (*Antología poética* 38-39).

[10] "Creacionismo" is only one of several poems in the "Evasión" section of *Imagen* which can be considered an *ars poetica*. It is also possible to regard "Salto del trampolín" and "San Juan" in this manner.

...Hagamos nuestro Génesis.
Con los tablones rotos,
con los mismos ladrillos,
con las derruidas piedras,
levantemos de nuevo nuestros mundos.
La página está en blanco.
'En el principio era...' (*Imagen* 1-17/139)

Diego purposely imitates Huidobro's poem, and the image of the blank page seems to suggest concurrence with the Chilean's insistence on breaking with the past. Yet Diego's "página en blanco" should be understood as an altogether different rallying cry to freedom–the liberty to fashion an idiosyncratic and temporally heterogeneous poetry. Suddenly, "Creacionismo" says something quite different than it had on first glance. The images of fragmentation and destruction characteristic of the avant-garde manifesto–"los tablones rotos," "los mismos ladrillos," "las derruidas piedras"–become constructive materials for the unrestrained poet as *bricoleur*. Diego turns this detritus into the building blocks for the musical architecture of *Imagen* and *Manual de espumas*.

To examine Diego's statements about modern poetry is to comprehend how different they were from the typically extreme formulations of the avant-garde. In a letter dated June 24, 1921, to José Ortega y Gasset, Diego departs considerably from Huidobro's *Creacionismo*, as well as from the revolutionary spirit with which the movement is infused: "¿A qué debe aspirar, pues, nuestra poesía? A ser verdaderamente ποίησις; A ser *creado* en una autonomía perfecta de todo. A ser el antípoda de la Literatura" (Letter to José Ortega y Gasset). In contrast to Huidobro, Diego envisions *Creacionismo* as only one path among many towards the goal of a new modern poetics–the creation of a *poesía joven* to match Ortega's *arte joven*. By the time Diego began his correspondence with Ortega in 1921, his dissenting perspective on the avant-garde's dialectical conception of history had already taken the form of a highly idiosyncratic view of poetry:

> Creo que el *creacionismo*, no en el sentido ortodoxo en que lo quiere su inspirador Vicente Huidobro, sino como nuevo horizonte amplio poético y artístico en el que quepa la mayor libertad individual, es algo tan verdaderamente puro y tan distinto de lo anterior, que por vez primera el poeta de nuestros días deja de

mirar al de la generación antecesora como el enemigo urgente e inmediato. Romanticismo = anticlasicista. Parnasiano = anti-romántico. Simbolista = anti–parnasiano, etc. Pues bien, yo creo que el poeta de hoy es compatible con todos y con todo. No le estorba el simbolismo, ni el futurismo, ni aún el romanticismo, porque no es una consecuencia de ellos (por reacción, como solía ser). No está más allá, ni más acá. Está simplemente en otro plano. En rigor, en el sentido tradicional de la palabra, esta poesía que querríamos hacer no es poesía. Por eso, los poetas son inofensivos y no se trata de combatir sino de construir. Es más, creo que el poeta creacionista puede ser a la vez romántico y simbolista, como el que fuma, come y bebe; y el que hace versos, hace también prosa. Yo, al menos, así lo entiendo y aún lo practico. (Letter to José Ortega y Gasset, June 24, 1921)[11]

Integral to Diego's analysis is precisely the "fault" of *heterocronismo* of which Larrea accuses him. By redefining "el poeta creacionista" as one who can be "a la vez romántico y simbolista, como el que fuma, come y bebe," Diego maintains the sharpness of all his stylistic tools. In a letter just prior to Larrea's communication of June 22, 1919, he anticipates his fellow poet's neologism, using the adjective *heterocrónica* to describe his own heterodox combination of styles, from the Romantic to *Creacionismo*:

---

[11] The letter of June 24, 1921, is Diego's second to José Ortega y Gasset. In his first letter to Ortega, dated June 5, 1921, Diego introduces himself, presents his credentials to the respected philosopher, and tells him to expect to receive the manuscript of *Imagen*. The first two paragraphs of this letter are as follows:

Muy Sr. mío y admirado maestro: por el mismo correo recibirá V. un paquete que contiene el manuscrito de mi libro de versos 'Imagen.' Acaso mi oscuro nombre no le sea del todo desconocido por habérselo encontrado en las revistas de poesía moderna 'Grecia,' 'Reflector,' 'Ultra,' 'España,' etc. Yo sé que V. mira con simpatía todos los esfuerzos nobles de la juventud que trabaja con alteza de ideales y además tengo algunos amigos (que creo lo serán suyos) y que me hacen buenas ausencias. Por todo ello me he atrevido a sorprenderle con este envío inspirado que quisiera justificar, o, al menos, disculpar. Las ideas que ocasionalmente ha expuesto V. sobre estética y arte en recientes artículos y conferencias coincidían con mis exploraciones poéticas y estéticas; y esto me hizo pensar que sería V. el exégeta ideal de mis ensayos. En los *programas* y *intenciones* que preceden a cada una de las partes de mi libro podrá V. ver sintéticamente expresada mis ideas estéticas. Si V. quiere, y no le causa molestia, le escribiré extensamente explicándole despacio mis ideales y mis procedimientos técnicos (Letter to Ortega).

Me parece muy acertado, en general tu juicio de mis cosas. Me preguntas ¿por qué explicar todo? Si lo hago en las de carácter nuevo, será por resabios e inercias que procuraré desterrar. Pero en los más de los casos sucede que no me he propuesto escribir en ultraísta, sino casi en clásico. . . . Yo pienso cada cosa con una forma determinada, romántica, novecentista o creacionista, según la naturaleza del asunto y mi estado de ánimo. Me parecería estúpido coaccionarme obligándome a versificar en una forma que no he sentido. Siempre procuro respetar la idea primaria que, como sabes, se suele presentar ya revestida de su forma definitiva. Y esa forma y esa idea me dan el módulo de la estrofa o lo que sea, y del carácter total. De aquí que simultanee cosas *heterocrónicas* (cosa que han hecho todos los grandes poetas: Verlaine, Rubén, Góngora, Garcilaso, Verhaeren, Hugo, Fray Luis, etc., etc.). Y no creo que esto perjudique; en cambio, estoy seguro por experiencia, que los avances y libertades de técnica depuran la inspiración y mejoran lo que luego se intente hacer con técnica clásica. ("To Juan Larrea," qtd. in Díaz de Guereñu 133; my emphasis)[12]

Temporal synthesis and the integration of anteriority constitute the ultimate paradigm of Diego's work; indeed time (the time-travel of memory and the temporal rhythm of music and lyric) becomes the main structural principle of his poetry. In *Imagen* and *Manual de espumas*–of Diego's first three mature poetry volumes the two that most clearly operate under the sign of Huidobro–the architecture of *Creacionismo* becomes more flexible. Diego loosens the joints that hold Huidobro's early poetry together: visual metaphor, experimental typography, and a Cubist-inspired way of treating the poetic image and the space of the page as three-dimensional.

It is the musico-poetic lyric that provides Diego with various means of imbuing *Imagen* and *Manual de espumas* with a sense of time. Rhythm and the flow of melody, common to music and poetry, turn

---

[12] On the subject of Diego and *Creacionismo*, see Bernal, "Gerardo Diego: Heterocronismo y visión del mundo"; José Simon Cabarga, *Historia del Ateneo de Santander*; J. G. Manrique de Lara, "Umbral del creacionismo"; and J. Díez de la Fuente, "Gerardo Diego y los orígenes de la literatura de vanguardia en España." Likewise consult Pedro Aullón de Haro, *La modernidad poética, la vanguardia y el creacionismo*; Francisco Javier Díez de Revenga, *Gerardo Diego en sus raíces estéticas*; Bernal, Manual de espumas: *La plenitud creacionista de Gerardo Diego*; Bernal, ed., *Gerardo Diego y la vanguardia hispánica*; and Samuel Porrata, *La poesía creacionista de Gerardo Diego*. Bernal's *La biografía ultraísta de Gerardo Diego* will prove a useful source of information about Diego with respect to *Ultraísmo*.

into ways of making poetry temporally heterogeneous and thus free from the dictates of an avant-garde loath to include the past:

> Yo quisiera que mis poemas tuvieran el aspecto real y corpóreo de los ilusionismos creados por espejos múltiples. Escamoteo perfecto del estímulo inicial, imposibilidad de traducción a la prosa, y contagio de la emoción sin que experimente la necesidad del ¿qué quiere decir? ¿Se preguntaría eso a una melodía? La emoción de una melodía está en el ritmo, en el intervalo, en el acento y en la armonía latente que la guía. (Letter to José Ortega y Gasset, June 24, 1921)

Subjectivity becomes reintroduced into the text through lyric's music, but not as a result of the pure emotion often attributed to music and poetry. Rather, in Diego, rhythmic time leads back to the common ancestor of these art forms, the sung lyric, which is at once formal, architectonic, and affective.

José Luis Bernal has described *Imagen* as a "libro de acarreo" (Introduction 11); in Diego's words, the collection was a way to "cartearme largamente con Larrea" (*Versos escogidos* 27). It also became, significantly, a means for setting his idiosyncratic poetic in counterpoint to Huidobro, *Creacionismo*, and the avant-garde. "Salto del trampolín," the first poem and arguably the *ars poetica* of *Imagen*, is consistent with this pattern of textual and meta-textual conversation.[13] In addition, "Salto del trampolín" provides an early glimpse into Diego's way of using time and lyric to distinguish himself from Huidobro. The pronounced rhythmic structure of the poem differs markedly from Huidobro's *Creacionismo*, which relies heavily on the visual order of the text:

> *Salto del trampolín.*
> *De la rima en la rama*
> *brincar hasta el confín*
> *de un nuevo panorama.*

---

[13] "Salto del trampolín" is the first poem of "Evasión," the first section of *Imagen*. *Imagen* is divided into three parts: "Evasión," "Imagen múltiple," and "Estribillo." There is a short sub-section, "Epigramas," which comes at the end of "Estribillo." Each part of *Imagen* has either its own *ars poetica* or *Intencionario*—or both. The poem "Salto del trampolín" explains "Evasión," while "Imagen múltiple" and "Paralelamente" provide perspective on "Imagen múltiple" and "Estribillo" respectively.

Partir del humorismo
funámbulo y acróstico,
a cabalgar el istmo
del que pende lo agnóstico.

La garganta estridente,
el corazón maduro
y desnuda la frente
ávida de futuro.

Y un asirse y plegarse
a la música hermana
para bienorientarse
en la libre mañana.

Repudiar lo trillado
para ganar lo otro.
Y hozar gozoso el prado
con relinchos de potro.

Y así ved mis diversos
versos de algarabía.
Versos
                versos
                        más versos
como canté algún día.

("Salto del trampolín," *Imagen* 1-24/103)

The hoofbeats of the galloping colt–the "relinchos del potro"–hammer out the base line of the text. We hear the "Versos / versos / más versos" in the regular metrical "feet" of the poem. Repeated amphibrachs imitate the sound of the cantering of a horse, and the *redondillas*, eight-syllable quatrains (in this instance) rhyming a-b-a-b, intensify the sensation of regular motion. The *redondilla*, a staple of Spanish poetry since the early modern period, draws heavily on the sonic properties of lyric, just as assonance and alliteration imbue "Salto del trampolín" with a melodic quality. The steady beat of the colt's canter foregrounds time and, by extension, time's relation to the rhythm of music. In the last stanza, the pounding *versos* of feet–metrical and equine–propel the reader back in time to the past tense of the verb *cantar*–"como canté algún día." Diego emphasizes that he is in fact singing–through rhythm he has returned to the roots of lyric poetry in music–as well as showing us how his lyric song creates opportunities for the time travel of memory. The hoofbeats of Diego's colt constitute a metapoetic expression of his recovery of musical and lyric time. Shifting to the rhythmic musicality of lyric gives Diego a way to "brincar hasta el confín / de un nuevo panorama"–to break out of the visual and architectonic confines of *Creacionismo*. "Partir del humorismo / funámbulo y acróstico, / a cabalgar el istmo / del que pende lo agnóstico": as if on a tightrope, he balances between Huidobro's poetic and his own unique vision. The isthmus, another metaphor for Diego's solitary position, becomes a pun on the "ismos" of the avant-garde, whose rough waters surround and threaten to engulf him. From "el istmo / del que pende lo agnóstico," he gallops to new poetic horizons, borne on the back of lyric's music.

The musicality of lyric transforms the architecture of Diego's poetry, starting with the basic building blocks of poetic language. He begins his influential 1919 article, "Posibilidades creacionistas," with a meditation on the advanced position of *Creacionismo* in the Spanish avant-garde: "El creacionismo es ya una realidad tangible; ha pasado del periodo inicial de gestación cerebral y teórica para ramificarse en espléndidos brotes de hermosura vital, concreta y diáfana" (23). Diego discusses the limitations of *Creacionismo* that prevent it from making a tuneful melody. "Creo que el creacionismo, con ser en sí tan interesante," he writes, "lo es más como pórtico o umbral de todo un Arte nuevo, que contenido en el germen ha de desarrollarse en floraciones impensadas." The reason that *Creacionismo* falls short of music's expressiveness is precisely its structural soundness; Diego finds that "faltaba camino de recorrer," because "en la práctica no hay que olvidar el factor esencial *emoción*" (24). And *emoción*, as he reminds his fellow poets, can be found in abundance in the flexible structures of music. The ideal becomes to "vaciar nuestras emociones en estos moldes diáfanos impalpables," or create forms sufficiently expressive to transcend their own constraints (28).

Diego argues for the synthesis of "ornamental" figure with the basic constructive material of the poetic text. This in itself was nothing new to the poets of *Creacionismo*, who were well-versed in the French Symbolists. Indeed Paul Valéry had long since proclaimed the end of ornament with the refined music of Symbolism. In a variation on Valéry, Diego puts forth the idea that poetry ought to aspire to musical status, amalgamating music's emotional qualities and its architectural order: "'De la musique avant-toute chose?' Sí. Pero no por la onomatopeya y el sonsonete bailable, sino por la calidad espiritual y la 'no-interpretación' de la carne lírica" (Letter to José Ortega y Gasset, June 24, 1921). In "Retórica y poética," an article published in 1924, Diego confirms the inseparability of figural "decoration" and the architectonic foundation of the text–"el mármol está en Venus y en Apolo, pero Apolo y Venus no están en el mármol. La Retórica es el material de la Poética. Como el Lenguaje es el material de la Poesía."

Both "Posibilidades creacionistas" and "Retórica y poética" posit poetic form, particularly the image, as a textual architecture that retains the expressive character of music:

> *Imagen múltiple.* – No explica nada; es intraducible a la prosa. Es la Poesía, en el más puro sentido de la palabra. Es también, y exactamente, la Música, que es substancialmente el arte de las imágenes múltiples; todo valor disuasivo, escolástico, filosófico, anecdótico, es esencialmente ajeno a ella... Cada uno pone su letra interior a la Música, y esta letra imprecisa, varía según nuestro estado emocional. Pues bien: con palabras podemos hacer algo muy semejante a la Música, por medio de las imágenes múltiples. (27)

Diego elaborates a progressive scale of poetic representation, focusing on the image. Each degree, from the "imagen directa" to the "imagen múltiple," measures an increased distance from mimesis, which Huidobro similarly rejected. Diego reduces the "imagen directa" to the mere word ("la palabra"), and the "imagen refleja o simple" to "la imagen tradicional estudiada en las retóricas." The "imagen doble," contrastingly, "aumenta el poder sugestivo" and, with the "imagen triple, cuádruple, etc.," we move even further from mimetic representation–"nos vamos alejando de la literatura tradicional." Put differently, he opposes the "imagen directa, imagen refleja o simple" and "imagen doble" to the more complex "imagen triple, cuádruple, etc." associated with *Creacionismo*, and his peculiar invention, the musical "imagen múltiple" (26-27). The musicality of the *imagen múltiple*, at the pinnacle of Diego's system, comes from the duality of its nature–architectonic and emotional–the same characteristics that define his musical architecture: "Una imagen múltiple, esto es, no refleja de la naturaleza, ni reflejo de reflejo, sino ilusión, creación de sí misma, es un verdadero acorde. Simultaneidad de notas; coincidencia de intervalos que nos da una emoción creada, absolutamente independiente de las parciales que nos darían las notas sueltas" (Letter to José Ortega y Gasset, June 24, 1921). Certainly, his language in "Posibilidades creacionistas" reflects the elegant mathematical ratios of both architecture and music. "Por qué, pues, no ensayar una nueva proporción?" Diego asks rhetorically, only to answer that, "La nueva proporción sería esta: cubismo es a la pintura tradicional lo que es a la Poesía tradicional es X"; so as to find the solution to this equation, "*a priori*, habíamos de concluir la posibilidad, la existencia virtual de esa X, o Poesía = Música" (24-25). The architectonic character of the equations and schemas of "Posibilidades creacionistas," including his description of the inherent musicality of the *imagen múltiple*, mirrors Diego's conviction that order and equilibrium increase rather than inhibit emotion.

It is no accident that the most substantial concept (and term) from "Posibilidades creacionistas," the *imagen múltiple*, becomes the title of the middle part of *Imagen*, the section in which Diego sets about modifying Huidobro's architectonics with the emotion of music and lyric. "Posibilidades creacionistas," written at approximately the same time as "Imagen múltiple," constitutes one of the first articulations of Diego's musical architecture. In his brief remarks prefacing this section, Diego makes the organic metaphors of Huidobro's "Arte poética," which stand for *creación*–"Por qué cantáis la rosa, ¡oh Poetas! / Hacedla florecer en el poema" and "Hacer un poema como la naturaleza hace un árbol"–sing–"Y que sea el símbolo (–Crear un poema como la naturaleza hace un árbol–dice Vicente Huidobro) el árbol que arraigado misteriosamente–pudor de la técnica–abre sus brazos infinitos y canta en todas sus hojas al son voluble de los vientos" (145).[14] Song leads back to lyric–especially lyric time. Diego's return to lyric's temporal rhythms also means a revival of other aspects of lyric tradition, including an expressive subjectivity. As Diego explains to Ortega, contrasting traditional methods of poetic creation with the new

---

[14] Diego quotes the poem "Arte poética" from Huidobro's *El espejo de agua*. Huidobro also uses the phrase, "Hacer un poema como la naturaleza hace un árbol," in his 1925 *Manifestes*, a collection of theoretical documents (*Obras completas* 22, 33, 255). Braulio Arenas comments on both "Arte poética" and *Manifestes* in his prologue to the *Obras completas*. Regarding the avant-garde aesthetics and poetics of Vicente Huidobro, see Bruce Dean Willis, *The Vanguard Poetics of Vicente Huidobro and Mário de Andrade*.

techniques of *Creacionismo, poesía joven* should be defined by a renewed attention to the subjective:

> Los caminos (métodos) eran cuatro. Lo subjetivo por lo subjetivo: lirismo cerrado, misticismo o revés del panteísmo.–O lo objetivo por lo objetivo: aspiración del realismo indiferente, y si se quiere espiritualizar del panteísmo insensible.–A lo objetivo por lo subjetivo: el más explorado y explotado (novela, drama, casi toda la lírica, psicología... En una palabra, literatura). Quedaba uno inédito. A lo subjetivo por lo objetivo. Ese será lo nuestro. (Letter to José Ortega y Gasset, June 24, 1921)

Diego advocates a subjective standpoint and a subjectivity that do not abandon the architectonics of abstraction. His musical architecture, just as the "imagen múltiple," rests on a firm foundation of poetic form, but the characteristics of this textual construction echo lyric's different concerns.

Crucial to Diego's contribution to the first Spanish avant-garde is the way in which he uses lyric's special performative properties to increase the presence of the poetic subject in the text. Within a certain history of lyric poetry, the phenomenalization of the "I" can be regarded as "voicing" subjectivity. However, in the context of post-structuralism, Paul de Man takes a stand against such a lyric phenomenology, claiming instead that "voice" is really the product of textual construction: according to him, the "principle of intelligibility, in lyric poetry, depends on the phenomenalization of the poetic voice" because our "claim to understand a lyric text coincides with the actualization of a speaking voice." In de Man's understanding, what the poet responds to is the reader's demand to hear: "Since this voice is in no circumstance immediately available as an actual, sensory experience, the poetic labor that is to make it manifest can take several forms and adopt a variety of strategies." Due to the pressing desire to have poetic subjectivity made manifest or "audible," the techniques that produce "voice" go underground, since "it is essential that the status of the voice not be reduced to being a mere figure of speech or play of the letter" (De Man, "Lyrical Voice" 55). For de Man, structure remains just that: attempts at voicing the subject–even from inside the figural architecture of the text–inevitably say more about our desire to find transcendence in lyric poetry rather than what actually occurs. In response to de

Man's and other analogous arguments, Leslie Dunn and Nancy Jones strategically substitute "vocality" for "voice," in order to disentangle the relevant terminology from notions of producing subjectivity or physical embodiment (1-4). Their move away from a transcendental concept of subjectivity and an over-emphasis on structure constitutes an advance towards properly considering performativity as both an ordering and expressive factor in the text. This concern with performance encompasses non-verbal communication, as well as the interaction between performer and audience: "'Vocality' also implies an emphasis on the performative dimension of vocal expression, that is, on the dynamic, contingent quality of both vocalization and audition, and on their vital interrelationship" (Dunn and Jones 2).[15]

Apart from recognizing the key role played by the extralinguistic and intersubjective aspects of voicing such as historical and cultural conditions, it is imperative to regard the performative as that which at once generates structure and defies recovery into this structure, thereby maintaining poetry's expressiveness. To say that lyric performs–beyond voicing–conveys the way in which it gestures towards its own expressivity without sacrificing order. Because the idea of pure lyric expression can be interpreted as suggesting a nonmaterial and therefore nontextual presence, it is essential to recognize the paradox of textual performance–an intangible that can never quite be nailed down. Diego neither posits a transcendent subject with an audible voice, nor does he rely on textual structure to create the semblance of voicing, instead sounding subjectivity in and around the architecture of his poetry. While still providing firm support for the poetic text, the musical architecture of *Imagen* and *Manual de espumas* keeps its emotional power and ability to articulate subjectivity.

The performative features of Diego's "Columpio" (*Imagen*)–end rhyme, syntactic parallelism, and the repetition of short motifs–build the framework of the text as well as striking a ludic tone. In combination with the poem's rhyme and rhythmic patterns, the reiterations of the motif "sí-no" construct a visual and sonic architecture. The gentle swing of the amphibrachs, end rhyme, asso-

---

[15] Roland Barthes's concept of the "grain of the voice" deals with the slippage between language and music, as well as between the materiality of the body and language.

nance, and alliteration, parallel the motion of a pendulum–the object that Diego depicts through his arrangement of the poetic lines on the page. Conversely, the pendulum's long lever would seem to move back and forth as if "a caballo en el quicio del mundo," obeying the pulse produced by the contraposition of open "a" and "o" vowel sounds with the dominant consonants "b" and "d":

> A caballo en el quicio del mundo
> un soñador jugaba al sí y al no
>
> Las lluvias de colores
> emigraban al país de los amores
>
>   Bandadas de flores
> Flores de sí   Flores de no
>
>   Cuchillos en el aire
>   que le rasgan las carnes
>   forman un puente
>
> Sí   No
>
>   Cabalga el soñador
>   Pájaros de arlequines
>
> cantan el sí   cantan el no
>
> ("Columpio," *Imagen* 1-13/191)

The oscillation of the pendulum, alternating between "yes" and "no" in Diego's rendition of the popular game "loves me-loves me not," reflects the emotional fluctuation between gratification and frustration during romantic courtship. Diego shows the humor of the situation portrayed in "Columpio"–the clumsy attempts at the realization of desire and the yearning for reciprocated affection–through textual structure. Although no first-person subject emerges in the text, the poem's structures nonetheless highlight the subjectivity of "el soñador"; it is articulated "en el quicio del mundo," the textual scaffolding that is at once form and expression.

Although in its surface-level meaning, "Motivo" (*Imagen*) describes the experience of lying awake at night, counting sheep in a vain attempt to fall asleep, the poem can also be read in terms of the relationship between poetic language and subjectivity. Language dissolves, only to be recovered in the linguistic, graphic, and rhythmic order of the poetic text:

Desfilaron por mi silencio
los rebaños celestes en un blanco atropello
    Oh qué hartura de ritos y de rezos
Toda la noche la pasé contando
        Y decía
                Para vencer un remo
                Para vencer dos remos
                Para vencer tres remos
Y contaba los remos con los dedos
Toda la noche la pasé rezando
                Para cantar un vástago
                Para cantar dos vástagos
                Para cantar
Y al despertar volaron todos los pájaros ("Motivo," *Imagen* 1-14/199)

Diego's phrasing, imitating sleepless incoherence, is comparable to the subject's struggle to come into being through language: "Oh qué hartura de ritos y de rezos // Toda la noche la pasé contando." Such attempts at self-expression inevitably break apart into fragments, "Ritos y rezos," and strophes of odd parallelisms: "Para vencer un remo / Para vencer dos remos / Para vencer tres remos"; "Para cantar un vástago / Para cantar dos vástagos / Para cantar." The motif–also the poem's title–is equivalent to language stripped down to its pre-communicative essence, which reflects the liminal status that the subject may have. *Contar* and *cantar*, key words in the strophes that contain motifs, form a double paronomasia. On the one hand, the pun on the meanings of *contar* ("to count") and *cantar* ("to sing") reflects how rhythm becomes a signifying force in the poetic text. On the other hand, when these verbs are understood, respectively, as meaning "to tell" and "to sing," they can be interpreted as referring to three ends of lyric–to perform, communicate, and endow the subject with a certain presence. Counting and singing produce repeated motifs, or σημειον–the distinctive mark, trace, figuration–that is fundamental to textual architecture.

In "Verbos," language becomes pure figuration and sound, as the reader tries to reproduce the tongue-twisting vowel and consonant combinations of Diego's conjugations:[16]

---

[16] Diego includes the Spanish *amar*, Latin *lego*, French *être*, Arabic *tithemi* and *qtl*, and the Hebrew *qal*.

Un gato ha hilado la abuela
y era una media la rueca
Yo amo   *tú amas*   *él ama*

De mis labios
vuela una bandada de balandros
Legite   *o*   *legitote*   *legunto*

Y esa sonora melena
me salpica desde el balcón
Nous serons vous serez ils seront (*Imagen* 1-9/193)

Diego pairs difficult mixtures of sounds with complex metaphors in which tenor and vehicle are inverted. The sonority of phrases such as "De mis labios / vuela una bandada de balandros" weave the comparisons and juxtapositions involved in metaphor more tightly, thus rendering sound, mark, and sense inseparable.

In *Imagen* and *Manual de espumas*, the refrain becomes the ultimate figure for Diego's musical architecture. Further, Diego uses the multiple potential of the refrain as structuring device, melodic core, and reflexive chorus, in order that it refines all contours of the poetic text. Putting the refrain into relief allows us to ask what roles lyric performs and, by extension, how lyric performativity connects with subjectivity and emotion in the poetic text. In his essay "Actualidad poética de Fray Luis de León" (1930), Diego compares the exquisite balance between form, including rhythmic structures such as the refrain, and lyricism in Spanish Renaissance poet Fray Luis de León. "Es la arquitectura–y su hermana la música," he writes, "la guía maestra de nuestras bellas artes" (26). His praise of Fray Luis–"Qué escultor de estrofas, qué músico de acentos" (20)–stems from his admiration of the Renaissance master's synthesis of form and the music of lyric–"Maravillas de exactitud expresiva, de transiciones y modulaciones gallardamente burladas, abundan en las liras de fray Luis, verdaderas obras maestras de ebanistería poética" (21).

According to John Hollander's work on the musico-poetic function of the refrain, its recapitulations serve a dual purpose: on one level, they produce agreement phatically among lyric "singers"; and on another level, especially in modern poetry, they allegorize subjectivity and intersubjective communication. Hollander argues, emphasizing the special reflexivity of modern poetry, that "lyrics from the Renaissance on–poems whose relation to song-text is itself figurative–have tended more and more to trope the scheme of refrain" so as to "propound a parable out of its structural role" (74). In other words, there is already a strong meta-lyric thrust to this sort of poetry, and the refrain has an important and specific part in lyric's self-explanation, which is to expound on its own constructive capacity. If we interpret Hollander's argument in relation to the idea of the refrain as musical architecture, or metapoetic principle, then we can come up with the following formulation: the performed response of one subject or group of subjects is shaped by an original iteration, and this interaction and its effects multiply exponentially with each interchange. Diego orchestrates a call and response in "Movimiento perpetuo" (*Imagen*), thus facilitating intersubjective communication and swelling the number and kinds of subjects potentially addressed:

> La sortija   La sortija
> Dame la mano   dice mi hija
>
> . . . .
>
> En mi garganta rueda la rueda
> El agua ha muerto en la alameda
>
> El agua ha muerto hija
> La enterrarán en una sortija (5-13/204)

The rhyme and rhythm of "Movimiento perpetuo" drive the poem forward like a wheel; repeated mention of "la rueda" refers to such motive forces, as well as to verbal cycles of exchange in traditional lyric. Transformation is built into not only each of the refrain's repetitions but also the performative architecture of the text.

The refrain serves as textual architecture, and a means of articulating subjectivity and expressing emotion, as well as constituting the figure that metapoetically signs all of these various functions. Each element of this architecture, simultaneously playing constructive and performative roles, supports the others. Integral to the poems of the "Estribillo" part of *Imagen*–"Estética," "Columpio," "Madrigal," "Verbos," "Barrio," "Motivo," and "Movimiento perpetuo"–the refrain foregrounds its connection with the musico-poetic lyric. In the "Estribillo" section, Diego makes reference to the sung lyric, in which we typically find repetition in particular stanzaic forms, end-stopped lines, simple syntax, paratactic or cumulative logical structures, parallelism, and conventional imagery; these

features of the song tend to be equally expressive and structural
(Dunn 108). "Madrigal" retains the traditional form of the pastoral
song that lends its name to Diego's poem; conventional madrigal
consists of ten to fourteen lines, ending with a rhyming couplet, and
portrays themes of love and pastoral life. In a series of metaphors,
Diego compares cities ("Todas las ciudades / lloraban por ti") to
flocks of animals, thus suggesting how the lover feels when con-
fronted with the frustrating unattainability of the beloved, who va-
nishes from sight just as an individual can disappear into the mass
movements of herds or urban crowds:

> Estabas en el agua
> > estabas que yo te vi
> Todas las ciudades
> > lloraban por ti
>
> > > Las ciudades desnudas
> > balando como bestias en manada
>
> A tu paso
> > las palabras eran gestos
> como ahora estos que te ofrezco
>
> Creían poseerte
> porque sabían teclear en tu abanico
> > > > Pero
> > > > > No
> Tú
> > no estabas allí
>
> Estabas en el agua
> > que yo te vi ("Madrigal," *Imagen* 1-10/192)

Diego's diction gestures towards desire's song, from the primitive
noise of the sustained vowels made by the flock, "balando como
bestias en manada," to the refined music of his own lyrics, "pala-
bras" that "Creían poseerte / porque sabían teclear en tu abanico."
"Madrigal" turns on the tension between the absence and presence
of the beloved, whom the lover (the *yo*) encounters fleetingly in the
reflective mirror of the water: "Estabas en el agua / estabas que yo
te vi"; "Tú / no estabas allí // Estabas en el agua / que yo te vi."
The lover's only possible hope of re-connecting with the object of
desire comes in the form of lyric gesture–"A tu paso / las palabras

eran gestos / como estos que ahora te ofrezco"–yet Diego ackno-
wledges the expressive inadequacy of both words and music, as
well as the difficulty of possessing the beloved through any langua-
ge at all. The poet nevertheless finds a way of approximating the *yo*
and *tú* together in the text's repeated structures–assonance, allitera-
tion, feminine rhyme, and the variations on the refrain "Estabas en
el agua / Que yo te vi"–that sound desire.

While still including elements from *Creacionismo* and pictorial
Cubism in the text of *Manual de espumas*, Diego further develops
the temporal aspects of music with which he began to experiment
in *Imagen*. "De balcón a balcón / los violines de ciego / tienden sus
arcos de pasión": in "Mirador," internal and end rhyme–for exam-
ple iterations of the sound "ón" in "balcón"–creates a rocking beat
that becomes the supporting bass line of the poem (1-3/79).[17] Even
as the vocalic and accentual patterns change, this basic rhythmic
pattern remains in place. Given Diego's increasing incorporation of
lyric time through rhythm, his association of violins with blind-
ness–"violines de ciego"–underscores music's non-visual character
and its significance for the direction of his poetry.[18] The suggestion
of beat time in "Mirador," as well as in the poems "Otoño" and
"Canción fluvial" (*Manual de espumas*), hearkens back to the way in
which traditional lyric organizes the quotidian into easily remembe-
red and communicated–because highly rhythmic–segments:

> Mujer cultivadora
> de semillas y auroras
>
> Mujer en donde nacen las abejas
> que fabriquen las horas
>
> Mujer puntual como la luna llena
> ("Otoño," *Manual de espumas* 15-19/91)

Just as in "Mirador" brisk iambs alert the reader to Diego's shift in
emphasis from the eye to the ear, in "Otoño" anaphoric structures
"fabriquen las horas" through their iterations, in a double analogy
with the way in which time passes during activity that is repeated,

---

[17] The phrase "violines de ciego" recalls the popular *Romances de ciego.*
[18] Of course, rhyme and accentual patterns have a visual component, yet in
Manual de espumas, there is a change of emphasis from Cubist architectonics to a
musical architecture.

and how the traditional sung lyric at once integrates and expresses this experience.[19]

In "Canción fluvial," the rhythmic and mnemonic character of lyric–"esa copla que cantan"–permeates the text, thereby emphasizing its intersubjective function (31/88).[20] The poem portrays the kind of daily group activity engaged in by women in Spanish rural communities, and in which singing plays an integral part (Cummins 22):

> Mirad las lavanderas
> nutriendo de colores las limpias faltriqueras
>
> La espuma que levantan
> sube a la misma altura
> que esa copla que cantan
>
> > La luna muele estrellas
> > sin música y sin agua
> > y el amor aburrido
> > > sube y baja
> > La marea es tu vientre
> > traspasado de gracia
> > y el amor desde el nido
> > > rueda rueda
> > > como el molino turbio
> > > de la arboleda

("Canción fluvial," *Manual de espumas* 27-41/88)

The rhythmic pattern of the washerwomen's exchanges, as well as their song, follows the running of the water and the turning of the mill wheel. Ebbing and flowing like the life cycles referenced in the women's lyrics, the poem takes on their rhythm–"rueda rueda / como el molino turbio / de la arboleda."[21] In the popular sung lyric of the Spanish tradition, rhythm and the iterations of the refrain are vehicles for lyric's transmission from person to person (Cummins 3-7; Alín 13-14). Motifs play a key role in the bequeathing of lyric tra-

---

[19] Juan Gris selected "Canción fluvial," "Rima," and "Otoño" from *Manual de espumas* for submission to the German journal *Querschnitt* (Cordero de Ciria 112).

[20] Diego's allusion to the Virgin Mary–"La marea es tu vientre / traspasado de gracia" (36-37)–accentuates the connection with popular lyric.

[21] *Canciones de rueda* accompany the circle games played by children.

ditions to new generations of singers; a simple phrase such as "La luna muele estrellas" can set off a chain of associations that reaches back across time ("Canción fluvial" 32). Diego imitates the style of popular lyrics and incorporates the mechanisms that help their perpetuation over time, with the result that intersubjective relationships and communication are built back into the architecture of the poetic text.[22]

Diego was an accomplished pianist–a talent that became an intellectual and creative resource not only for his poetry but also for the frequent concert-recitals that he gave. He gained extensive knowledge of the music of Richard Wagner, Igor Stravinsky, and Claude Debussy through his friendship with Spanish composer Manuel de Falla (1876-1946), who had been a student of Stravinsky and Debussy in pre-World War I Paris, and who corresponded with Diego from 1921 until his death. Spanish musical modernism (of which Falla was a primary theorist) can be characterized in terms of a stylistic *heterocronismo* that integrates cultural memory into abstract form. As a matter of fact, the *heterocronismo* of Diego's idiosyncratic poetry parallels Falla's cultivation of multiple styles from diverse historical periods.

Falla and the composers in his Madrid circle sought to inflect music with the sound of the past, filtering by-gone musical idioms through the complex architectonics of modern music (Hess, *Manuel de Falla* 46-86).[23] From the lyric-theatrical *La vida breve* (1904-1905; revised version 1905-1913) to *El retablo de Maese Pedro* (1923) and the Harpsichord Concerto (1926), Falla actively looked

---

[22] Both the terms "poesía popular" and "poesía de tipo tradicional" have been used to describe lyrics from the medieval vernacular to the present. According to J. G. Cummins, *poesía popular* does not reflect the body of work by literate and courtly poets, in which popular lyrics are transformed. He proposes using the inclusive *poesía de tipo tradicional* to refer both to popular material and *culto* (literary) examples (1).

[23] The *Sociedad Nacional de Música*, founded by Manuel de Falla, the critic Miguel Salvador, and the musicologist Adolfo Salazar, was inaugurated on February 8, 1915, with a concert at the Hotel Ritz in Madrid. The Madrid musical circle that made this notable event possible can be characterized as liberal and cosmopolitan in orientation; anti-war remarks were made at the first concert. Despite its pacifism, the group favored France and French culture. As a result, Falla et al. leaned towards the neo-classicism of Claude Debussy and other composers of pre-World War I France. Yet at the same time, they wished to counter the orientalist vision of Spain with an authentic sound that stemmed from the country's musical and poetic traditions–*cante jondo*, *flamenco*, and the popular lyric.

for ways to combine musical modernism with representations of Spanish identity (Hess, *Sacred Passions* 73-74, 137).[24] During Falla's *andalucista* period, in which he composed *La vida breve*, *El amor brujo*, and *Noches en los jardines de España*, he translated popular idioms from Spain's southernmost region to the concert hall. *El amor brujo* mixed *flamenco* with lyric drama in a score that balances symphonic writing for strings, the harmonies of Impressionism, and other styles. For the premiere of *El amor brujo* in April 1915, Pastora Imperio, a Roma (*gitana*) woman born in Seville, sang the principal female role in the *flamenco* style, in order to increase the authenticity of the work and as a gesture of genuine respect for *flamenco* music's origins. The plot of a woman's emotional triumph over the lover who spurned her forms part of Falla's artistic affirmation of Spain's popular culture. At the same time, *El amor brujo* came under attack from particular quarters of the Spanish press, not only for its shocking (for the time) incorporation of *flamenco* elements, but also for its use of French and Russian modernist styles (derived from Debussy, Maurice Ravel, and Stravinsky). *Noches en los jardines de España* similarly nods to the history of musical modernism, for instance when Falla follows a deliberately obvious quote of Richard Wagner's "Tristan" chord with an impressionist A-b 9th chord (Hess, *Sacred Passions* 78-81, 85-87, 92).

Even as Falla, with his protégé, the young Federico García Lorca, was organizing the 1922 *Concurso de Cante Jondo*, which was aimed at preserving Andalusian popular song, he became more and more neo-classicist in his leanings, in keeping with post-World-War-I trends in music composition. *El retablo de Maese Pedro* and the Harpsichord Concerto, fruits of this phase of Falla's work, turn from *cante jondo* to pre-seventeenth-century Spanish musical styles and instruments, and such genres as the baroque *concerto grosso*. In *El retablo de Maese Pedro*, modern instrumentation contrasts with Falla's use of the lute and harpsichord, as well as with his drawing on the Arabic and medieval tradition of the *trujamán/pregonero* (boy town crier), and the *cancioneros*, lyrics collected in book form (examples exist from the Middle Ages to Falla's time). Falla infuses *El retablo de Maese Pedro* with popular forms from the Spanish Renaissance: *gallardas*, *tonadas*, carols and madrigals. A sixteenth-cen-

---

[24] Diego references *El retablo de Maese Pedro* in *Imagen* with the poem "Retablo."

tury song, "De los álamos vengo madre" by Juan Vásquez, inspires the first movement of the Harpsichord Concerto; the second movement includes the plainchant associated with the feast of Corpus Christi; and the third movement alludes to Domenico Scarlatti's (1685-1757) harpsichord virtuosity, and compositions that incorporate polyphony, popular lyrics, and sacred music. In *El retablo de Maese Pedro* and the Harpsichord Concerto, Falla chooses not to merely blend past and present, instead juxtaposing them strategically so as to champion their coexistence (Hess, *Sacred Passions* 137-43, 160-61).

Falla provided Diego with information about the techniques of musical modernism, including innovative ways of using the refrain or refrain-like fragments of music. Diego mentions Debussy several times in his early correspondence with Falla, expressing knowledge of the French composer and Falla's artistic debt to him, and the poet indicates in a letter of January 20, 1926, that they had discussed Debussy's music: "Ya lo creo que he leído las cartas de Debussy a Chausson! Admirables! Cuando nos veamos charlaremos sobre esta *curiosa* correspondencia" (*Correspondencia* 65; emphasis in the original). The abstract motifs of Debussy, as well as Wagner's thematic "leitmotifs,"[25] became models for Diego's poetics of the refrain. In his first letter to Falla, dated February 12, 1921, he asks permission to dedicate the poem "Estética" (*Imagen*) to his "admirado maestro":

> 'Estética' no tiene otra intención que la de definir por imágenes mi concepto de la Poesía (tan unido al de la Música) tratando de conseguir además el equilibrio, la fuerza y la pureza del ritmo. No sé si lo habré conseguido. Por su carácter, pues, semi-doctrinal pienso reservarlo para encabezamiento de la última parte de mi libro, que se publicará. . .
>
> La dedicatoria no es caprichosa; era obligada. Puesto que los versos son consecuencia directa del 'Mouvement' de Debussy y de ciertos compases de 'El Amor Brujo.' (*Correspondencia* 12)[26]

---

[25] We can define a "leitmotif" as a repeated theme or idea in music that remains identifiable while metamorphosing. A leitmotif (leitmotiv in German) undergoes changes in harmony, rhythm, orchestration, and accompaniment; other themes can be juxtaposed or combined with a leitmotif. In a musical work, leitmotifs symbolize or otherwise represent abstract ideas, places, characters, and emotions.

[26] By "mi libro," Diego means *Imagen*.

"Estética" can be considered an *ars poetica* of the "Estribillo" part of *Imagen*, since it has pride of place as the first selection of the section. The poem exemplifies the way in which the refrain, or *estribillo*, forms the architecture of *Imagen* and *Manual de espumas*:

> Estribillo   Estribillo   Estribillo
> El canto más perfecto es el canto del grillo
>
> Paso a paso
>   se asciende hasta el Parnaso
> Yo no quiero las alas de Pegaso
>
>   Dejadme auscultar
>   el friso sonoro que fluye la fuente
>
>   Los palillos de mis dedos
>   repiquetean ritmos ritmos ritmos
>   en el tamboril del cerebro
>
> Estribillo   Estribillo   Estribillo
> El canto más perfecto es el canto del grillo

("Estética," *Imagen* 1-12/187)

The ludic quality and repetitiveness of "Estética" almost hide the seriousness of Diego's statement of poetics, yet the mention of code words for Parnassianism indicates that something else entirely is going on: "Paso a paso / se asciende hasta el Parnaso / Yo no quiero las alas de Pegaso." Diego ascends the heights of creation "Paso a paso" with each iteration of the "Estribillo / Estribillo / Estribillo." He deftly substitutes his poetics of the *estribillo* for the sculptural poetics of Parnassianism by means of the play on the near homophones "auscultar" and "esculpir": "Dejadme *auscultar* el friso sonoro que fluye la fuente" (my emphasis).[27] The Parnassians, whose ranks included Théodore de Banville, Charles Baudelaire, Théophile Gautier, and Charles Laconte de Lisle, thought that impassive form, including the structure of rhyme, was the essence of poetry. The impossibility of completely fulfilling desire was often represented in Parnassian poetry as the love of a statue; for example, Gautier gives a rationale for this penchant for the hard beauty of sculpture in the preface to his novel *Mademoiselle de Maupin* (1835)

---

[27] Diego is perhaps nodding to poet Rubén Darío, and his *Cantos de vida y esperanza.* The poem of the volume entitled *Nocturno* opens with the line, "Los que auscultasteis el corazón de la noche" (*Obras completas* 5: 931).

(Johnson 744-45).[28] Each sounding of the refrain brings Diego closer to his alternative musical Parnassus–"El canto más perfecto es el canto del grillo"–thereby opposing the Parnassian ideal of contained beauty to the expressive emotion of lyric and song.[29] Diego's tweaking of Parnassianism also involves an implicit comparison with the highly structured poetics of *Creacionismo*, especially its emphasis on visual metaphor and experimental typography. The parallel graphic and sonic structures of "Estética"–the blank spaces between each iteration of the word *estribillo* as well as the repetition of the refrain–perform the production of sound and feeling "en el tamboril del cerebro."

The reasons for the titles of "Estribillo" and "Estética"–and Diego's dedication of "Estética" to Falla–now come into sharper focus. Just as the *estribillo* becomes the framework for some kinds of musical modernism, the refrain turns into the main constructive principle of Diego's textual architecture. As a musician-poet, Diego must have been aware of the refrain's role in the two art forms that occupied him: it simultaneously releases and interrupts (as an act of formal restraint) the flow of lyric and music (Hollander 75).[30] The refrain also serves as self-conscious sign and reminder of its own dual function–melody in form and form in melody.

Diego takes a page from the book of Falla, Debussy, and Wagner, and adapts the refrain, or leitmotif, so that it becomes textual architecture and lyric music. "D'après Debussy" (*Imagen*) can be considered an intertext of Debussy's ballet *Jeux*, composed in 1912

---

[28] The first edition of *Le Parnasse Contemporain*, the journal of the Parnassian movement, appeared in 1866. Diego had great knowledge of French art and literature, and was fluent in the language. He married the French student Germaine Marin in 1934.

[29] Interestingly, Antonio Gallego notes in the Introduction to his edition of Diego's *Poemas musicales* that the poet referred to Falla's "'estética del grillo'" in writings for a lecture on the composer (41-43).

[30] Both Diego and Larrea experimented with a musical *Creacionismo*, although Diego's pianism and advanced knowledge of music led him to achieve greater heights than Larrea in this regard (Bernal, Introduction 43). Diego came out with "D'après Debussy" in the August 10, 1919 issue of *Grecia*, just before Larrea's publication of another poem of musical inspiration. "Improntu al grillo," subtitled "Andante," takes as its dominant theme the repetitive "song" sung by the cricket, familiar from Diego's "Estética." The "Estribillo / Estribillo / Estribillo" of the *grillo* is likewise found in Larrea's "Improntu al grillo": "Vámonos, grillo; / el taladro / de tu cantar / me enargolla un cascabel / en cada auricular" (Diego; "Estética," *Imagen* 1-2/187; Larrea, "Improntu al grillo" 26-30/5).

for the *Ballets Russes*.[31] The dance steps and shifting tonalities of *Jeux* portray the meeting of young men and women engaged in ludic (as thinly disguised romantic and sexual) pursuits. Two women and one man play tennis in the park, during which time romance and jealousy arise; coupling and uncoupling, they kiss, embrace, and eventually retreat after the unwanted intrusion of a stray ball. Game-playing is likewise the theme of Diego's "D'après Debussy," which depicts children engaging in a popular Spanish version of Blind Man's Bluff, or *jugar a las cuatro esquinas*. Diego's evocative phrasing imitates the sensibility and atmosphere of the children's play, as well as the sounds and particular phrases associated with Blind Man's Bluff. The refrain articulated in the first two lines of "D'après Debussy"–"No le hallábamos el nido. / No le hallábamos" (*Imagen* 1-2/138)–works in a way similar to Debussy's characteristic transformation of leitmotifs. In Debussy's music, sonic motifs are linked with the development of characters, themes, and symbolism–but gradually over time and not necessarily by means of obvious psychological links (Smith 78-84).

Debussy raised the status of sound from decorative element to structural principle, starting with the opera *Pelléas et Mélisande* (1902) and continuing with his last major compositions. Replacing harmonic progression as the primary means of ordering tonality broke with the temporal system conventional in Western music of the common practice period (1600-1900). Sound techniques such as diatonic saturation, *ostinato*, pedal points, and the creation of new tonal patterns paved the way for conceiving the development of musical ideas in a global rather than linear fashion.[32] Changing the evolutionary patterning of sound and tone refocused attention from resolution–getting to the end–to the present moment and the temporal organization of the music. Fully articulated leitmotifs, instead of being used only to create individual effects of sonority, become discrete structures of varying size that take on functional importance in the composition (Wenk 115, 120).

---

[31] Laurence Berman notes that the exact month of 1912 in which Sergei Diaghilev commissioned *Jeux* from Debussy remains uncertain. (It might have been June, July, or early August.) As he points out, it is likewise difficult to know whether the idea for the ballet began with Diaghilev or Vaslav Nijinsky (225).

[32] "Diatonic" refers to an octave of seven notes (or eight-note scale), in contrast with chromatic or other types of scales. The term "ostinato" describes the musical technique of repeating a pattern numerous times while other parts of the composition are changing. A "pedal point" is a long note sustained for multiple bars, during which time the rest of the music undergoes transformation (Oxford Music Online).

In each section of *Jeux*, Debussy employs a different motif, which then repeats and changes. For instance, in the first section two major motifs can be identified, in addition to three accompanimental figures which provide variety of timbre. Debussy uses the same basic structure in the minor figures as in the principal motifs, except that this time he alters the rhythmic pattern: at the close of the initial section, he breaks down the regular 3/8 rhythm by introducing an implied duple time (Pasler 61-63).[33] To take another example, the *pianissimo* floating melody in the piccolos, flutes, oboes, and clarinets in the opening "Très lent" recurs at several intervals: first, in the "Mouvement du Prélude" that follows the articulation of a second major motif in the "Scherzando"; second, transformed into various forms throughout the composition; and third, returning briefly before the playful ending, the recognizable bounce of a tennis ball in a three-note figure in the woodwinds, brass, xylophone, celesta, and strings.[34] The bringing in of different motifs and their metamorphoses produce neither exactly a melodic line nor a formal pattern; instead, they shift the listener's attention to the temporal and instrumental contexts in which they appear. Since the individual leitmotifs tend to be short, normally two measures in length, the changes from one to another seem abrupt, thus deftly retuning the ear to focus on rhythm rather than melody.[35] De-

---

[33] In the elaborate part of the ballet during which the young man and two women characters engage in *pas de deux* and *pas de trois*, Debussy introduces up to four of a dozen motifs in the space of fifty or sixty measures, while shifting at a different rate from 3/4 and 3/8 to 2/4 and 4/8 time (Pasler 65-68).

[34] In *Jeux*, Debussy fragments the chordal and tonal paradigm that he developed from *Pelléas et Mélisande* to *Jeux de vagues* (1905), thereby expanding the number of layers in each harmonic unit. Alterations in orchestration show that structural shift has replaced thematic variation as the ordering device of the composition. One example of such a shift in orchestration is the emergence of major seconds in repetitions of initial dominant seventh chords (Wenk 67-91).

[35] Debussy builds a continuous pulse into *Jeux* by maintaining the eighth note constant. For instance, the indication "mouvement initial" at rehearsal number 51, when Debussy alters the tempo marking from 3/4 to 3/8, effectively means that the quarter note will stay the same; therefore, the measure will proceed at the same speed as the preceding quarter note, without the beat changing. The pulse remains constant until the end–the eighth note of the 3/8 equals the sixteenth note of the beginning of the composition's 4/4–with the exception of a short period of 3/4 at rehearsal 78. In the third and last major section, duple and triple rhythms contrast with each other, occasionally expanding into hemiolas. (A hemiola is defined as the overlaying of three notes in the time of two, or two in the time of three [Oxford Music Online]).

bussy makes these rhythmic transformations, as well as the alternation and variation of motifs, the formal structure of the composition (Pasler 71, 72, 61).

Fracturing the refrain into ever-smaller expressive pieces gives Diego's "D'après Debussy" its basic arc, in a similar way as the reiteration of interconnected series of chords in Debussy creates harmonically coherent modules. Debussean sonorities pervade the text:

> No le hallábamos el nido.
> No le hallábamos.
> La lluvia devanaba
> su moaré de raso
> y cuchicheaba
> entre los verdes muslos de las hierbas.
> El nido estaba próximo.
> No le hallábamos.
> Jugamos a las cuatro esquinas.
> Jugamos a la gallina ciega.
> Nos esponjábamos como sauces
> y picoteábamos el granizo.
> No le hallábamos.
> Pasó silbando un pajarraco negro.
> El pequeñín no sabía volar
> y se cayó al pozo.
> Y el nido
> no le hallábamos.
> La lluvia abría su abanico tornasol.
> En esto. . . . ("D'après Debussy" 1-20/138)

Diego scatters the same vowels and consonants throughout the poem in a micro-structural reflection of the main idea; the *ll, m, n, d* and *o* recombine to bring about variations in the poem's "instrumentation"; and sounds such as the *ll* recall the sonic repetitions of Debussy's later compositions. Surfacing after four- and five-line intervals, the sound motifs of "D'après Debussy" acquire phatic and organizational functions akin to legislated pauses in a rule–bound game or breaths in a sung musical composition. The iterations of sound develop in the poem in a manner analogous to Debussy's *Jeux*, since the variations on the leitmotifs structure the composition, shaping the text and providing it with a steady rhythm.

Accentual, alliterative, and onomatopoetic patterns turn into new motifs. The *ll* of *ll*uvia emerges as the dominant sound, deluging the text like rain, and the most elaborate images and visual metaphors of the poem follow the sonic downpour that they produce. Diego marks the first motif–"No hallábamos el nido. No le hallábamos" (1-2/138)–with the highly accented *esdrújulo* (proparoxytone), stressed on the antepenultimate syllable, in order to draw the reader into the rhythm of the game.[36] The motif's strong rhythmic pulse captures the reader's attention, centering it on the lines that follow: "La lluvia devanaba / su moaré de raso / y cuchicheaba / entre los verdes muslos de las hierbas." The sound of the imperfective verbs "devanaba" and "cuchicheaba" recall that of the *esdrújulo* "hallábamos"; the rest of the variation on this rhythmic theme plays on the difficult accentual patterns suggested by the proparoxytone. Accentuating the word *moaré* directs both ear and eye towards the metaphors used to describe the Blind Man's Bluff game. *Moaré* is a near-barbarism of the French *moiré*, a type of fabric which, when held up to direct light and moved back and forth, two distinct motifs become discernible, yet these different designs go back to being one and the same if they are regarded from an alternate perspective. The transformation of *moiré* fabric perfectly describes the structure and function of the motif in the poem.

The recapitulation and variation of sound patterns tell the reader when something new lies around the corner. The first section ends with a restatement of the initial theme–"El nido estaba próximo / No le hallábamos"–then changes abruptly to a second motif–"Jugamos a las cuatro esquinas. / Jugamos a la gallina ciega" (7-8/138). Although this motif retains some of the features of the first–the *ll* and the amphibrachs–it is different enough to signal the arrival of another metaphor, in which the game-playing children are compared to weeping willows and hens: "Nos esponjábamos como sauces / y picoteábamos el granizo" (11-12/138). A brief return of the original motif in fragmented form–"No le hallábamos" (13/138)–distinguishes the next section of the text, which is similarly characterized by exaggerated accentuation and arduous sounds–"Pasó silbando un pajarraco negro. / El pequeñín no sabía volar / y se cayó al pozo"

---

[36] Diego's use of proparoxytones, in comparison with Torre's, is primarily geared towards his poetics of the refrain and refrain's role in jogging memory, rather than defamiliarization or the renovation of language for its own sake. Yet at the same time, as an avant-garde poet involved with *Creacionismo*, Diego certainly remained interested in "making it new" on a number of different levels, including that of poetic language.

(14/138). The consonants *rr* and *ñ*, as well as the quasi-onomatopo-
eia *pajarraco* and the diminutive *pequeñín*, create an emphatic yet
odd rhythm that ends suddenly in calm meditation: "La lluvia abría
su abanico tornasol" (19/138). Rain dries up into sunshine as the
driving accentual pattern of the *ll* motif relaxes into the gentle roc-
king motion of repeated amphibrachs. Visually speaking, the longer,
hard-to-pronounce words dissolve into easily formed vowel and con-
sonant combinations, including the *sol* in *tornasol*–a pun on the
sun's emergence after the rain. Sound and its visual articulation form
the structural backbone of the text, while simultaneously producing
its melodic line of images and metaphors.

Diego looked not only to Debussy's but also to Wagner's con-
version of rhythmic patterns into an expressive compositional struc-
ture. In both Wagner's *Die Meistersinger* (1845) and Diego's "San
Juan: Poema sinfónico en el modo wagneriano" (*Imagen*), form and
expression become interchangeable through the combinatory wor-
kings of the leitmotif/refrain. Different themes form the harmonic
foundation of "San Juan," while the transformation of these basic
motifs creates unifying melodic lines. So as to sound the right emo-
tional note, Diego breaks apart and re-orchestrates lines of poetry
just as Wagner composes variations on the leitmotifs in the musical
score. He follows the Wagnerian paradigm by introducing the five
main leitmotifs in the "Tabla temática" that prefaces "San Juan,"
then varying their form as newly-added motifs collide with existing
themes in each of five stanzas. In a similar way as in Wagnerian mu-
sic-drama, in "San Juan," the convergences that produce the emo-
tional language of the poem occur over time: the degree of meta-
morphosis of each leitmotif increases as the dramatic action moves
towards climax. By the time of the introduction of the final theme
in the last stanza of the poem, the mutually transformative impact
of the leitmotifs has generated a sense of rhythmic ecstasy, articula-
ted though a series of rapid-fire phrases:

> Viva la moza. Viva la Juana.
> Viva el espliego y la mejorana.
> Ronda de mozos, flor en la oreja,
> mejillas rojas de las hogueras.
> Arcos de flores. El tamboril
> –viva el espliego repica –crí–crí.
> Campanero, toca las campanas.

Viva la moza. Viva la Juana.
Danzas druídicas. Corros de estrellas.
Rondas de mozos. Viva la fiesta.
Abren los ojos las margaritas.
Curvan sus alas las golondrinas.
San Juan. San Juan. San Juan.
Grillos. Estrellas. Rondas. Cohetes.
Humo. Amapolas. Tin-tan. Tin-tan. ("San Juan," *Imagen* 61-75/137)

The ecstatic sensibility of "San Juan," occasioned by the modification and interaction of the different motifs, reflects the heightened emotion felt on Saint John's Day, a traditional celebration of the summer equinox.[37]

Seen through Diego's eyes, Wagner's *Die Meistersinger* becomes a parable about the preservation of emotion in abstraction. In the opera, a group of apprentices vie for entry into the guild of Master Singers and the prize of marriage with the beautiful young Eva. Since *Die Meistersinger* affirms the need for form and inspiration to temper each other, the plot turns on the way in which the different apprentices, particularly the hero, the knight Walther von Stolzing, strike this balance. Master Singer and cobbler Hans Sachs embodies the Aristotelian values of the artisan-poet who is able to incorporate

---

[37] *Die Meistersinger* takes place in and around St. John's Day, when the carnivalesque festivities of the equinox resolve into the harmony of Christian marriage and the reestablishment of order. In the Wagner, *Hans* Sachs receives the congratulations demanded by tradition on his saint (or name) day and, following the plot of the opera, Diego dedicates "San Juan" to his own *Juan* Larrea on the occasion of Larrea's name day. The dedication–"A Juan Larrea, en el día de San Juan–1919"–is found below the poem's full title, "San Juan: Poema sinfónico en el modo wagneriano" (131). "San Juan" is a measure of the weight that Diego placed on his relationship with Larrea, particularly with regard to the genesis of *Imagen.* Prior to inclusion in the volume, "San Juan" appeared in the July 10, 1919 issue of the journal *Grecia (Año* II, no. XXI), prefaced by a stronger dedication–"A Juan Larrea, en el día de su santo, con un fraterno abrazo"–as well as a clearer allusion to the poem's musical source. Next to the "Dedicatoria" appears the following note ("Lema"): "'Tema de S. Juan en *Los Maestros cantores de Nuremburg.* (Wagner)'" (Bernal, Introduction 130). "Evasión," *Imagen's* first section and the place where most of Diego's meta-textual conversations with Larrea take place, begins with an epigraph from Larrea's poem "Cosmopolitano," which was published in the journal *Cervantes* in November, 1919: "Mis versos ya plumados / aprendieron a volar por los tejados / y uno solo que fue más atrevido / una tarde no volvió a su nido" (Diego, *Imagen* 101; Larrea, "Cosmopolitano"). Diego may well have had in mind also the "Canciones de San Juan" and the "Seguidillas de la noche de San Juan" of Félix Lope de Vega (*Poesías líricas* 1: 86-88, 89).

emotion into the techniques of master craftsmanship. *Poiesis*, from the perspective of Sachs, consists in fitting the inspirational raw material of dreams with the order of form, as if the soles and uppers of a finely-fashioned leather boot.[38] The comparison between poetry and dreams in the dialogue of the Act III, scene 2 duet between Walther and his mentor Sachs shows how rules and inspiration come together to engender true art. The scene can also be understood as an explanation of the creative and constructive potential of Wagner's leitmotifs:

WALTHER	How to begin, I scarcely know.
SACHS	Tell me your morning dream.
WALTHER	Through the good precepts of your rules, I would feel as if it were tarnished.
SACHS	Then take poetry to your hand now: using it, many found what was thought lost.
WALTHER	So rather than a dream, it may be poetry?
SACHS	The two are friends, standing shoulder to shoulder.
WALTHER	How do I begin according to the rules?
SACHS	Make them yourself, then follow them. Think of your beautiful morning dream; Hans Sachs will take care of the rest! (Wagner; Page et al. 218)

To the questioning Walther, "poetry" initially means "the good precepts of your rules," but the interventions of Sachs persuade him to think of the form of his verses as inspired by the emotion of dreams. Master and apprentice negotiate the definition of poetry until they conclude together that poetry is indeed the making of rules, yet these rules have their origin in the subjective world of the psyche and so are not imposed from without as Walther had originally and erroneously assumed.

At the climax of *Die Meistersinger*, Walther achieves artistic maturity by following Sachs' example of balance. The Prize Song that earns Walther membership in the guild of Master Singers comes to

---

[38] The entire opera is full of such productive oppositions: Hans Sachs represents the moderate opposite of Sixtus Beckmesser's pedantic Marker (the Master Singer charged with enforcing the law of verse and melodic structure); Walther's aristocratic knight contrasts with the social ideal of the *Meistersinger* as *burgher*; young Eva is the eternal feminine alternative to Walther's creative masculinity. All the binary oppositions of characters in the opera exemplify the tension that Wagner creates between structure and the uncontrolled emotion of dreams.

him in a dream–a moment of creative imagination that contrasts with the rigid organization of the Bar Form–the basic unit of composition according to the rule book of the Master Singers.[39] *Die Meistersinger* is thus about the reconciliation of rules–or form–with the dreamlike flow of creative ideas (Marvin 414-16, 422, 458). This synthesis pervades every level of the opera, from the matrimony of Walther and Eva in the *finale*, to the interplay of leitmotifs and the "marriage" of music and drama in the Wagnerian *Gesamtkunstwerk*, or total work of art. Diego wrestles with the same issues as Walther and Sachs in *Die Meistersinger*: How is it possible to invent a form that does not cause art to lose emotional power? When not spontaneously invented, form, however modern, can dampen the expression of subjectivity. In *Die Meistersinger*, although Walther reconciles his art with the rules of the guild, he does not by any means adhere to the six essential rules articulated by Fritz Kothner in Act I; in fact, none of the four original compositions that he sings in the opera conform completely to the prototype of Master Song (Marvin 415-17, 422). The tradition that Kothner and Beckmesser, the pedantic Marker of the song competition, attempt to uphold becomes less of a desired solution than the attunement of form with the innocent emotion of Walther's dream. This is the synthesis that Diego desires–the harmonization of structure and emotive subjectivity. His new way of ordering the text, based on flexibility and the potential for variation, raises suggestive possibilities for the expressivity of the modern lyric and the poetry of the Spanish avant-garde.[40]

Diego finishes the blueprint for his musical architecture in *Manual de espumas*. While of all of his early poetic works, *Manual de espumas* remains the closest to Cubism, in this volume, Diego departs from Cubist architectonics by incorporating the temporal quality of music into the visual structure of the text:

> *Manual de espumas* es mi libro clásico dentro de la poética creacionista. Largas conversaciones con Vicente Huidobro y Juan Gris, y además con María Blanchard, Léger y otros artistas, críticos y poetas en el París de aquel año hicieron posible

---

[39] See the extensive discussion of Wagnerian leitmotivs in Camille Benoit, H. M. Brown, Mary A. Cicora, and Carl Dahlhaus.

[40] Although Diego does not in any way share Wagner's nationalistic aesthetic ideology, his dilemma about synthesizing form, lyric, and emotion is similar to the one presented by the German composer in *Die Meistersinger*.

que yo aprendiese cuanto necesitaba. Escuchándoles, no obstante, yo pensaba siempre en mi música y en mis músicos, y traducía mentalmente los términos plásticos a vocabulario temporal y sucesivo que por serlo era más idóneo para 'componer' poesía. Los 'rapports,' las gradaciones desde el tema u objeto de la naturaleza hasta su transfiguración en unidad, y calidades autónomas plásticas y cromáticas, ya en sentido abstraedor, ya por el contrario concretador si se partía de lo geométrico, me abrían cada día inéditas perspectivas que luego en la paz feliz de la playa cantábrica encontraban su armoniosa poetización. (*Versos escogidos* 37)

Diego developed *Manual de espumas* in conversation with Huidobro and the Cubist painters, especially Juan Gris, during his 1922 residency in Paris. In order to emphasize the Cubist connection, Diego included Gris's canvases in the volume as illustrations, as well as dedicating certain of the poems to prominent figures in the world of Cubism ("Canción fluvial" to Juan Gris, and "Cuadro" to the French art critic Maurice Raynal). The architectonic structure of the poetic texts of *Manual de espumas* recalls the arrangement of different perspectives in Gris. At the same time, Diego transposes the "ensayos más musicales que plásticos" (185) of *Imagen* into a chromatic architecture that includes time within the spatial harmony of the text, thereby adding a third, non-visual and musical dimension to Gris' *rapports*, or the pictorial expression of synaesthesia (Arizmendi, 11-12, 18, 32).[41] The musicality of lyric and the lyricism of music transform the architecture of Diego's poetry.

In "Primavera," the first poem in *Manual de espumas*, Diego combines the poetics of the refrain with an expressive subjectivity. He evokes the beauty of the spring season, following a traditional theme of lyric poetry. Yet contrary to custom, Diego identifies spring with disappointment rather than happiness in love, and compares the season of renewal with the brute machinery of modernity–"la más bella grúa"–instead of nature (9/77):

---

[41] In her introduction, Milagros Arizmendi discusses *Manual de espumas* in relation to Cubism, Gris, and the associative character of Diego's images. See also Juan Manuel Díaz de Guereñu, Andrés Soria Olmedo ("Cubismo y creacionismo: matices del gris"), and Enrique Cordero de Ciria.

Ayer   Mañana
Los días niños cantan en mi ventana

Las casas son todas de papel
y van y vienen las golondrinas
doblando y desdoblando esquinas

Violadores de rosas
Gozadores perpetuos del marfil de las cosas
Ya tenéis aquí el nido
que en la más bella grúa se os ha construido

Y desde él cantaréis todos
en las manos del viento

                        Mi vida es un limón
                  pero no es amarilla mi canción
                        Limones y planetas
                        en las ramas del sol
                     Cuántas veces cobijasteis
                     la sombra verde de mi amor
                     la sombra verde de mi amor

La primavera nace
y en su cuerpo de luz la lluvia pace

El arco iris brota de la cárcel

Y sobre los tejados
mi mano blanca es un hotel
para palomas de mi cielo infiel

("Primavera," *Manual de espumas* 1-24/77-78)[42]

The performance of memory in "Primavera" responds to the rhythm of its textual architecture. Diego builds the poem around repeated dactyls, as well as aa-bb and a-b-a-b rhyme patterns. Just as in a refrain, this rhythm seems to jog memory, giving order to its impressions. "Ayer Mañana / Los días niños cantan en mi ventana": poetic expression and recollection are comparable to the lyric "singing" in the window. In Diego, remembrance continues to be connected with the articulation of a poetic subject and the representation of sensations belonging to it. The graphic separation between

---

[42] Diego's use of the word "golondrinas" is reminiscent of one of Bécquer's famous *Rimas*, "Volverán las oscuras golondrinas."

the words *ayer* and *mañana* creates an opening for the perceptions of the first-person subject to enter the window of memory and of the text. Diego sets the section with the remembered refrain on the right side of the page, placing it in the middle of two left-aligned stanzas. Consequentially, he makes the graphic structure of the poem resemble the window that is the first and most important image of time and space in "Primavera." Combining the temporally heterogeneous impressions of the poetic subject in this material aperture reflects the way in which lived experience exists in the psyche, in the interstices of past, present, and future. The architectural spaces in "Primavera"–the houses and window–are also metaphors for the mechanism–"la más bella grúa"–that orders the images and impressions in the text. "Doblando y desdoblando esquinas," the swallows turn down the pages of Diego's book: one meaning of the Spanish verb *doblar* refers to the folding of paper; *desdoblar* can actually signify the reverse, to unfold. The bending and unbending of the paper parallel the workings of the inner gears of Diego's poetry, which depend on the yes/no and forward/reverse movements characteristic of the refrain. His musical architecture works along similar lines as memory–forward and back in time.

Diego locates the source of yesterday's memories in "las golondrinas" and the first-person subject who listens to their song. The swallows, just as the songbird in popular lyric, constitute a traditional stand-in for the subjectivity of the poet or poetic "I." Addressing "las golondrinas" through apostrophe intensifies their subjectivity and the subjectivity of the textual subject that addresses them, both of which the songbirds represent: "Ya tenéis aquí el nido / Que en la más bella grúa se os ha construido // Y desde él cantaréis todos / en las manos del viento." The swallows' song is transformed into the expressive melody of experience which, carried by memory, floats out over and above the architecture of the text's paper house. Diego's diction in the refrain is redolent of the "poesía tradicional" of Spain: mention of lemons and the "sombra verde de [mi] amor" recalls the language of the Spanish popular lyric. In this type of poetry, devices such as the refrain and syntactic parallelism generate a rhythmic connection among singers. In Diego, the production of communicative relationships conventional in lyric–between the first-person subject and the swallows, and among the different voices singing the refrain–translates into the return of subjectivity to avant-garde poetry. Diego's incorporation of the refrain also brings his peculiar *heterocronismo* into the picture: the link with such older forms of lyric as popular poetry, and the similarity with the complex temporal workings of memory.

According to Diego, in "Actualidad poética de Fray Luis de León," "todos los poetas de hoy se afanan por dar perdurabilidad a su obra, torneándola amorosamente, solícitamente, infatigablemente, seguros de que no basta licenciar el chorro de la fluente espontaneidad" (20). The spontaneity of Diego's poetry softly erodes this constructivism, as if a river wearing down its own banks over time. In "Paralelamente," the statement of intentions (*Intencionario*) prefacing the "Estribillo" section of *Imagen*, Diego compares his poetry at once to music and the flow of water in time:

> Paralelamente, estos otros ensayos más musicales que plásticos, dejándose ir cauce abajo en un deleitoso entresueño cerebral. Aspiran a una perfección más tersa que construida, y más que forma quisieran ser materia pura. Poesía de vacaciones cantada entre siestas perezosas y lejanos ritornelos infantiles. Estribillos, repetidos o no, que aun estos quisieran serlo por su ingenua espontaneidad involuntaria. El ademán, el gesto, la intención solamente, que se colme y se desagüe en un solo suspiro.
>
> Y esta vez el símbolo será el agua, fugaz, eterna y transparente, capaz de todas las melodías sobre su ritmo infinito y torpe, friso corriente siempre en la misma deliberada postura. (185)

The apparent oxymoron "friso corriente" expresses the temporal and spatial flexibility–the potential for movement and transformation–in Diego's musical architecture. The structure of his poetry is not merely *like* music; rather, the material of the poem functions in the same way as a musical phrase or leitmotif. "El ademán, el gesto, la intención solamente, que se colme y se desagüe en un solo suspiro": this gestural quality approximates the expressive subjectivity of the musical and poetic lyric. Suggestively, Diego uses his own poetry as epigraph to "Estribillo"; the lines "A tu paso / las palabras eran gestos" stress the gesture made by lyric ("Madrigal," *Imagen* 7-8/192). The gestural or performative character alluded to by the epigraph to "Estribillo" and the metaphor "friso corriente" in "Paralelamente" becomes the figure of subjectivity and the means for the phenomenalization of the poetic subject in Diego.

In "Gesta" (*Imagen*) just as in "Primavera," Diego plays with the complex interconnections between the tempo of memory and subjectivity. In the first of several variations on the refrain that appears throughout the poem, the irruption of the poetic "I" into the text draws attention to the presence of a subject: "A la luz pensativa de mis manos / todo lo voy contemplando" (11-12/149).[43] The poet's variation on the theme of the refrain parallels the way in which, in Bergson, memory connects different images and moments, repeating and ordering them in time. Past and present meet in the refrain as if the result of the processing of memory; the iterations of the refrain unfold like the pattern governing the subject's consciousness of itself. To recall Machado's formulation in "Sobre el libro *Colección* del poeta andaluz José Moreno Villa," the function of rhythm is to situate poetic language in time, where time is conceived as lived experience with a particular emotional tenor (1365). In "Gesta," from each recapitulation of the refrain, or refrain-like passages that foreground the repetitive act of contemplation, spirals out a series of images of sensory impressions:

> Por vez primera entre la lluvia muerta
> cantaban los tranvías zozobrantes.
>
> Y en la sala del piano
> un esqueleto
> jugaba al ajedrez con guantes negros.
>
> Golondrinas precoces recitaban sus versos.
>
> La abuela junto al tiempo
> rezaba su rosario de nietos.
>
> Y el rumor de las sombras en la estancia
> encendía romanzas sin palabras.
>
> A la luz pensativa de mis manos
> todo lo voy contemplando. (*Imagen* 1-12/149)

---

[43] I refer to the following structural and semantic variations on a theme, repeated throughout "Gesta": "A la luz pensativa de mis manos / todo lo voy contemplando" (11-12); "Voy midiendo las millas con mis rimas" (55); "Yo le fui desnudando / beso a beso / sin notar que se apagaba / entre mis brazos" (91-94); "Entre mis dedos / ríe el mundo transparente" (131-32); "voy quemando uno a uno los instantes" (136); "Todo lo voy contemplando / la luz soñadora de mis manos" (150-51); "A la luz de mis dedos / que arden como cirios / lo veo" (160-62). Diego also gestures towards the idea of the refrain in such lines as "La abuela junto al tiempo / rezaba su rosario de nietos. // Y el rumor de las sombras en la estancia / encendía romanzas sin palabras" (7-8); and "Y doncellas sin novio / me esposan las manos / con un rosario de versos" (165-67). Repetition and variation are built into both the structure and expressive language of the poem.

Both the grandmother's prayers as she says the rosary and the reciting of poetry by the "golondrinas precoces" emphasize the kind of iterative repetition characteristic of the refrain.[44] Sound–the noise of "los tranvías zozobrantes," the piano, the rhythmic recitations of the grandmother and the swallows–binds together impressions from distinct temporal periods, since *represented* sound is necessarily *recalled* sound. Juxtaposed across the reaches of time, the musical recollections contained in the images of the text become accessible once again to the subject. The poem's voicing of memory demands interpretation, which in turn requires the presence of a mediating subjectivity. From this *heterocronismo*–defined as temporal shift rather than a trans-historic borrowing of styles–emerges a more flexible and provisional "poem" that defies its own status as "text." Representation no longer equals static inscription; instead the musical architecture of the text develops performatively through time. Playing the psychic sound recording revives the poetic subject's consciousness of the present by transferring sensation from the reified text–anteriority–to the now of interpretation: "Y el rumor de las sombras en la estancia / encendía romanzas sin palabras."

The dynamic exchange between the recursive form of the text and the immediacy of perception acts as metaphor for the movement of time that generates the image (as the common unit of the poetic text and the subject's experience). Images are nothing if not temporally synthetic: in the act of perceiving, the psyche brings past perceptual knowledge and the anticipation of future events to the experience of every present moment. Building the temporal character of image formation–bringing what Maurice Merleau-Ponty calls the "pre-history" of the representation of perceptual experience into the text–becomes Diego's strategy for developing subjectivity in the poetic text (278-79):

La retreta de sueños
                    y papeles pintados
desfilando a compás
                    sobre los puentes del ocaso

---

[44] Diego's phrasing has a very nineteenth-century feel in this passage of the text. His diction again recalls Bécquer's "Volverán las oscuras golondrinas" (*Rimas*) which, in Diego's heyday, every schoolchild could recite. Given Diego's musical knowledge, there is also the suggestion of Felix Mendelssohn's piano miniatures, "Romances sans paroles."

Y un día
    la cometa
        que desaté en mi regazo
y ancló desorientada en el pasado

      En la ciudad dormida
    salían retozando de la escuela
      los signos ortográficos

      Y los ángeles de la guarda
    en el pico traían las estampas
      ("Gesta" 17-29/149-50)

The perceptual t(r)ail of "la cometa" inscribes memory with the "signos ortográficos" of the past–creating the impressionistic "estampas" that provide the subject access to the pattern of its previous existence. The body, or more precisely, the perceptual mechanism, takes on the function of what Bergson refers to as the "hyphen between the subject and the exterior world." Bergson's hyphen connects diverse temporal moments into a psychic web; this is also true of Diego's poem (*Matter* 102-103, 133). In a meditation on the way in which the perceptual mechanism fixes past experience in memory, Bergson argues that, "every *attentive* perception truly involves a *reflection*, in the etymological sense of the word, that is to say the projection, outside ourselves, of an actively created image, identical with, or similar to, the object on which it comes to mold itself" (102; emphasis in the original). According to him, "we are constantly creating and reconstructing," because our "distinct perception is really comparable to a closed circle, in which the perception-image, going toward the mind, and the memory-image, launched into space, careen the one behind the other" (103). Bergson considers the image both in the literal sense of visual perception and in the more abstract sense of memory. Perception never simply consists of the encounter between the subject and external object; rather, it is composed of "memory-images" that at once structure and interpret the object (133). Situating the poetic subject in its own perceptual experience means locating the subject in time: the subject becomes as such when it has, so to speak, a history.

In "Gesta," the dynamic exchange between perceptual immediacy and the inscription of sensation in memory is analogous to the balance between the temporal fluidity of the image and the recursive form of the text:

> Los verbos irregulares
> brincan como alegres escolares
>
> Por el termómetro trepa la emoción
>
>   En una sonata blindada
>   me embarqué con la brújula imantada
>
>   Las campanas vuelan en mi cabellera (47-52/151)

Metapoetic references to image production throughout the text–its "signos ortográficos" and "verbos irregulares"–create a parallel between the temporal alternation of memory and the writing of poetry. The shape taken on by the images in "Gesta" depends on the construction of time in the text; the image is generated along the same lines as the arrangement of sensory impressions in the space of the psyche. In a way similar to memory, in the poem, the juxtaposition of past and present sensations orders experience into a succession of images:

> Voy midiendo las millas con mis rimas
>
>   A la hora del té
>   los abanicos bailan un minué
>
> Para apagar mi sed
> fumé todas las islas
> La lámpara del estío
>
>   abrió
>   su sombrilla
>
> Y un hálito de playa
> atraviesa la lona de campaña
>
>   De   tienda   a   tienda
>   el   oasis   cuelga sus   hamacas
>   (55-66/151)

    Diego's diction suggests that poetry's peculiar capacity to beat time–"voy midiendo las millas con mis rimas"–increases the temporal heterogeneity of the image and, in consequence, likeness to the reality of perception and memory-formation. Constant shifting among verbal tenses, rhythmic and rhyme patterning, and the spatial gaps between strophes all contribute to the feeling of being in the middle of the mind's attachment of new impressions to old memories. The peculiar structuring mechanisms of the mind parallel the slightly off-kilter "rimas" of "Gesta." "A la hora del té / los abanicos bailan un minué": the exaggerated, almost comical rhyme suggests the instability of perception itself. "Y un día / la cometa / que desaté en mi regazo / ancló desorientada en el pasado" (21-24/150): the kite's tail metaphorically represents the trace of past experience recorded in memory and, by extension, the poetic subject's powers of recollection.

The patterning of memory in "Gesta" turns temporal gaps into the complex architecture of selfhood. Through temporal heterogeneity, Diego returns avant-garde poetry to lived experience, since the subject knows itself phenomenologically as a series of images (Merleau-Ponty 476-503). As Gilles Deleuze argues, recollection and perception become one in the images created by the psyche, and existence is defined by the effort to locate the self within these impressionistic combinations of past and present (25-27). Alternating between the moment of recollection and an anterior time of perception causes the "I" to read its own image in the trace of representation. The mock death of the "meses muertos" in "Gesta" becomes the means for the poetic subject's resurrection through the writing of poetry. "Los signos ortográficos" and "las estampas" are the autobiography of the subject–constructed in the reflective space of perception (27, 29/150). Left by the passage of time, they metamorphose into implements for writing the history of the poetic subject in reverse–from the end (the moment of remembrance or metaphorical death) to the beginning (the original moment of perception):

> Sobre vuestros disfraces arrugados
> yo nevaré mis versos
>
> Aquel corro de niñas
>
> Para la primavera
> los besos maduros caerán de sus trenzas
>
> Por entonces Mambrú volverá de la guerra
>
> En las revistas ilustradas
> las efemérides
> se han convertido en alas disecadas
>
> Y el lápiz que planté
> alumbra la calle como un farol (33-43/150)

The articulation of memory in "mis versos" provides access to the "life history" of the writing (authorial and poetic) subject: recalling "la primavera" of existence makes childhood games–"aquel corro de niñas"–and the refrain from the old tune about the Duke of Marlborough–"Por entonces Mambrú volverá de la guerra"–graspable by memory as well as textually legible. The text of "Gesta" is therefore transformed into a double biography: *ars poetica* and lyric poem. In the written pages filled with images of the past, the "alas disecadas" of the "revistas ilustradas," we read the paradox of representation. This memorial, just as any, inevitably becomes a *memento mori*, or token of the inescapable forgetting that is death:

> Todo lo voy contemplando
>   a la luz soñadora de mis manos
>
> Mi   gesta   encadenada
>
> se   alzará   arco   tras   arco
>
> como el gran acueducto de los siglos
>
> Y allá   Tras las murallas
>   Anclada en el silencio
>   La biblioteca
>
> El tiempo sabe a cloroformo (150-59/155-56)

The poet and his legacy remain forever perched on the edge of oblivion–"anclada en el silencio" of "la biblioteca"–but the mnemonic power of the "rosario póstumo" (167/156)–the text–calls them back from the abyss.

Diego's chains of images–"mi gesta encadenada"–are comparable to the synthesis of diverse sensations in synaesthesia–"el rumor de las sombras en la estancia / encendía romanzas sin palabras." Like the traces inscribed in memory and poetic writing, they are the figure of time and time's performance through remembrance and, by means of this figuration, the reader of "Gesta" experiences the shift between recalling and forgetting that is constitutive of being. The image as trace is analogous to the architecture of memory and of the text. Both are designed to be performed back into existence, in a similar way as playing a musical score:

Sembrando mis imágenes
me hallaréis olvidado entre la nieve

La mujer paisaje
desnuda como un circo
canta tardes antiguas
en las trémulas gargantas del ramaje

En las aguas del piano
se ha ahogado aquel recuerdo
sin dejar rastro ni de sus cabellos

La sirena aúlla
como un perro lejano (137-47/155)

Shifting between recollection and the present-tense interpretation of memory's recorded music, "las aguas del piano" sound experience into audible range. Their glassy surface mirrors the subject–"Sembrando mis imágenes / me hallaréis entre la nieve"–and the way in which the subject's interpretation of anterior moments in time constructs its self-image. Traces of the past stay incomplete without the complementary gesture of remembrance that performing–writing and reading–the text sets in motion: "Mi gesta encadenada / se alzará arco tras arco / como el gran acueducto de los siglos." The black and white keys of the piano recall the black and white text of "Gesta"; these triggers for remembrance perform the past and subjectivity into being.

The promise of immortality offered by memory and poetic writing comes to be a grand performative gesture in which the past approximates the present and future. Contained in the title of "Gesta" is a double pun: *gesta* alludes to the medieval *cantares de gesta* that inscribed the heroic deeds of the knights of the Reconquest in Spanish cultural memory; the word also functions as a paronomasia of *gesto*, or *gesture*. For Diego, representation must be an act of heroism and a sign of belief in the possibility of the preservation of subjectivity in memory and the modern lyric. His poetry of remembrance is always already gestural–a reach back in time and the stretching of time towards the present moment of representation and the future of interpretation.

Diego's inclusive attitude towards tradition gives his poetry a different stamp than the rest of the first Spanish avant-garde. Yet his nod to the past does not simply include incorporation of past styles, but instead generates a real transformation of the structure of the poetic text. Diego's musical architecture draws on the temporal character of lyric to approximate the movement of time in memory. The musico-lyric refrain parallels memory, regarding the way in which the web of remembered traces in the psyche at once forms a complex architecture and functions as recording device; this combination of the structural and gestural constructs the frame of *Imagen* and *Manual de espumas.* The recorded music of Diego's poetry sounds the past–in the form of lyric tradition–back into audible range. Reintroducing the rhythm of the past is of enormous consequence for avant-garde poetry, especially in the Spain of the 1910s and early 1920s, where *vanguard* was often synonymous with rebellion against tradition, and *new* meant the suppression of subjectivity in the text. Diego turns lyric's manifestation of subjectivity through temporal structures into an ingenious strategy for returning to the past while still marching towards an avant-garde future. As a result, Diego manages to have it both ways: his emphasis on architecture remains in keeping with avant-garde aesthetics, while the lyricism of his poetry transcends formalist preoccupations. The performativity of *Imagen* and *Manual de espumas*, as a consequence of Diego's revival of lyric, becomes highly suggestive with respect to modern and contemporary experimental poetics. Moving to the music of lyric, avant-garde structure in Diego takes on a new expressivity and lyric expression acquires an architectonic form truly worthy of poetry's front line.

CONCLUSION

But every *attentive* perception truly involves a *re-flection*, in the etymological sense of the word, that is to say the projection, outside ourselves, of an actively created image, identical with, or similar to, the object on which it comes to mold itself. If, after having gazed at any object, we turn our eyes abruptly away, we obtain an 'afterimage' of it: must we not suppose that this image existed already while we were looking?

Henri Bergson, *Matter and Memory* (102-103)

I N Sonia Delaunay-Terk's *Le Bal Bullier*, simultaneous form replicates the sensations produced by a Paris dance hall's rhythms and electric lights. The sensory experiences of the dancers depicted in the painting–fictive subjects–stand in for the viewer's perception–the way in which rhythms and lights become colors and abstract shapes through the process of perceiving. Such remnants of the figurative as the dancers in Delaunay-Terk's *Le Bal Bullier* have been completely converted into abstract form in Robert Delaunay's *Fenêtres ouvertes simultanément 1ère partie, 3e motif, Formes circulaires, Soleil no. 1*, and *Formes circulaires, Soleil no. 2* (see figs. 3.1, 3.2, and 3.3). Yet in Delaunay just as in Delaunay-Terk, form at once recapitulates the experience of perceptual simultaneity and induces it in the viewer, teaching the eye to assimilate many sensations at the same time. It has been my argument that the relationship between form and perception–how form both represents and reduplicates perception, encoding the operation of perceiving within its structure–in the art of Delaunay and Delaunay-Terk (*Simultaneisme*), becomes paradigmatic of a certain type of avant-garde aesthetic. This aesthetic, in which perceptual simultaneity plays a crucial role, inspires and shapes the first Spanish avant-garde, in particular Guillermo de Torre's *Ultraísmo*. Perceptual simultaneity, in Torre, becomes the psychic means by which to cross the boundaries of spaces marked as national or regional, and thus move towards the cosmopolitan. What I have called Torre's perceptual cosmopolitanism is precisely this vehicle for breaking out of the confines of *lo castizo*, remapping Spain in relation to the rest of Europe and the European avant-garde.

In Torre's poem "Ariadna" (*Hélices*), for instance, perceptual simultaneity turns the textual landscape into a hyperbolic cosmic space in which sensations bombard the psyche:

> Se iluminan sonoramente
>   los jardines
>   pendientes del horizonte
>   rayado por asteroidales trolleys
>
> Hay una inversión planista
>
> Se irisa un sol de media noche
>
> Y adviene una metarritmización total (lines 14-20/27)

The synaesthesia and visual metaphors suggested in the phrase, "Se iluminan sonoramente / los jardines / pendientes del horizonte / rayado por asteroidales trolleys," sets going the "inversión planista," or transformation of perception, augured by the "sol de media noche." It is this perceptual simultaneity–the "metarritmización total"–that generates the outpouring of images that follow:

> Los panoramas viajeros   afluyen
>   al vórtice de la red ariádnica
>
> Las naves perforan
> los túneles de la atmósfera
>
> Sobre los ríos emergen
> Las locomotoras jadeantes
>
> ("Ariadna," *Hélices* 21-26/27)

Perceptual simultaneity makes the subject, like the viewer of paintings by Delaunay and Delaunay-Terk, forget everything but the sensations converging upon the psyche in the present moment. Torre's calligrammatic arrangement of the poetic lines on the page mirrors the psychic hyperactivity and consequential temporal amnesia brought on by the maximizing of sensory stimulation:

> Qué nube ha borrado
> > los itinerarios?
> He perdido la clave del
> > del laberinto arácnido
> ("Ariadna" 30-33/28)

Memory has been erased by the multiplicity of sensations, causing the verbal hiccup that Torre ingeniously works into lines 32 and 33: "He perdido la clave *del / del* laberinto arácnido" (my emphasis). The maze-like feeling produced by the sensorial barrage recalls the famous labyrinth of Greek mythology referred to in the poem's title, from which Theseus escapes using Ariadne's thread. (This dread prison, built by Daedalus on the orders of Minos, the oppressive King of Crete, contained the monster known as the Minotaur, who devoured the Athenian youths exacted by Minos as his annual tribute.) In Torre, the subject loses itself in the labyrinth of perceptual simultaneity, but instead of the destructive sort of disorientation that we might imagine, the subject's ramped-up sensory capacity sets in motion a positive psychic metamorphosis that reveals extraordinary perspectives.

In the course of reordering the textual landscape through perceptual simultaneity, Torre deconstructs the mechanisms used–characteristically in Antonio Machado's *Campos de Castilla*–to configure the *castizo*. Machado's ethical purpose to have the reader identify with the national and regional as a means of promoting unity in the face of Spain's turn-of-the-century crisis (the "Disaster" of 1898) manifests itself by means of the perspectival and perceptual framing devices which he employs in *Campos de Castilla*. Torre's response to the location of identity in the *castizo* landscape necessarily involves disrupting the framing strategies that make this positioning possible.

Crucial to the reader's identification with the landscape in *Campos de Castilla* is how Machado's framing of the landscape facilitates the kind of meditative psychic attitude which synthesizes present sensations and past impressions, for it is this temporal bridge that joins perception to subjectivity and subjectivity to collective identity. To take an example, in "Orillas del Duero," the removed perspective conducive to contemplation, as well as the evocative representation of sensation and focus on detail, jog the reader's memory of similar perceptual experiences:

> ¡Campillo amarillento,
> como tosco sayal de campesina,
> pradera de velludo polvoriento
> donde pace la escuálida merina!
>
> ¡Aquellos diminutos pegujales
> de tierra dura y fría,
> donde apuntan centenos y trigales
> que el pan moreno nos darán un día!
>
> Y otra vez roca y roca, pedregales
> desnudos y pelados serrijones,
> la tierra de las águilas caudales,
> malezas y jarales,
> hierbas monteses, zarzas y cambrones.
>
> (*Campos de Castilla* CII 5-17/110)

The recollection spurred by centering on detail receives additional stimulation by various exclamations, conjoined with apostrophe, which attract attention not only to the features of the landscape (belonging at once to present perceptions and past impressions), but also to Machado's regenerationist message. The reader is called upon to answer the rhetorical questions comprising the apostrophe of the last strophe and, in doing so, becomes implicated in the acts of remembering a brighter past and comparing this anterior time with Spain's present degenerated condition. Machado thus couples nostalgia–which the landscape is carefully constructed to engender–with the ethical considerations demanded by national conditions:

> ¿Y el viejo romancero
> fue el sueño de un juglar junto a tu orilla?
> ¿Acaso como tú y por siempre, Duero,
> irá corriendo hacia el mar Castilla?
>
> ("Orillas del Duero" 49-52/112)

Machado's diction, specifically the words "romancero" and "juglar," point to the special role that he envisions for poetry and the poet in Spain's renascence. It is the poet's grave responsibility to bear witness to the country's present ruin and awaken memory of what once made it great, which Machado, in a similar way to Miguel de Unamuno, understands as originating in the truly *castizo*.

Torre's uprooting of the subject from the *castizo* landscape means interfering with the contemplative perception that connects the sensations of the now to memory. Such a psychic disruption is effected through perceptual simultaneity, which collapses time into a present that has become detached from the past. This temporal compression opens new horizons to the subject, which are portrayed as aerial or otherwise elevated perspectives; space expands as time contracts in Torre. He turns such "vertical" perspectives into the equivalent of crossing the borders of *castizo* Spain, in this way translating perceptual simultaneity into perceptual cosmopolitanism.

The poem "Madrigal a bordo" (*Hélices*) typifies the way in which Torre shifts from perceptual simultaneity to perceptual cosmopolitanism. We may compare the syncopated rhythms of jazz and the fragmented visual organization of the poetic lines (perceptual simultaneity) to the varied vistas seen from an ocean-liner (a representation of the cosmopolitan):

> Mar sincopado
> > Olas efervescentes
> > > Un transatlántico
> > Oh mujer enredada en gestos enigmáticos
> > Tú desnuda sobre cubierta
> > > rimas la cadencia del silencio
>
> . . . .
>
> Sobre tus muslos rueda
> > la bola de los hemisferios
> En tus miradas emergen
> > paisajes submarinos
> Un collar de ciudades
> > ciñe tus senos hesperidios
> Tus palabras
> > resumen las perspectivas inholladas
> > > (Torre, "Madrigal a bordo," *Hélices* 1-18/79)

Having become the structural paradigm of the psyche, liberating the subject from all bounds, perceptual simultaneity has turned "cosmopolitan" in a much more far-reaching way than the fashionable tastes, international travel, and intrigues of the ocean liner's privileged set: "El barco danza un vals nostálgico / Nostalgia de tu psíquis cosmopolita / que ha visto el revés de los horizontes" ("Madrigal a bordo" 27-29/80). However, in converting perceptual simultaneity into a paradigm for a cosmopolitanism that would transcend the national and regional, uprooting the subject and preventing its identification with *castizo* places, Torre creates a disconcerting sensation of existential disconnect. As I have emphasized, short-circuiting memory with an eye towards radically expanding the experience of the present cuts off the psychic pathways that permit the construction of a coherent self, as well as the association of subjectivity with a collective identity.

One of the fundamental issues that I have addressed in this book is the series of problems that perceptual simultaneity poses for subjectivity. Henri Bergson's observation that "every *attentive* perception truly involves a *reflection*," indicates the importance of time to perception according to his perspective; in view of this idea, we can imagine the temporal vacuum that simultaneous perception creates (*Matter and Memory* 102; emphasis in the original). In contrast with the way in which perceptual simultaneity, in *Ultraísmo* and *Simultaneisme*, remains narrowly concentrated on the now, temporal multiplicity remains central to Bergson's phenomenology of perception. His explanation of what he terms the "actively created image" underscores the concept that all images are actually projected from the psyche rather than being merely passive perceptions, and highlights the similitude of these images to "the object on which it comes to mold itself" (102). Put differently, what we believe to be our momentary perception of an object turns out to be the convergence of past and present perceptions. Our perception of the object is really a compendium of various impressions produced over time and then combined at the instant in which we perceive. The act of reflection is therefore temporally complex by definition, in that the perception of an object is always derived, at least in part, from that which has already been perceived and assimilated into the psyche and memory. From Bergson's standpoint, informed by his knowledge of the physiology of perception, the past bears heavily on the production of images in the present:

The recent discovery of centrifugal fibers of perception inclines us to think that this is the usual course of things and that, beside the afferent process which carries the impression to the center, there is another process, of contrary direction, which brings back the image to the periphery. It is true that we are dealing here with images photographed upon the object itself, and with memories following immediately upon the perception of which they are but the echo. But, behind these images, which are identical with the object, there are others, stored in memory, which merely resemble it, and others, finally, which are only more or less distantly akin to it. All these go out to meet the perception, and, feeding on its substance, acquire sufficient vigor and life to abide with it in space (*Matter and Memory* 103)

My perspective has been that the "contrary direction" indicated by Bergson is essential not only to perception, but also to subjectivity, given that the relationship between perception and subjectivity turns precisely on memory. By hindering the engagement of perception with memory, perceptual simultaneity–and perceptual cosmopolitanism–blocks one of the most important conduits to any definition of self–past experience.

Walter Benjamin seizes on what Bergson terms an "afterimage," or impression, making this concept emblematic of Bergson's philosophy, which for him, "represents an attempt to give the details of this afterimage and to fix it as a permanent record" ("Some Motifs" 157). While Benjamin's remarks more accurately characterize his own project than Bergson's, they do show a key aspect of the philosophy articulated in *Matter and Memory*–the part played by time and memory in both perception and subjectivity. In his brief but suggestive analysis of *Matter and Memory* in "On Some Motifs in Baudelaire," Benjamin links perception with memory and that which he calls "the philosophical pattern of experience" (157). He contextualizes this paradigm of experience, at once individual and collective, in the historical changes that created the type of modern urban existence first (in his estimation) portrayed in the poetry of Charles Baudelaire. The "emancipation from experiences" produced by these historical shifts is part and parcel of the related transformation in the way in which perception functions; conversely, the metamorphosed workings of perception become a factor in the development of the circumstances of history (162).

I have suggested that the perceptual simultaneity in Torre, Delaunay, and Delaunay-Terk (as well as the poet Blaise Cendrars) at once reflects and fosters the emancipation from experiences that Benjamin delineates, although it should be noted that Benjamin's consciousness of such an emancipation's social and political consequences is largely absent from *Ultraísmo* and *Simultaneisme*. Nonetheless, as I would insist, the perceptual simultaneity in play in *Ultraísmo* and *Creacionismo* is connected with the erasure of memory, and by extension, the alterations in the structure of experience described by Benjamin. For simultaneity's reduction of perception's usual temporal complexity breaks down the way in which perception itself works, as envisioned by Bergson, because memory is integral to the production of psychic images. There can be no real reflection, in the true sense of the word, without remembrance, and when remembrance finds itself interrupted, the foundations of subjectivity disintegrate as well. While perceptual simultaneity in *Ultraísmo* and *Simultaneisme* may or may not have the same far-reaching consequences as Benjamin imagined for Baudelaire's readers, what remains certain is that the narrowing of perception's temporal window impacts the construction of subjectivity and the communicability of experience.

Gerardo Diego's taking up of the musico-poetic lyric constitutes a return to time and memory, as well as to the potential for intersubjective communication embedded in the musico-poetic lyric's peculiar structures. In the volumes *Imagen* and *Manual de espumas*, the refrain (*estribillo*), chorus, call and response, and syntactic parallelism jog memory and provide a common language by means of their iterative and rhythmic essence. Such constructive devices lay the foundation of what I have identified as Diego's musical architecture, which accords with the prevailing aesthetics and poetics of the first Spanish avant-garde while at the same time creating an aperture for recollection–the psychic bridge to subjectivity and collective identity.

In *Imagen*, the musical and lyric counterbalance the architectonic *Creacionismo* that Diego adapted in his poetry in conversation with Vicente Huidobro and Juan Larrea. The same is true of *Manual de espumas*, but in this volume, musical and lyric devices not only serve as counterpoint to the structured character of *Creacionismo*, but also of pictorial Cubism–the result of Diego's contact with Juan Gris in Paris in 1922. The title of the poem "Nocturno funambulesco" (*Imagen*), for instance, summons to mind the musical genre known as the "nocturne," as well as Rubén Darío's "Nocturno," Chopin's *Nocturnes*, and Diego's tribute to the Romantic composer, *Nocturnos de Chopin* (1918; publ. 1963). In *Imagen* and *Manual de espumas* we "hear" Diego's shift to the musico-poetic lyric, just as the sonority of Darío's "Nocturno" ("Silencio de la noche, doloroso silencio"), generated by assonance, alliteration, and onomatopoeia, voices the way in which sensation and emotion tie together in his poetry: "Oigo el zumbido de mi sangre, / dentro mi cráneo pasa una suave tormenta" (*Obras completas* 5: 3-4/1018). It is important to recall that, in a musical context, one of the primary significations of "nocturne" is a nineteenth-century Romantic piano piece in which the left hand articulates a broken-chord pattern while the right hand plays a slow and dream-like melody–Chopin's *Nocturnes*, to give an example that would have particularly resonated with Diego (Oxford Music Online). The word "nocturno," in "Nocturno funambulesco," describes the musical architecture of *Imagen*–equal parts expressive lyric and architectonic support. Diego, a pianist and admirer of Chopin, probably meant the word as a comparison with how carefully constructed chords simultaneously offset and create soaring melodies in Chopin's *Nocturnes*. The exaggerated rhyme and rhythm of "Nocturno funambulesco" (*Imagen*) reflect Diego's metapoetic intentions, magnifying them as if in a fun-house mirror:

> El muelle es el escenario.
> Desde allí diviso el vario,
> brumario y extraordinario
> panorama.
> (1-4/105)

The rocking motion of the amphibrachs, and the internal and end rhyme recall the *Intencionario* (*ars poetica*) to the first section ("Evasión") of *Imagen*, "Salto del trampolín," which foregrounds time and repeated structures as a way of reviving avant-garde poetry's expressiveness and communicability.

Juxtaposing "Nocturno funambulesco" with "Salto del trampolín," which immediately precedes it in *Imagen*, demonstrates Diego's sly humor with respect to his own attempt at writing poetry that is both lyrical and vanguard:

Sobre el silencio terrestre
se abre el blanco circo ecuestre
en el paisaje rupestre
     de la luna.
Mis visiones de noctámbulo
acrobatizo sonámbulo
en equilibrio funámbulo
     una a una.
     ("Nocturno funambulesco" 9-15/105)

In light of the metapoetic significance of "Nocturno funambules-
co" and "Salto del trampolín," the extended circus trope becomes
metaphor for the balance that Diego strikes between the architec-
tonics of Huidobrian *Creacionismo* and the expressive flexibility of
the musico-poetic lyric. The second word in the title "Nocturno
funambulesco" should be regarded as a quasi-paronomasia, an
amalgamation of "funambulesco"–the extravagant and grotes-
que–and "funámbulo"/"funambulista"–a tight-rope walker. This
last part of the pun strengthens the connection to "Salto del tram-
polín," which is remarkably similar to "Nocturno funambulesco"
in terms of diction:

> *Partir del humorismo*
> *funámbulo y acróstico,*
> *a cabalgar el istmo*
> *del que pende lo agnóstico.*
> ("Salto del trampolín," *Imagen* 5-8/103)

In a way analogous to "Salto del trampolín," Diego emphasizes the
equilibrium that he is determined to maintain between the architec-
tonic–the avant-garde–and the lyric and musical, in order to achieve
his idiosyncratic poetic.

Diego makes another nod towards the nocturne in *Manual de es-
pumas*. He dedicates "Nocturno" to Manuel Machado, the *moder-
nista* poet and brother of Antonio, for whom symbolism was a major
influence; this gesture becomes significant because Diego, like the
Symbolists, thought that poetry must strive towards the condition of
music, in which architectonic and emotional expression merge in a
flexible form. As Diego writes in the *Intencionario* prefacing "Ima-
gen múltiple," the second section of *Imagen*: "Las palabras no dicen
nada, pero lo cantan todo; y se engarzan en una libre melodía de ar-

monías" (145). In other words, the multiple image (the multifaceted image at the heart of Diego's poetic) is, to follow his musical metaphor, simultaneously melodic and harmonic, since its form is as much expressive as it is structural. The alliterative reiteration of "l" and "ll" sounds in "Nocturno" (*Manual de espumas*) at once provide constructive support and an emotive sonority:

> Son sensibles al tacto las estrellas
> No sé escribir a máquina sin ellas
>
> Ellas lo saben todo
> Graduar el mar febril
> y refrescar mi sangre con su nieve infantil
> (5-9/115)

At the same time, Diego incorporates visual metaphor, reminiscent of Huidobro and Juan Gris, into the poem: "La noche ha abierto el piano / y yo . . . digo adiós con la mano" ("Nocturno," *Manual de espumas* 10-11/115). He compares nighttime's expansive darkness to the open lid of a grand piano and the hand of the pianist in the midst of playing (a metonym for Diego as a poet-musician) to a wave good-bye.

The metaphor of the piano player's hand waving good-bye in "Nocturno" resembles another in "Carnaval" (*Imagen*): "Los dedos de los árboles / empiezan a ejercitarse en el doigté" (3-4/162). By means of his diction and, above all, through his use of the iterative musico-poetic devices syntactic parallelism, assonance, and alliteration, Diego underlines the dual capacity of the structural in his poetry:

> En mi bolsillo
> se me ha extraviado la ciudad
>
> Era bello en los mármoles
> ver danzar los desfiles de las calles
>
> Era bello y perfecto
> como un andamio aéreo de arquitecto
> ("Carnaval," *Imagen* 20-25/163)

The architectural scaffolding–the "andamio aéreo de arquitecto"–of *Imagen* and *Manual de espumas* is built by devices which have meta-lyrical and meta-musical roles in structuring the poetic text, lending integrity to the text while retaining their expressivity. Similar to a piano keyboard or a nocturne, each component of the "scaffold" plays a constructive, "harmonic" part while simultaneously articulating an emotive "melody." Indeed, in Diego just as in a nocturne, harmony becomes inseparable from melody–an idea that is mirrored in Diego's seeming oxymoron, "libre melodía de armonías," in the *Intencionario* to the "Imagen múltiple" section of *Imagen*.

I have established a contrast among the temporal disorientation and fragmented subjectivity associated with perceptual simultaneity–embraced by *Ultraísmo* and *Simultaneisme*–and the coherent subjectivity and layered time of Diego's idiosyncratic *Creacionismo*. While Torre's perceptual cosmopolitanism creates the necessary psychic conditions for breaking out of the *castizo* spaces of which Machado's Castilian landscapes are characteristic, it leaves the problem of rupturing with memory unresolved. The framing devices that Machado employs in *Campos de Castilla* are designed to situate the subject in a landscape coded as national and regional, and encourage identification with this landscape as an intimate part of individual and collective selfhood, but despite Machado's ethical motivation, these common spaces of remembrance prove uncomfortably confining to the experimentally and internationally oriented first avant-garde. Yet to rupture these spaces is to sever ties to subjectivity and common identity, which comes at the enormous cost of the atrophy of experience. Torre's avant-garde textual landscapes, contoured by perceptual cosmopolitanism, can be just as restrictive as *castizo* landscapes, since the psychic movements required for their navigation shut off the flow between past and present that Bergson finds natural to perception. By blocking access to the past through memory–the memory inherently involved in perception–the subject's self-conception and way of identifying with others becomes irrevocably fractured. What Diego accomplishes with his musical architecture is to revive memory by restoring the bridge to anterior experience, which must be understood as the basis of subjectivity and identity. The musico-lyric structures composing the musical architecture of *Imagen* and *Manual de espumas*, by means of their iterative and expressive nature, act as these essential temporal connections. In bringing time back to the text's construction, Diego generates a viable model for an avant-garde poetry in which recollection has a place, and where, through memory, there may emerge a coherent subjectivity, as well as links between this subjectivity and the collective. He thus provides a road map for negotiating both the *castizo* and the cosmopolitan in conjunction with the avant-garde–a map which gives us an advance glimpse of Spain's second vanguard wave–the Generations of 1925 and 1927.

WORKS CITED

Abel, Richard. *French Film Theory and Criticism, 1907-1939: A History/Anthology.* Vol. 1. Princeton: Princeton UP, 1988. 2 vols.

Albornoz, Aurora de. *La presencia de Miguel de Unamuno en Antonio Machado.* Madrid: Gredos, 1968.

Alín, José María. *El cancionero español de tipo tradicional.* Madrid: Taurus, 1968.

Alonso, Dámaso. *Poetas españoles contemporáneos.* Madrid: Gredos, 1969.

Alpers, Paul. "The Eclogue Tradition and the Nature of Pastoral." *College English* 34.3 (Dec. 1972): 352-71.

Anderson, Andrew A. *El veintisiete en tela de juicio: examen de la historiografía generacional y replanteamiento de la vanguardia histórica española.* Madrid: Gredos, 2005.

Apollinaire, Guillaume. *Méditations esthétiques: les peintres cubistes.* Intro. and notes by L.-C. Breunig and J.-Cl. Chevalier. Paris: Hermann, 1965.

———. "The New Spirit and the Poets." *Selected Writings of Guillaume Apollinaire.* Trans. and intro. Roger Shattuck. New York: New Directions, 1971. 227-37.

———. *Œuvres poétiques.* Paris: Gallimard, 1965.

———. "Réalité, peinture pure." 1912. *Chroniques d'art 1902-1918.* Ed., preface, and notes by L.-C. Breunig. Paris: Gallimard, 1960. 344-49.

———. "Les reformations du costume." *Mercure de France* (Jan. 1, 1914): 219-20.

Arenas, Braulio. Prologue. *Obras completas de Vicente Huidobro.* By Vicente Huidobro. Santiago de Chile: Zig-Zag, 1963. 15-42.

———. "Vicente Huidobro y el creacionismo." 1964. Costa 177-208.

Arias Angles, Enrique. "La pintura de paisaje en España en el siglo XIX." *Tres grandes maestros del paisaje decimonónico español: Jenaro Pérez Villaamil. Carlos de Haes. Aureliano de Beruete.* Madrid: Ayuntamiento de Madrid-Concejalía de Cultura, Centro Cultural del Conde Duque, 1990. 111-72.

Arizmendi, Milagros. Introduction. *Manual de espumas; Versos humanos.* By Gerardo Diego. Ed. Milagros Arizmendi. Madrid: Cátedra, 1986. 11-65.

Aullón de Haro, Pedro. *La modernidad poética, la vanguardia y el creacionismo.* Ed. and prol. Javier Pérez Bazo. Malaga: Universidad de Málaga, 2000.

Azorín: see entries for Martínez Ruiz, José.

Bajarlía, Juan-Jacobo. "La leyenda negra contra Huidobro." 1964. Costa 167-76.

Baroja, Pío. *Camino de perfección.* 1902. Madrid: Caro Raggio, 1974.

Barón, Javier. "El paisaje en España en el siglo XIX." *Carlos de Haes (1826-1898).* August-September 2002. Santander: Fundación Marcelino Botín, 2002. 15-65.

Barrera López, José María. *El Ultraísmo de Sevilla.* Seville: Alfar, 1987. 2 vols.

Barrera Morate, José Luis. "Biografía de José Macpherson y Hemas (1839-1902)." *Boletín de la Institución Libre de Enseñanza* 45 (July 2002). 17 Dec. 2010 <http://www.fundacionginer.org/boletin/bol_nn_barrera.htm>.

Barthes, Roland. "The Grain of the Voice." 1972. *Image. Music. Text.* Trans. Stephen Heath. New York: Hill and Wang, 1978. 179-89.

Beauduin, Nicolas. Letters to Guillermo de Torre. 1921-1925. Ms. 22819/45. Cervantes Collection. Biblioteca Nacional de España, Madrid, Spain.

Beceiro, Carlos. "Antonio Machado y su visión paradójica de Castilla." *Celtiberia* 15 (1958): 127-42.

Bécquer, Gustavo Adolfo. "Volverán las oscuras golondrinas." *Rimas.* Ed. Rafael Montesinos. 5th ed. Madrid: Cátedra, 1999. 145-46.

Benjamin, Walter. "The Image of Proust." *Illuminations.* Ed. and intro. Hannah Arendt. New York: Schocken Books, 1968. 201-15.

———. "On Some Motifs in Baudelaire." *Illuminations* 155-200.

———. "The Work of Art in the Age of Mechanical Reproduction." *Illuminations* 217-51.

Benoit, Camille. *The Typical Motives of the Master-Singers of Nuremberg, a Musical Comedy.* New York: G. Schirmer, 1889.

Berckelaers, Fernand. Letter to Guillermo de Torre. 1919. Ms. 22830/6. Cervantes Collection. Biblioteca Nacional de España, Madrid, Spain.

Bergmann, Emilie L. *Art Inscribed: Essays on Ekphrasis in Spanish Golden Age Poetry.* Cambridge, MA: Harvard UP, 1997.

Bergson, Henri. *Duration and Simultaneity: Bergson and the Einsteinian Universe.* Ed. and intro. Robin Durie. Trans. Leon Jacobson. Manchester, Eng.: Clinamen P, 1999.

———. *Matter and Memory.* Trans. N. M. Paul and W. S. Palmer. New York: Zone, 2002.

———. *Time and Free Will: An Essay on the Immediate Data of Consciousness.* Trans. F. L. Pogson. Mineola, NY: Dover, 2001.

Berman, Laurence D. "*Prelude to the Afternoon of a Faun* and *Jeux*: Debussy's Summer Rites." *19th-Century Music* 3.3 (Mar. 1980): 225-38.

Bernal, José Luis. *La biografía ultraísta de Gerardo Diego.* Caceres: Universidad de Extremadura, 1987.

———. "Gerardo Diego: heterocronismo y visión del mundo." *Ínsula: Revista de Letras y Ciencias Humanas* 597-98 (1996): 6-8.

———. Introduction. *Imagen.* By Gerardo Diego. Ed. José Luis Bernal. Malaga: Centro Cultural de la Generación del 27, 1989. 7-92.

———. *Manual de espumas: la plenitud creacionista de Gerardo Diego.* Valencia: Pre-Textos; Santander: Fundación Gerardo Diego, 2007.

———. *El Ultraísmo. ¿Historia de un fracaso?* Caceres: Universidad de Extremadura, 1988.

———, ed. *Gerardo Diego y la vanguardia hispánica.* Caceres: Universidad de Extremadura, 1987.

Blanco Aguinaga, Carlos. *Juventud del 98.* Madrid: Siglo XXI de España Editores, 1970.

Bochner, Jay. *Blaise Cendrars: Discovery and Re-Creation.* Toronto: U of Toronto P, 1978.

———. Introduction. *Complete Poems.* By Blaise Cendrars. Trans. Ron Padgett. Berkeley: U of California P, 1992.

Bohn, Willard. *The Aesthetics of Visual Poetry 1914-1928.* London and New York: Cambridge UP, 1986.

Boletín de la Institución Libre de Enseñanza. Año I-Año XI (Years 1-11) (1877-1887).

Bonet, Juan Manuel. *Diccionario de las vanguardias en España (1907-1936).* 1995. Madrid: Alianza, 1999.

Botstein, Leon. "Modernism." Grove Music Online. Oxford UP. 12 Mar. 2013 <http://www.oxfordmusiconline.com:80/subscriber/article/grove/music/40625>.

Braga, Dominique. Letter to Guillermo de Torre. September 9, 1921. Ms. 22820/33. Cervantes Collection. Biblioteca Nacional de España, Madrid, Spain.

Branciard, Laetitia. "Guillermo de Torre et l'œuvre de Robert Delaunay." *Peinture et écriture.* Paris: Éditions de la Différence, 1996. 155-61.

Bratton, Jean. "Antonio Machado y el lenguaje de la intuición." *Ínsula* 158.1 (Jan. 1960): 8.

Brown, H. M. *Leitmotiv and Drama: Wagner, Brecht, and the Limits of 'Epic' Theatre.* Oxford and New York: Clarendon P and Oxford UP, 1991.

Buckberrough, Sherry A. *Robert Delaunay: The Discovery of Simultaneity.* 1978. Studies in the Fine Arts. The Avant-Garde 21. Ann Arbor, MI: UMI Research P, 1982.

Busto Ogden, Estrella. *El creacionismo de Vicente Huidobro en sus relaciones con la estética cubista.* Madrid: Playor, 1983.

Calderón, Salvador. "La meseta central de España: resumen de algunas investigaciones orográficas." *Boletín de la Institución Libre de Enseñanza* 1.200 (June 15, 1885): 169-70.

Calvo Serraller, Francisco. "La teoría del paisaje en la pintura española del siglo XIX: de Villaamil a Beruete." *Tres grandes maestros del paisaje decimonónico español: Jenaro Pérez Villaamil. Carlos de Haes. Aureliano de Beruete.* Madrid: Ayuntamiento de Madrid-Concejalía de Cultura, Centro Cultural del Conde Duque, 1990. 49-62.

Campbell, Timothy C. *Wireless Writing in the Age of Marconi.* Electronic Mediations Ser. 16. Minneapolis and London: U of Minnesota P, 2006.

Cansinos-Assens, Rafael. *El movimiento V.P.* Madrid: Mundo Latino, 1921.

———. *El movimiento V.P.* Ed. and prol. Juan Manuel Bonet. Pamplona: Peralta, 1978.

———. *La nueva literatura.* Vol. 1. Madrid: Editorial Paez, 1925. 2 vols.

———. "Vicente Huidobro y el Creacionismo." *Cosmópolis* 1.1 (Jan. 1919): 68-73.

Cassou, Jean. Letter to Guillermo de Torre. August 21, 1919. Ms. 22821/19. Cervantes Collection. Biblioteca Nacional de España, Madrid, Spain.

Castro Cardús, Santiago. Aureliano de Beruete: Consideraciones sobre el pintor y su pintura: Conferencia pronunciada por Don Santiago Castro Cardús el 10 de marzo de 1970. Madrid (Fernán González, 20): S. Castro, 1970.

Cendrars, Blaise. *Complete Poems.* Trans. Ron Padgett. Intro. Jay Bochner. Berkeley: U of California P, 1992.

———. "Delaunay: le contraste simultané." *La Rose Rouge* 1-15 (July 24, 1919): 204.

———. *La Prose du Transsibérien et de la petite Jeanne de France. Œuvres complètes.* 1947. Vol. 1. Paris: Le Club Français du Livre, 1980. 16-32.

———. "Tour." *Complete Poems.* Trans. Ron Padgett. Intro. Jay Bochner. Berkeley: U of California P, 1992. 260-61.

Cervantes Saavedra, Miguel de. *Rinconete y Cortadillo y La ilustre fregona.* Ed., study, and notes by Angel González Palencia. 14th ed. Zaragoza: Editorial Ebro, 1982.

Chevreul, M. E. *The Principles of Harmony and Contrast of Colors and their Applications to the Arts.* 1854. Intro. and notes by Faber Birren. New York: Reinhold, 1967.

Cicora, Mary A. *Modern Myths and Wagnerian Deconstructions: Hermeneutic Approaches to Wagner's Music-Dramas.* Westport, CT: Greenwood P, 2000.

Cordero de Ciria, Enrique. "Cinco cartas inéditas de Gerardo Diego." *Cuadernos Hispanoamericanos* 439 (1987): 109-14.

Cordero de Ciria, Enrique, and Juan Manuel Díaz de Guereñu, eds. *Juan Larrea: cartas a Gerardo Diego, 1916-1980.* San Sebastian: Cuadernos Universitarios, 1986.

Costa, René de, ed. *Vicente Huidobro y el creacionismo.* Madrid: Taurus, 1975.

Crary, Jonathan. *Techniques of the Observer: On Vision and Modernity in the Nineteenth Century.* Cambridge, MA, and London, Eng.: MIT P, 1990.

Crispin, John. *La estética de las generaciones de 1925.* Valencia: Pre-Textos; Nashville, TN: Vanderbilt UP, 2002.

Culler, Jonathan D. "Apostrophe." *On Deconstruction: Theory and Criticism after Structuralism.* By Jonathan Culler. Ithaca: Cornell UP, 1982. 135-54.

Cummins, J. G. *The Spanish Traditional Lyric.* Oxford and New York: Pergamon P, 1977.

Dahlhaus, Carl. *Richard Wagner's Music Dramas.* Trans. Mary Whittall. Cambridge and New York: Cambridge UP, 1979.

Darío, Rubén. *Cantos de vida y esperanza. Obras completas.* By Rubén Darío. Vol. 5. Madrid: Afrodisio Aguado, 1953. 861-88. 5 vols.

———. "Nocturno" ("Los que auscultasteis el corazón de la noche"). *Obras completas.* By Rubén Darío. Vol. 5. Madrid: Afrodisio Aguado, 1953. 931-32. 5 vols.

———. "Nocturno" ("Silencio de la noche, doloroso silencio"). *Obras completas.* By Rubén Darío. Vol. 5. Madrid: Afrodisio Aguado, 1953. 1018. 5 vols.

Delaunay, Robert. *Du cubisme à l'art abstrait.* Ed. Pierre Francastel. Guy Habasque, Catalogue of the *œuvre* of Robert Delaunay. Paris: École Pratique des Hautes-Études/SEVPEN, 1957.

———. Letter to Guillermo de Torre. *Lettres.* 1918-1919. Microfilm 7151. Fond Delaunay, Bibliothèque Nationale de France, Paris, France.

———. Letter to Guillermo de Torre. October 18, 1923. Ms. 22822/5. Cervantes Collection. Biblioteca Nacional de España, Madrid, Spain.

———. *Lettres.* Microfilm 7151. Fond Delaunay, Bibliothèque Nationale de France, Paris, France.

———. "La lumière." *Du cubisme à l'art abstrait.* Ed. Pierre Francastel. Guy Habasque, Catalogue of the *œuvre* of Robert Delaunay. Paris: École Pratique des Hautes-Études/SEVPEN, 1957. 146-50.

———. *Projets de couverts de livres et revues, notamment* Destruction construction *et* Du nord a sud. *Ecrits I: 1911-1924.* Microfilm 7149. Fond Delaunay, Bibliothèque Nationale de France, Paris, France.

Delaunay, Sonia. "4 minutes de lettres. 1919-1920." *Lettres.* Microfilm 7160. Fond Delaunay, Bibliothèque Nationale de France, Paris, France.

Delaunay, Sonia, with Jacques Demase and Patrick Reynaud. *Nous irons jusqu'au soleil.* Ed. André Coutin. Paris: Éditions Robert Laffont, 1978.

Deleuze, Gilles. *Bergsonism.* 1991. Trans. Hugh Tomlinson and Barbara Habberjam. New York: Zone, 2002.

Demase, Jacques. *Sonia Delaunay.* Ed. Edouard Mustelier. Paris: Galerie de Varenne, 1971.

Dermée, Paul. Letters to Guillermo de Torre. Ms. 22822/8. Cervantes Collection. Biblioteca Nacional de España, Madrid, Spain.

Derrida, Jacques. *The Truth in Painting.* 1978. Trans. Geoff Bennington and Ian McLeod. Chicago and London: U of Chicago P, 1987.

Dessy, Mario. Letter to Guillermo de Torre. August 20, 1920. Cervantes Collection. Biblioteca Nacional de España, Madrid, Spain.

Dessy, Mario. Letter to Guillermo de Torre. September 23, 1920. Cervantes Collection. Biblioteca Nacional de España, Madrid, Spain.

Díaz de Guereñu, Juan Manuel. *Poetas creacionistas españoles.* Malaga: Centro Cultural de la Generación del 27, 1999.

Díaz-Plaja, Guillermo. "El modernismo, cuestión disputada." *Hispania* 48.3 (Sept. 1965): 407-12.

——. *Modernismo frente a noventa y ocho.* 1951. Madrid: Espasa-Calpe, 1966.

Diego, Gerardo. "Actualidad poética de Fray Luis de León." *Crítica y poesía.* By Gerardo Diego. Madrid: Júcar, 1984. 9-45.

——. *Antología poética (1918-1969).* Madrid: Dirección General de Enseñanza Media y Profesional, 1969.

——. *Antología. Primer cuaderno (1918-1940).* Salamanca: Ediciones Anaya, 1958.

——. "Bilingüismo poético." *Memoria de un poeta. Obras completas.* Vol. 4. Ed. and intro. José Luis Bernal. Madrid: Alfaguara, 2000. 596-98.

——. *Biografía incompleta.* La Encina y el Mar 11. Madrid: Ediciones de Cultura Hispánica, 1953.

——. *Imagen.* Ed. José Luis Bernal. Malaga: Centro Cultural de la Generación del 27, 1989.

——. "To Juan Larrea." June 14, 1919. Díaz de Guereñu 133.

——. Letter to José Ortega y Gasset. June 5, 1921. ID 1102. Sig. C-10/2. Archivo José Ortega y Gasset. Fundación Ortega y Gasset, Madrid, Spain.

——. Letter to José Ortega y Gasset. June 24, 1921. ID 1103. Sig. C-10/3. Archivo José Ortega y Gasset. Fundación José Ortega y Gasset, Madrid, Spain.

——. *Manual de espumas; Versos humanos.* Ed. Milagros Arizmendi. Madrid: Cátedra, 1986.

——. "To Manuel de Falla." February 12, 1921. *Correspondencia Gerardo Diego-Manuel de Falla.* Notes by Federico Sopeña Ibáñez. Santander: Fundación Marcelino Botín, 1988. 12.

——. "To Manuel de Falla." January 20, 1926. *Correspondencia Gerardo Diego-Manuel de Falla.* Notes by Federico Sopeña Ibáñez. Santander: Fundación Marcelino Botín, 1988. 65.

——. *Nocturnos de Chopin (Paráfrasis románticas); Alondra de verdad; La luna en el desierto y otros poemas.* Madrid: Editorial Bullón, 1963.

——. *Poemas mayores (antología).* Madrid: Alianza, 1980.

——. *Poemas menores (antología).* Madrid: Alianza, 1980.

——. *Poesía de creación.* Barcelona: Seix Barral, 1974.

——. "Posibilidades creacionistas." *Cervantes* (Oct. 1919): 23-28.

——. *Primera antología de sus versos.* Madrid: Espasa-Calpe, 1941.

——. "Retórica y poética." 1924. *Prosa literaria.* Vol. 6 of *Obras completas.* 174-80.

——. *Segunda antología de sus versos.* Madrid: Espasa-Calpe, 1967.

——. *Soria. Galería de estampas y efusiones.* Valladolid: Librería Viuda de Montero, 1923.

——. *Versos escogidos.* Madrid: Gredos, 1970.

Díez de la Fuente, J. *Las vanguardias. Renovación de los lenguajes poéticos.* Ed. T. Albaladejo, F. J. Blasco, and R. de la Fuente. Madrid: Júcar, 1992.

Díez de Revenga, Francisco Javier. *Gerardo Diego en sus raíces estéticas.* Valladolid: Secretariado de Publicaciones e Intercambio Editorial, Universidad de Valladolid, 2006.

Dorival, Bernard. Preface. *Robert Delaunay: Sonia Delaunay.* Ottawa, National Gallery of Canada, 1965.

Driever, Steven L. "The Signification of the Sorian Landscapes in Antonio Macha-
do's *Campos de Castilla.*" *Isle: Interdisciplinary Studies in Literature and Envi-
ronment* 4.1 (1997): 43-70.

Drucker, Johanna. *The Visible Word: Experimental Typography and Modern Art,
1909-1923*: Chicago and London: U of Chicago P, 1994.

———. "Visual Performance of the Poetic Text." *Close Listening: Poetry and the
Performed Word.* Ed. Charles Bernstein. New York and Oxford: Oxford UP,
1998. 131-61.

Dunn, Leslie. "Poetry and Song." *The New History of Literature: English Poetry
and Prose.* 1970. Ed. Christopher Ricks. New York: Peter Bedrick, 1987. 107-
19.

Dunn, Leslie C., and Nancy A. Jones. Introduction. *Embodied Voices: Representing
Female Vocality in Western Culture.* Ed. Dunn and Jones. Cambridge: Cambrid-
ge UP, 1994. 1-13.

Durán, Manuel, ed. *Ortega y Gasset: sus mejores páginas.* Englewood Cliffs, NJ:
Prentice-Hall, 1966.

Durey, Jill Felicity. "The State of Play and Interplay in Intertextuality." *Style* 25.4
(1991): 616-35.

Epstein, Jean. *Esprit de cinéma.* Geneva and Paris: Jeheber, 1955.

———. Letter to Guillermo de Torre. September 20, 1921. Ms. 22822/38. Cervan-
tes Collection. Biblioteca Nacional de España, Madrid, Spain.

———. Letter to Guillermo de Torre. October 10, 1921. Ms. 22822/38. Cervantes
Collection. Biblioteca Nacional de España, Madrid, Spain.

———. "Magnification." Abel 235-41.

———. "On Certain Characteristics of *Photogénie.*" Abel 314-18.

———. *La poésie d'aujourd'hui, un nouvel état d'intelligence. Lettre de Blaise Cen-
drars.* Paris: Éditions de la Sirène, 1921. 22 July 2008 <http:// books. google.
com/>.

———. "The Senses I (b)." 1921. Abel 241-46.

"Excursión a la Sierra del Guadarrama." *Boletín de la Institución Libre de Enseñan-
za* 9.225 (June 30, 1886): 190-92.

"Excursiones proyectadas para el verano de 1881." *Boletín de la Institución Libre de
Enseñanza* 5.104 (Jun. 16, 1881): 86.

Falcó, José Luis. *El Ultraísmo: teoría, y practica poética.* Valencia: Ariadna, 1993.

Ferreira, Paulo. *Correspondance de quatre artistes portugais: Almada-Negreiros, José
Pacheco, Souza-Cardoso, Eduardo Vianna avec Robert et Sonia Delaunay.* Paris:
Presses Universitaires de France; Fondation Calouste Gulbenkian; Publications
du Centre Culturel Portugais, 1981.

"Foliated." *The Oxford English Dictionary.* 11 May 2013 <http://www.oed.com.ez-
proxy.fiu.edu/view/Entry/72515?redirectedFrom=foliated#eid>.

Galland-Szymkowiak, Mildred. "Le 'symbolisme sympathique' dans l'esthétique de
Victor Basch." *Revue de métaphysique et de morale* 2.34 (2002): 61-75.
<http://www.cairn.info/article.php>.

Gallego, Antonio. Introduction. *Poemas musicales (antología).* By Gerardo Diego.
Ed. Antonio Gallego. Madrid: Cátedra, 2012. 15-156.

Gallego Roca, Miguel. *Poesía importada. Traducción poética y renovación literaria en
España (1909-1936).* Almería, Sp.: Universidad de Almería, 1996.

García, Carlos, ed. *Correspondencia Juan Ramón Jiménez/Guillermo de Torre, 1920-
1956.* Madrid: Iberoamericana; Frankfurt am Main: Vervuert, 2006.

———. *Correspondencia Rafael Cansinos Assens/Guillermo de Torre: 1916-1955.*
Madrid: Iberoamericana; Frankfurt am Main: Vervuert, 2004.

———. *Federico García Lorca/Guillermo de Torre: correspondencia y amistad.* Ma-
drid: Iberoamericana; Frankfurt am Main: Vervuert, 2009.

García, Carlos, ed. *Las letras y la amistad: correspondencia (1920-1958), Alfonso Reyes-Guillermo de Torre*. Valencia: Pre-Textos, 2005.

García, Carlos, and Martín Greco, eds. *Escribidores y náufragos: correspondencia Ramón Gómez de la Serna/Guillermo de Torre, 1916-1963*. Madrid: Iberoamericana; Frankfurt am Main: Vervuert, 2007.

García-Suárez, José Antonio. *La Institución Libre de Enseñanza: perspectiva histórica y comentario*. Esplugues de Llobregat, Sp.: Círculo Editor Universo, 1978.

Gibson, Ian. *Ligero de equipaje: la vida de Antonio Machado*. Madrid: Aguilar, 2006.

Gicovate, Bernardo. "El concepto de la poesía en la poesía de Juan Ramón Jiménez." *Comparative Literature* 8.3 (Summer 1956): 205-13.

Gifford, Paul, ed. *Reading Paul Valéry*. Cambridge, Eng.: Cambridge UP, 1998.

Giner de los Ríos, Francisco. "La crítica espontánea de los niños en bellas artes." *Boletín de la Institución Libre de Enseñanza* 9.192 (Feb. 15, 1885): 41-42.

———. "Excursión a la Sierra del Guadarrama el 19 de junio de 1886." *Boletín de la Institución Libre de Enseñanza* 10.225 (June 30, 1886): 190-92.

———. "Excursiones geológicas." *Boletín de la Institución Libre de Enseñanza* 9.198 (May 15, 1885): 131-34.

———. "El paisaje." *La Lectura* 1 (1915): 361-70.

Glendinning, Nigel. "The Philosophy of Henri Bergson in the Poetry of Antonio Machado." *Revue de Littérature Comparée* 36 (Jan.-May 1962): 50-70.

Gómez de la Serna, Ramón. *Greguerías*. Ed., intro., and notes by Antonio A. Gómez Yerba. Madrid: Castalia, 1994.

———. *Pombo*; *La sagrada cripta de Pombo*. Prol. Andrés Trapiello. Madrid: Visor, 1999. 2 vols.

González Egido, Luciano. Introduction. *En torno al casticismo*. By Miguel de Unamuno. 1902. Madrid: Espasa-Calpe, 1943. 12th ed. 1998. 9-27.

Graham, John T. *The Social Thought of Ortega y Gasset: A Systematic Synthesis in Postmodernism and Interdisciplinarity*. Columbia: U of Missouri P, 2001. <http://books.google.com/>.

Granjel, Luis S. *La generación literaria del noventa y ocho*. Salamanca: Ediciones Anaya, 1966.

Gutiérrez Márquez, Ana. "Carlos de Haes (1826-1898). Biografía y trayectoria artística." *Carlos de Haes (1826-1898)*. 69-127.

Gutting, Gary. *French Philosophy in the Twentieth Century*. Cambridge, Eng.: Cambridge UP, 2001.

Haes, Carlos de. "Discurso de Don Carlos de Haes, leído en Junta pública de 26 de febrero de 1860. De la pintura de paisaje antigua y moderna." *Carlos de Haes (1826-1898)*. 339-46.

Hagstrum, Jean H. *The Sister Arts: The Tradition of Literary Pictorialism and English Poetry from Dreyden to Gray*. 1958. Chicago and London: U of Chicago P, 1968.

Heffernan, James A. W. *Museum of Words: The Poetics of Ekphrasis from Homer to Ashbery*. Chicago and London: U of Chicago P, 1993.

———. *Wordsworth's Theory of Poetry: The Transforming Imagination*. Ithaca and London: Cornell UP, 1969.

"Hesperidio." *Diccionario de la Lengua Española*. Real Academia Española. 22nd ed. 11 May 2013 <http://lema.rae.es/drae/?val=hesperidio>.

Hess, Carol A. *Manuel de Falla and Modernism in Spain, 1898-1936*. Chicago: U of Chicago P, 2001.

———. *Sacred Passions: The Life and Music of Manuel de Falla*. Oxford and New York: Oxford UP, 2005.

Hollander, John. "Breaking into Song: Some Notes on Refrain." Hošek, Parker, and Arac 73-89.

Hoog, Michel. "Quelques précurseurs de l'art d'aujourd'hui." *La Revue du Louvre et des Musées de France* 16.3 (1966): 165-72.

———. *Robert Delaunay.* Trans. Alice Sachs. New York: Crown, 1976.

Hošek, Chaviva, Patricia Parker, and Jonathan Arac, eds. *Lyric Poetry: Beyond New Criticism.* Ithaca: Cornell UP, 1985.

Huidobro, Vicente. *Antología poética.* Ed., intro., and notes by Hugo Montes. Madrid: Castalia, 1970.

———. "La creación pura." *Obras completas de Vicente Huidobro.* Prol. Braulio Arenas. Santiago de Chile: Zig-Zag, 1964. 656-61.

———. "La création pure." *L'Esprit Nouveau* (Apr. 1921): 769-76.

———. Letter to Gerardo Diego. April 28, 1920. Archivo Gerardo Diego. Private Collection of Elena Diego.

———. Letter to Gerardo Diego. December 2, 1922. Archivo Gerardo Diego. Private Collection of Elena Diego.

———. Letter to Gerardo Diego. July 3, 1922. Archivo Gerardo Diego. Private Collection of Elena Diego.

———. Letter to Gerardo Diego. August 15, 1922. Archivo Gerardo Diego. Private Collection of Elena Diego.

———. Letter to Gerardo Diego. August 16, 1922. Archivo Gerardo Diego. Private Collection of Elena Diego.

———. Letter to Guillermo de Torre. February 24, 1920. Ms. 22825/25. Cervantes Collection. Biblioteca Nacional de España, Madrid, Spain.

———. Letter to Guillermo de Torre. August 17, 1920. Ms. 22825/25. Cervantes Collection. Biblioteca Nacional de España, Madrid, Spain.

———. "Non serviam." *Obras completas de Vicente Huidobro.* Santiago de Chile: Zig-Zag, 1963. 653-54.

———. *Obras completas de Vicente Huidobro.* Santiago de Chile: Zig-Zag, 1963.

"Hyaline." Def. A. *The Oxford English Dictionary.* 11 May 2013 <http:// www. oed. com.ezproxy.fiu.edu/view/Entry/89790?redirectedFrom=hyaline#eid>.

Iglesia, José Luis de la, Ana Lucas, Juan Manuel Martínez, Francisco José Martínez, Luis Martínez de Velasco. *Antonio Machado y la filosofía.* Madrid: Orígenes, 1989.

"Ignivomous." *The Oxford English Dictionary.* 9 May 2013 <http:// www. oed. com.ezproxy.fiu.edu/view/Entry/91218?redirectedFrom=Ignivomous#eid>.

Jakobson, Roman. "Two Aspects of Language and Two Types of Aphasic Disturbances." *On Language.* By Roman Jakobson. Ed. Linda R. Waugh and Monique Monville-Burston. Cambridge, MA and London, Eng.: Harvard UP, 1990. 115-33.

Jiménez, Juan Ramón. *El modernismo: notas de un curso (1953).* Ed., prol., and notes by Ricardo Gullón y Eugenio Fernández Méndez. Mexico: Aguilar, 1962.

Johnson, Barbara. "The Dream of Stone." *A New History of French Literature.* Ed. Denis Hollier. Cambridge and London: Harvard UP, 1994. 743-48.

Johnson, R. Stanley. *Cubism and La Section D'Or: Reflections on the Development of the Cubist Epoch 1907-1922.* Chicago and Düsseldorf: Klees/Gustorf, 1991.

Johnson, W. R. *The Idea of Lyric: Lyric Modes in Ancient and Modern Poetry.* Berkeley, Los Angeles, and New York: U of California P, 1982.

Jongh-Rossel, Elena M. de. *El krausismo y la generación de 1898. Hispanófila 38.* Valencia, Sp., and Chapel Hill, NC: Albatros Ediciones, 1985.

Jurkevich, Gayana. *In Pursuit of the Natural Sign: Azorín and the Poetics of Ekphrasis.* Lewisburg, PA: Bucknell UP; London: Associated UP, 1999.

Kern, Stephen. *The Culture of Time and Space 1880-1918.* Cambridge, MA: Harvard UP, 1983.

Kolocotroni, Vassiliki, Jane Goldman, and Olga Taxidou, eds. *Modernism: An Anthology of Sources and Documents*. Chicago: Chicago UP, 1998.

Kracauer, Siegfried. "Cult of Distraction: On Berlin's Picture Palaces." *The Mass Ornament: Weimar Essays*. 1963. Trans., ed., and intro. Thomas Y. Levin. Cambridge, MA, and London, Eng.: Harvard UP, 1995. 323-28.

Kramer, Hilton. Introduction. *Abstraction and Empathy*. By Wilhlem Worringer. 1953. Trans. Michael Bullock. Chicago: Elephant Paperback, 1997. vii-xiv.

Krauss, Rosalind E. *The Picasso Papers*. New York: Farrar, Straus and Giroux, 1998.

———, ed. *October: The Second Decade, 1986-1996*. Cambridge, MA: MIT P, 1997.

Krieger, Murray. *Ekphrasis: The Illusion of the Natural Sign*. Baltimore and London: Johns Hopkins UP, 1992.

Krough, Kevin. *The Landscape Poetry of Antonio Machado. A Dialogical Study of Campos de Castilla*. Lewiston, NY: Edwin Mellen P, 2001.

Lafuente Ferrari, Enrique. "Antonio Machado y su mundo visual." *Antonio Machado y Soria: homenaje en el primer centenario de su nacimiento*. Madrid: Patronato José María Quadrado, Consejo Superior de Investigaciones Científicas, Centro de Estudios Sorianos, 1976. 71-112.

Larrea, Juan. "Cosmopolitano." *Cervantes* (Nov. 1919): 22-28.

———. "To Gerardo Diego." June 22, 1919. Cordero de Ciria and Díaz de Guereñu 92-95.

———. "Improntu al grillo." *Grecia* 2.25 (Aug. 20, 1919): 5.

Lázaro, Blas. "El arte de las excursiones instructivas." *Boletín de la Institución Libre de Enseñanza* 5.114 (Nov. 15, 1881): 163-65.

———. "Historia de la flora ibérica (I)." *Boletín de la Institución Libre de Enseñanza* 10.217 (Feb. 28, 1886): 51-54.

———. "Historia de la flora ibérica (I)." *Boletín de la Institución Libre de Enseñanza* 10.218 (Mar. 15, 1886): 76-79.

———. "Historia de la flora ibérica (I)." *Boletín de la Institución Libre de Enseñanza* 10.219 (Mar. 31, 1886): 89-93.

León, Luis de. [Fray Luis de León]. *Poesía*. Ed., study, and notes by Antonio Ramajo Caño. Madrid: Real Academia Española, 2012. Biblioteca Clásica de la Real Academia Española 38.

Llera, Esteban de. "J. Ortega Gasset e le avanguardie." *Trent'anni di avanguardia spagnola: da Ramón Gómez de la Serna a Juan-Eduardo Cirlot*. Ed. Gabriele Morelli. Milan: Jaca, 1987. 55-75.

Llorens, Tomàs. Personal interview. Nov. 2002.

Llorens, Tomàs, Brigitte Léal, and Pascal Rousseau. *Robert y Sonia Delaunay 1905-1941*. Museo Thyssen-Bornemisza, October 8, 2002-January 12, 2003. Madrid: Museo Thyssen-Bornemisza, 2002.

Machado, Antonio. "Autobiografía escrita en 1913 para una proyectada antología de Azorín." *Campos de Castilla*. By Antonio Machado. 1912, 1917. Ed. Geoffrey Ribbans. 6th ed. Madrid: Cátedra, 1995. 283-85.

———. *Campos de Castilla*. 1912, 1917. Ed. Geoffrey Ribbans. 6th ed. Madrid: Cátedra, 1995.

———. "Canciones a Guiomar." *Poesías completas*. By Antonio Machado. 13th ed. Madrid: Espasa-Calpe, 1971. 276-78.

———. "Don Francisco Giner de los Ríos." *Campos de Castilla*. By Antonio Machado. 1912, 1917. Ed. Geoffrey Ribbans. 6th ed. Madrid: Cátedra, 1995. 295-97.

———. "Fragmentos de una carta de Antonio Machado a Miguel de Unamuno, publicados por éste en 1904." *Cartas de Antonio Machado a Miguel de Unamuno*. Intro., comp., and biographical sketch by José Ramón Arana. Mexico: Monegros, 1957. 9-10.

Machado, Antonio. *Nuevas canciones. 1917-1930. Poesías completas.* By Antonio Machado. 13th ed. Madrid: Espasa-Calpe, 1971. 180-228.

———. *Poesías completas.* By Antonio Machado. 13th ed. Madrid: Espasa-Calpe, 1971.

———. "Prólogo de *Páginas escogidas* (1917): Campos de Castilla." *Campos de Castilla.* By Antonio Machado. 1912, 1917. Ed. Geoffrey Ribbans. 6th ed. Madrid: Cátedra, 1995. 274-75.

———. "Sobre el libro *Colección* del poeta andaluz José Moreno Villa." *Poesía y prosa.* By Antonio Machado. Ed. Oreste Macrì with Gaetano Chiappini. Vol. 3. Madrid: Espasa-Calpe; Fundación Antonio Machado, 1989. 1358-373.

Macrì, Oreste. Introduction. *Poesía y prosa.* By Antonio Machado. Ed. Oreste Macrì with Gaetano Chiappini. Madrid: Espasa-Calpe, 1989. 13-185.

Man, Paul de. "Literary History and Literary Modernity." *Blindness and Insight: Essays in the Rhetoric of Contemporary Criticism.* By Paul de Man. Intro. Wlad Godzich. 2nd ed. Rev. Theory and History of Literature 7. Minneapolis: U of Minnesota P, 1983. 142-65.

———. "Lyrical Voice in Contemporary Theory: Riffaterre and Jauss." Hošek, Parker, and Arac 55-72.

Manrique de Lara, J. G. "Umbral del creacionismo." *Gerardo Diego.* By Manrique de Lara. Madrid: Espesa, 1970. 137-56.

Marinetti, F. T. "The Founding and Manifesto of Futurism 1909." *Modernism: An Anthology of Sources and Documents.* Ed. Vassiliki Kolocotroni, Jane Goldman, and Olga Taxidou. Chicago: U of Chicago P, 1998. 249-53.

Martín González, Juan José. "Poesía y pintura en el paisaje castellano de Antonio Machado." *Curso en homenaje a Antonio Machado.* Ed. Eugenio de Bustos. Salamanca: Universidad de Salamanca, 1975. 179-93.

Martín i Ros, Rosa M. "La *Casa Sonia* y la obra textil y decorativa de Sonia Delaunay-Terk entre 1917 y 1921." *Robert y Sonia Delaunay.* Musée National D'Art Moderne, Centre Georges Pompidou, Museu Picasso; Museu Tèxtil D'Indumentària, Barcelona, October 20, 2000-January 21, 2001. Barcelona: Carroggio-Institut de Cultura de Barcelona; Museu Picasso, 2000. 71-83.

Martínez Ruiz, José [Azorín]. *El alma castellana (1600-1800). 1900. Obras completas.* Vol. 1. Madrid: Aguilar, 1947. 575-686. 9 vols.

———. *Castilla.* Madrid: Biblioteca Nueva, 1969. 9th ed.

———. *Clásicos y modernos.* Madrid: Renacimiento, 1913.

———. *España.* 1909. 3rd ed. Madrid: Espasa-Calpe, 1967.

———. *Fantasías y devaneos. 1920. Obras completas.* Vol. 4. Madrid: Aguilar, 1948. 31-140. 9 vols.

———. "La Generación de 1898." *Clásicos y modernos.* By Azorín. Buenos Aires: Editorial Losada, 1958. 5th ed. 1959. 174-91.

———. *Lecturas españolas.* Buenos Aires: Espasa-Calpe Argentina, 1938.

———. *El libro de Levante. 1929. Obras completas.* Vol. 5. Madrid: Aguilar, 1948. 343-441. 9 vols.

———. *Al margen de los clásicos. 1914. Obras completas.* Vol. 3. Madrid: Aguilar, 1947. 171-276. 9 vols.

———. *Obras completas.* Madrid: Aguilar, 1947-1954. 9 vols.

———. *El paisaje de España, visto por los españoles. 1917. Obras completas.* Vol. 3. Madrid: Aguilar, 1947. 1115-245. 9 vols.

———. "El paisaje en la poesía." *Clásicos y modernos.* By Azorín. Madrid: Renacimiento, 1913. 117-24.

———. *Un pueblecito-Ríofrío de Ávila. 1916. Obras completas.* Vol. 3. Madrid: Aguilar, 1947. 527-95. 9 vols.

Martínez Ruiz, José [Azorín]. *La ruta de Don Quixote*. 1905. Ed., intro., notes, and critical study by H. Ramsden. Manchester, Eng.: Manchester UP, 1966.

———. *Valencia*. 1941. *Obras completas*. Vol. 6. Madrid: Aguilar, 1948. 25-178. 9 vols.

———. *Visión de España – Páginas escogidas*. 1941. *Obras completas*. Vol. 6. Madrid: Aguilar, 1948. 311-15. 9 vols.

———. *La voluntad*. 1902. Ed., intro., and notes by E. Inman Fox. 5th ed. Madrid: Castalia, 1989.

Marvin, William S. "The Function of 'Rules' in *Die Meistersinger von Nürnberg*." *The Journal of Musicology* 20.3 (2003): 414-60.

Merleau-Ponty, Maurice. *Phenomenology of Perception*. 1945. Trans. Colin Smith. London and New York: 2002.

Molinari, Danielle. *Robert et Sonia Delaunay*. Paris: Nouvelles Éditions Françaises, 1987.

Molinero Cardenal, Marcos. *Antonio Machado y Soria: ideología y estética, 1907-1939*. Madrid: Terciarias Ediciones, 1993.

Morand, Paul. Letter to Guillermo de Torre. Ms. 22827/66. Cervantes Collection. Biblioteca Nacional de España, Madrid, Spain.

Morelli, Gabriele, with the collaboration of Carlos García. *Vicente Huidobro. Epistolario. Correspondencia con Gerardo Diego, Juan Larrea y Guillermo de Torre, 1918-1947*. Madrid: Residencia de Estudiantes, 2008.

Mostaza, Bartolomé. "El paisaje en la poesía de Antonio Machado." *Cuadernos Hispanoamericanos* 11-12 (1949): 623-41.

"Muequear." *Diccionario de la Lengua Española*. Real Academia Española. 22nd ed. 11 May 2013 <http://lema.rae.es/drae/?val=muequear>.

"Myriapod." Def. A. *The Oxford English Dictionary*. 11 May 2013 <http://www.oed.com.ezproxy.fiu.edu/view/Entry/124544?redirectedFrom=myriapod#eid>.

"Opinions sur Robert Delaunay." *Robert Delaunay (1885-1941)*. Musée National d'Art Moderne, May 25-September 30, 1957. Paris: Éditions des Musées Nationaux. 35-44.

Ortega Cantero, Nicolás. "Paisaje e identidad. La visión de Castilla como paisaje nacional (1876-1936)." *Boletín de la A.G.E.* [Asociación de Geógrafos Españoles] 51 (2009): 25-49. 17 Dec. 2010 <http://age.ieg.csic.ed/boletin/51/02-ORTEGA.pdf>.

Ortega y Gasset, José. *La deshumanización del arte*. 1925. Madrid: Revista de Occidente and Alianza, 2002.

———. "Meditación del marco." El Espectador *de José Ortega y Gasset*. Madrid: Biblioteca Nueva, 1950. 415-24.

Ortega Morales, Natividad Isabel. *La enseñanza-aprendizaje del arte: una innovación educativa de la Institución Libre de Enseñanza*. Granada: Grupo Editorial Universitario, 2002.

Ostriker, Alicia. "The Lyric." *The New History of Literature: English Poetry and Prose*. 1970. Ed. Christopher Ricks. New York: Peter Bedrick, 1987. 91-119.

Owre, J. Riis. "Un cursillo de poesía con Juan Ramón Jiménez." *Hispania* 51.2 (May 1968): 320-26.

Oxford Music Online. Oxford UP. 26, 28, 29 June 2008 and 22 Apr. 2013 <http://www.oxfordmusiconline.com>.

Padgett, Ron. Translator's Preface. *Blaise Cendrars: Complete Poems*. Trans. Ron Padgett. Intro. Jay Bochner. Berkeley: U of California P, 1992. vii-xi.

———, trans. "The Prose of the Trans-Siberian and of the Little Jean of France." *Blaise Cendrars: Complete Poems*. Intro. Jay Bochner. Berkeley: U of California P, 1992. 15-29.

Page, Tim, Ward Marston, Gottfried Kraus, and Harvey Sachs. Notes. *Die Meister-singer von Nürnberg*: Salzburg Festival 1937. By Richard Wagner. Cond. Arturo Toscanini. Perf. Philharmoniker Wiener and Staatsopernchor Konzertvereini-gung Wiener. Notes by Tim Page, Ward Marston, Gottfried Kraus, and Harvey Sachs. Admin. Festspiele Salzburger. Andante, 2003.

Pao, Maria. "The View from the Wheel: De Torre, Salinas, and Hinojosa." *Revista Hispánica Moderna* 54 (2001): 88-107.

Pasler, Jann. "'Jeux': Playing with Time and Form." *Nineteenth Century Music* 6:1 (Summer 1982): 60-75.

Peiper, Tadeusz. Letter to Guillermo de Torre. December 16, 1921. Ms. 22828/60. Cervantes Collection. Biblioteca Nacional de España, Madrid, Spain.

———. Letter to Guillermo de Torre. August 22, 1923. Ms. 22828/60. Cervantes Collection. Biblioteca Nacional de España, Madrid, Spain.

Pena, María del Carmen. "Aureliano de Beruete y Moret, personaje y paisajista es-pañol de fin de siglo." *Aureliano de Beruete 1845-1912. Exposición organizada por la Obra Cultural de la Caja de Pensiones*. Madrid, March 22-May 14, 1983. Madrid: Obra Social de la Caja de Pensiones, 1983. 12-22.

Peña, Manuel de la. *El ultraísmo en España.* Madrid: Colección Clásicos y Moder-nos, Librería Concesionaria Fernando Fè, 1925.

Pérez de Ayala, Ramón. *Las máscaras. Obras completas.* By Ramón Pérez de Ayala. Select. and comp. J. García Mercadal. Vol. 3. Madrid: Aguilar, 1964. 11-600.

Pérez Bazo, Javier. "Tres poemas franceses de Gerardo Diego y el problema de la traducibilidad del texto creacionista." *Círculos de lumbre: estudios sobre Gerar-do Diego.* Ed. F. J. Díez de Revenga and Mariano de Paco. Murcia: Caja Murcia, 1997. 121-52.

Pérez-Rioja, José Antonio. "Soria, en la poesía de Antonio Machado." *Antonio Ma-chado y Soria: homenaje en el primer centenario de su nacimiento.* Madrid: Pa-tronato José María Quadrado, Consejo Superior de Investigaciones Científicas, Centro de Estudios Sorianos, 1976. 33-53.

Persin, Margaret H. *Getting the Picture: The Ekphrastic Principle in Twentieth-Cen-tury Spanish Poetry.* Lewisburg, PA: Bucknell UP; London: Associated UP, 1997.

"Pleonectic." *The Oxford English Dictionary.* 9 May 2013 <http://www.oed.com.ez-proxy.fiu.edu/view/Entry/145718?redirectedFrom=Pleonectic#eid >.

"Pleonexia." *The Oxford English Dictionary.* 9 May 2013 <http://www.oed.com.ez-proxy.fiu.edu/view/Entry/145719?redirectedFrom=Pleonexia#eid >.

Poema de Mio Cid [*Poema del Cid*]. 3rd ed., corrected and with notes by Ramón Menéndez Pidal. Madrid: La Lectura, 1929.

"Poma." *Diccionario de la Lengua Española.* Real Academia Española. 22nd ed. 11 May 2013 <http://lema.rae.es/drae/?val=poma>.

Porrata, Samuel. *La poesía creacionista de Gerardo Diego.* Potomac, MD: Scripta Humanistica, 2007.

Puente, Joaquín de la. "Paisaje, paisajes, y lo paisajístico: 1901-1936." *Tres grandes maestros del paisaje decimonónico español: Jenaro Pérez Villaamil. Carlos de Haes. Aureliano de Beruete.* Madrid: Ayuntamiento de Madrid-Concejalía de Cultura, Centro Cultural del Conde Duque, 1990. 83-107.

Quiroga, Francisco. "Estructura uniclinal de la Península Ibérica." *Boletín de la Ins-titución Libre de Enseñanza* 5.97 (Mar. 8, 1881): 50-52.

———. Estructura uniclinal de la Península Ibérica." *Boletín de la Institución Libre de Enseñanza* 5.100 (Apr. 20, 1881): 50-52.

———. Estructura uniclinal de la Península Ibérica." *Boletín de la Institución Libre de Enseñanza* 5.101 (Apr. 30, 1881): 57-59.

Quiroga, Francisco. "Excursiones geológicas en los alrededores de Madrid." *Boletín de la Institución Libre de Enseñanza* 9.205 (Aug. 31, 1885): 248-51.
———. "Excursiones geológicas en los alrededores de Madrid." *Boletín de la Institución Libre de Enseñanza* 9.206 (Nov. 15, 1885): 263-65.
———. "Sociedad para el estudio del Guadarrama. Excursión al cerro de Almodovar y á San Fernando (7 febrero 1887)." *Boletín de la Institución Libre de Enseñanza* 11.241 (Feb. 28, 1887): 59-60.
———. "Sociedad para el estudio del Guadarrama. Otra excursión á Torrelodones (I)." *Boletín de la Institución Libre de Enseñanza* 11.239 (Jan. 31, 1887): 30-31.
Ramsden, H. *The 1898 Movement in Spain: Towards a Reinterpretation with Special Reference to* En torno al casticismo *and* Idearium español. Manchester, Eng.: Manchester UP, 1974.
"Rheophore." *The Oxford English Dictionary.* 11 May 2013 <http:// www. oed. com.ezproxy.fiu.edu/view/Entry/243420?redirectedFrom=rheophore#eid>.
Ribas, Pedro. "El *Volksgeist* de Hegel y la intrahistoria de Unamuno." *Cuadernos de la Cátedra Miguel de Unamuno* 21 (1971): 23-33.
Ribbans, Geoffrey. Introduction. *Campos de Castilla.* By Antonio Machado. Ed. Geoffrey Ribbans. 6th ed. Madrid: Cátedra, 1995. 13-88.
———. Introduction. *Soledades. Galerías. Otros poemas.* 1983. Ed. Geoffrey Ribbans. Madrid: Cátedra, 2000. 15-53.
Ricks, Christopher, ed. *The New History of Literature: English Poetry and Prose 1540-1674.* New York: Peter Bedrick, 1987.
Le Rider, Jacques. "L'Héritage de Goethe: Romantisme et expressionisme." *Aux origines de l'abstraction 1800-1914.* Musée D'Orsay, November 3, 2003-February 22, 2004. Paris: Éditions de la Réunion des Musées Nationaux, 2003. 111-20.
Rodríguez Forteza, Adela. *La naturaleza y Antonio Machado.* San Juan, PR: Editorial Cordillera, 1965.
Romains, Jules. *La vie unanime: Poème 1904-1907.* Paris, Gallimard, 1983.
Rood, Ogden. *Modern Chromatics, with Applications to Art and Industry.* New York: D. Appleton, 1879. 4 Dec. 2009 <http://books.google.com>.
Roque, Georges. "Les vibrations colorées de Delaunay: une des voies de l'abstraction." *Robert Delaunay 1906-1914: De L'Impressionnisme à l'abstraction.* Centre Georges Pompidou, June 3-August 16, 1999. Paris: Éditions Centre Georges Pompidou, 1999. 53-74.
Rosenfeld, Daniel, and Robert G. Workman. *The Spirit of Barbizon: France and America.* San Francisco: The Art Museum Association of America, 1986.
Rousseau, Pascal. "'El arte nuevo nos sonríe': Robert y Sonia Delaunay en Iberia (1914-1921)." *Robert y Sonia Delaunay.* Musée National D'Art Moderne, Centre Georges Pompidou, Museu Picasso; Museu Tèxtil D'Indumentària, Barcelona, October 20, 2000-January 21, 2001. Barcelona: Carroggio-Institut de Cultura de Barcelona; Museu Picasso, 2000. 40-70.
———. "'L'œil solaire': Une généalogie impressionniste de l'abstraction." *Aux origines de l'abstraction 1800-1914.* Musée D'Orsay, November 3, 2003 - February 22, 2004. Paris: Éditions de la Réunion des Musées Nationaux, 2003. 123-39.
———. "El vértigo de la mirada: La pintura abstracta de Robert Delaunay bajo el 'reino de la imagen.'" *Robert y Sonia Delaunay 1905-1941.* Museo Thyssen-Bornemisza, October 8, 2002-January 12, 2003. Madrid: Museo Thyssen-Bornemisza, 2002. 33-55.
Rubinger, Krystyna, ed. and comp. *Robert Delaunay.* Galerie Gmurzynska, May 13-July 30, 1983. Cologne, Ger.: Galerie Gmurzynska, 1983.
Salinas, Pedro. "El concepto de generación literaria aplicado a la del 98." *Revista de Occidente* (Dec. 1935): 249-59.

Salinas, Pedro. "El concepto de generación literaria aplicado a la del 98." *Literatura española siglo XX*. By Pedro Salinas. Madrid: Alianza, 1970. 26-33.

———. "Navacerrada, abril." *Seguro azar. Poesías completas*. By Pedro Salinas. Prol. Jorge Guillén. Barcelona: Barral, 1971. 116.

Salmon, André. "Le Salon." Numéro Consacré au XXXe Salon des Artistes Indépendants. Spec. issue of *Montjoie!* 2.3 (Mar. 1914): 21-28.

Salvador Jofré, Alvaro. "La dialéctica vestido/desnudo en la poesía de Juan Ramón Jiménez." *Criatura afortunada: estudios sobre la obra de Juan Ramón Jiménez*. Granada: Universidad de Granada, Departamento de Literatura Española, 1981. 195-213.

Sánchez Barbudo, Antonio. *Estudios sobre Unamuno y Machado*. Madrid: Ediciones Guadarrama, 1959.

Sarabia, Rosa. "Una aproximación a los poemas pintados como reflexión del signo artístico." *Vicente Huidobro y las artes plásticas*. By Juan Manuel Bonet et al. Madrid: Museo Nacional Centro de Arte Reina Sofía, 2001. 55–65.

Seeleman, Rosa. "The Treatment of Landscape in the Novelists of the Generation of 1898." *Hispanic Review* 4.3 (July 1936): 226-38.

Serrano Poncela, Segundo. *Antonio Machado: su mundo y su obra*. Buenos Aires: Editorial Losada, 1951.

Sesé, Bernard. *Claves de Antonio Machado*. Collaboration and trans. Soledad García Mouton. Madrid: Espasa Calpe, 1990.

Shaw, Donald L. *The Generation of 1898 in Spain*. London and Tonbridge: Ernest Benn; New York: Barnes and Noble, 1975.

Sidoti, Antoine. *Genèse et dossier d'une polémique:* La Prose du Transsibérien et de la Petite Jehanne de France. *Blaise Cendrars-Sonia Delaunay. Novembre-décembre 1912-juin 1914*. Archives des Lettres Modernes 224. Paris: Lettres Modernes, 1987.

El siglo XIX en el Prado. Madrid: Museo Nacional del Prado, 2010.

Silverman, Renée M. "La Prose du Transsibérien et de la petite Jehanne de France (1913): Abstraction, Materiality, and an Alternative Simultaneisme." Ed. Irene Chytraeus-Auerbach and Elke Uhl. *Der Aufbruch in die Moderne. Herwarth Walden und die europaeische Avantgarde*. Berlin: LIT Verlag, 2013. 55-77.

———. "Questioning the Territory of Modernism: *Ultraísmo* and the Aesthetic of the First Spanish Avant-Garde." *Romanic Review* 97.1 (Jan. 2006): 51-71.

Simón Cabarga, José. *Historia del Ateneo de Santander*. Madrid: Editorial Nacional, 1963.

Smith, Richard Langham. "Motives and symbols." *Claude Debussy: Pelléas et Mélisande*. By Roger Nichols and Richard Langham Smith. Cambridge and New York: Cambridge UP, 1989. 78-106.

Soria Olmedo, Andrés. "Cubismo y creacionismo: matices del gris." *Boletín de la Fundación Federico García Lorca* 9 (1987): 38-49.

———. "Juan Ramón Jiménez, crítico del vanguardismo." *Criatura afortunada: estudios sobre la obra de Juan Ramón Jiménez*. Granada: Universidad de Granada, Departamento de Literatura Española, 1981. 214-28.

Sotelo Vázquez, Adolfo. "Miguel de Unamuno y la forja de la poesía desnuda de Juan Ramón Jiménez." *Hispanic Review* 55.2 (Spring 1987): 195-212.

Soupault, Philippe. Letters to Guillermo de Torre. Ms. 22831. Ms micro. 13140. Cervantes Collection. Biblioteca Nacional de España, Madrid, Spain.

Spate, Virginia. *Orphism: The Evolution of Non-Figurative Painting in Paris, 1910-1914*. Oxford: Clarendon P; New York: Oxford UP, 1979.

"Tarsus." Def. 1a. *The Oxford English Dictionary*. 11 May 2013 <http:// www. oed. com.ezproxy.fiu.edu/view/Entry/197924?redirectedFrom=tarsus#eid>.

"Tegmen." Def. D. *The Oxford English Dictionary*. 11 May 2013 <http:// www. oed.com.ezproxy.fiu.edu/view/Entry/198607?redirectedFrom=tegmen#eid>.

Torner, Eduardo M. *Lírica hispánica: relaciones entre lo popular y lo culto*. Prol. Homero Serís. Madrid: Castalia, 1966.

Torre, Guillermo de. *El arte decorativo de Sonia Delaunay-Terk*. 1921. Ms. 22843/ 13. Cervantes Collection. Biblioteca Nacional de España, Madrid, Spain.

———. "El arte decorativo de Sonia Delaunay-Terk." *Alfar* 35 (1925). Rpt. in *Robert y Sonia Delaunay*. Fundación Juan March, April-May, 1982. Madrid: Fundación Juan March, 1982. [N. pag.].

———. *Blaise Cendrars*. Ms. 22843/10. N. d. Cervantes Collection. Biblioteca Nacional de España, Madrid, Spain.

———. "El cinema y la novísima literatura: sus conexiones." *Cosmópolis* 9.34 (Sept. 1921): 97-107.

———. *Destrucción-Reconstrucción: la pintura de Robert Delaunay*. 1920. Ms. 22843/14. Cervantes Collection. Biblioteca Nacional de España, Madrid, Spain.

———. *Hélices*. Madrid: Mundo Latino, 1923.

———. *Hélices*. 1923. Ed. and intro. José María Barrera López. Vol. 1. Malaga: Centro Cultural de la Generación del 27, 2000.

———. "La imagen y la metáfora en la novísima lírica." *Alfar* 45 (Dec. 1924): 218-24.

———. "Itinerario noviespacial del paisaje." *Cervantes* (1920): 81-93.

———. "Juan Gris y Robert Delaunay: Reminiscencias personales." *Minorías y masas en la cultura y el arte contemporáneo*. Barcelona: EDHASA, 1963. 231-55.

———. "Juan Gris y Robert Delaunay: Reminiscencias personales." *Revista de Ideas Estéticas* 21, no. 84 (Oct.-Dec. 1963): 295-316.

———. Letter to José Ortega y Gasset. January 4, 1922. ID 1236. Sig. C-73/7a. Archivo José Ortega y Gasset. Fundación Ortega y Gasset, Madrid, Spain.

———. Letter (Dedication) to José Ortega y Gasset. 1925. ID 10558. Sig. C-73/7ch. Archivo José Ortega y Gasset. Fundación Ortega y Gasset, Madrid, Spain.

———. Letter to José Ortega y Gasset. April 2, 1928. ID 2096. Sig. C-73/7b. Archivo José Ortega y Gasset. Fundación Ortega y Gasset, Madrid, Spain.

———. Letter to José Ortega y Gasset. September 25, 1929. ID 2274. Sig. C-73/7c. Archivo José Ortega y Gasset. Fundación Ortega y Gasset, Madrid, Spain.

———. Letter to Robert Delaunay. December 13, 1920. *Lettres, Guillermo de Torre et Robert et Sonia Delaunay*. 1920-1937. Fond Delaunay, Bibliothèque Kandinsky, Musée Nationale D'Art Moderne, Paris, France.

———. Letter to Robert Delaunay. February 5, 1921. *Lettres, Guillermo de Torre et Robert et Sonia Delaunay*. 1920-1937. Fond Delaunay, Bibliothèque Kandinsky, Musée Nationale D'Art Moderne, Paris, France.

———. Letter to Robert Delaunay. June 23, 1921. *Lettres, Guillermo de Torre et Robert et Sonia Delaunay*. 1920-1937. Fond Delaunay, Bibliothèque Kandinsky, Musée Nationale D'Art Moderne, Paris, France.

———. Letter to Robert Delaunay. July 24, 1921. *Lettres, Guillermo de Torre et Robert et Sonia Delaunay*. 1920-1937. Fond Delaunay, Bibliothèque Kandinsky, Musée Nationale D'Art Moderne, Paris, France.

———. Letter to Robert Delaunay. March, 1922. *Lettres, Guillermo de Torre et Robert et Sonia Delaunay*. 1920-1937. Fond Delaunay, Bibliothèque Kandinsky, Musée Nationale D'Art Moderne, Paris, France.

———. *Lettres, Guillermo de Torre et Robert et Sonia Delaunay*. 1920-1937. Fond Delaunay, Bibliothèque Kandinsky, Musée Nationale D'Art Moderne, Paris, France.

Torre, Guillermo de. *Literaturas europeas de vanguardia*. Ed. José María Barrera López. Seville: Renacimiento, 2001.
———. "Manifiesto vertical ultraísta." Suppl, *Grecia* 3.50 (1920).
———. "Poemas fotogénicos." *Cosmópolis* 11.42 (June 1922): 94-97.
———. "La poesía creacionista y la pugna entre sus progenitores." *Cosmópolis* 20 (Aug. 1920): 589-605.
———. "La polémica del Creacionismo: Huidobro and Reverdy." 1962. Costa, *Vicente Huidobro y el creacionismo* 151-65.
———. Postal Card to Robert Delaunay. October 24, 1921. *Lettres, Guillermo de Torre et Robert et Sonia Delaunay*. 1920-1937. Fond Delaunay, Bibliothèque Kandinsky, Musée Nationale D'Art Moderne, Paris, France.
———. "Problemas teóricos y estética experimental del nuevo lirismo. 'La poesía de hoy' por el teorizante Jean Epstein." *Cosmópolis* 8.33 (Aug. 1921): 585-607.
———. "Rasgos polémicos: réplica a Vicente Huidobro." *Alfar* 2.39 (Apr. 1924): 26-30.
———. *Ultraísmo, existencialismo y objetivismo en literatura*. Madrid: Ediciones Guadarrama, 1968.
———. *Walt Whitman, poète cosmique*. Ms. 22843/27. [N.d.] Cervantes Collection. Biblioteca Nacional de España, Madrid, Spain.
Torres Campos, R. "La enseñanza de la geografía." *Boletín de la Institución Libre de Enseñanza* 7.159 (Sept. 30, 1883): 283-85.
La Tourette, Gilles de. *Robert Delaunay*. Paris: Charles Massin, 1950.
Turvey, Malcolm. "Jean Epstein's Cinema of Immanence: The Rehabilitation of the Corporeal Eye." *October* 83 (Winter 1998): 25-50.
Unamuno y Jugo, Miguel de. *Andanzas y visiones españolas*. 1922. *Obras completas*. Ed. Manuel García Blanco. Vol. 1. Madrid and Barcelona: Afrodisio Aguado; Vergara, 1958. 599-847.
———. *En torno al casticismo*. 1902. Madrid: Espasa-Calpe, 1943. 12th ed. 1998.
———. *España y los españoles* (I. 1897-1919). *Obras completas*. Ed. Manuel García Blanco. Vol. 4. Madrid and Barcelona: Afrodisio Aguado; Vergara, 1958. 1017-168.
———. *Obras completas*. Ed. Manuel García Blanco. Madrid and Barcelona: Afrodisio Aguado; Vergara, 1958.
———. *De mi país. Descripciones, relatos y artículos de costumbres*. 1903. *Obras completas*. Ed. Manuel García Blanco. Vol. 1. Madrid and Barcelona: Afrodisio Aguado; Vergara, 1958. 85-231.
———. *Paisajes*. 1902. *Obras completas*. Ed. Manuel García Blanco. Vol. 1. Madrid and Barcelona: Afrodisio Aguado; Vergara, 1958. 43-84.
———. *Paz en la guerra*. Intro. Juan Pablo Fusi. Madrid: Alianza, 2003.
———. *Poesías*. 1907. *Obras completas*. Ed. Manuel García Blanco. Vol. 13. Madrid and Barcelona: Afrodisio Aguado; Vergara, 1958. 193-496.
———. *Por tierras de Portugal y de España*. 1911. *Obras completas*. Ed. Manuel García Blanco. Vol. 1. Madrid and Barcelona: Afrodisio Aguado; Vergara, 1958. 349-597.
———. *El porvenir de España*. *Obras completas*. Ed. Manuel García Blanco. Vol. 4. Madrid and Barcelona: Afrodisio Aguado; Vergara, 1958. 951-1015.
———. *Rosario de sonetos líricos*. 1911. *Obras completas*. Ed. Manuel García Blanco. Vol. 13. Madrid and Barcelona: Afrodisio Aguado; Vergara, 1958. 497-646.
Valle-Inclán, Ramón del. *Flor de santidad*. 1904. Ed. María Paz Díez Taboada. 2nd ed. Madrid: Cátedra, 1999.
Vázquez, Francesca. "Traductología de vanguardia." *La vanguardia en España: arte y literatura*. Ed. Javier Pérez Bazo. Toulouse: CRIC, Université de Toulouse-Le Mirail; Paris: Ophrys, 1998. 81-99.

Vega, Félix Lope de. "Canciones de San Juan." *Poesías líricas*. By Félix Lope de Vega. Ed., intro., and notes by José F. Montesinos. Madrid: Espasa-Calpe, 1968. 86-88. 2 vols.

———. "Seguidillas de la noche de San Juan." *Poesías líricas*. By Félix Lope de Vega. Ed., intro., and notes by José F. Montesinos. Madrid: Espasa-Calpe, 1968. 89. 2 vols.

Videla, Gloria. *El Ultraísmo: estudios sobre movimientos poéticos de vanguardia en España*. Madrid: Gredos, 1963.

Videla de Rivero, Gloria. "Huidobro en España." *Revista Iberoamericana* 45.106-107 (Jan.-June 1997): 37-48.

Vila-Belda, Reyes. "Paisajismo e impresionismo en *Campos de Castilla*, de Antonio Machado." *Revista Canadiense de Estudios Hispánicos* 28.1 (Fall 2003): 281-97.

Wagner, Richard. *Die Meistersinger von Nürnberg*: Salzburg Festival 1937. Cond. Arturo Toscanini. Perf. Philharmoniker Wiener and Staatsopernchor Konzertvereinigung Wiener. Notes by Tim Page, Ward Marston, Gottfried Kraus, and Harvey Sachs. Admin. Festspiele Salzburger. Andante, 2003.

Wenk, Arthur B. *Claude Debussy and Twentieth-Century Music*. Boston, MA: Twayne Publishers, 1983.

Wheelen, Guy. "Los Delaunay en España y Portugal." *Goya* 48 (1962): 420-29.

Whitman, Walt. *Leaves of Grass. The Complete Poems*. Ed. Francis Murphy. 1975. Harmondsworth, Middlesex: Penguin, 1986.

Wilcox, John C. "'Naked' versus 'Pure' Poetry in Juan Ramón Jiménez, with Remarks on the Impact of W. B. Yeats." *Hispania* 66.4 (Dec. 1983): 511-21.

Willis, Bruce Dean. *The Vanguard Poetics of Vicente Huidobro and Mário de Andrade*. West Lafayette, IN: Purdue UP, 2006.

Worringer, Wilhelm. *Abstraction and Empathy*. 1953. Trans. Michael Bullock. Chicago: Elephant Paperback, 1997.

Zuleta, Emilia de. *Guillermo de Torre*. Buenos Aires: Ediciones Culturales, 1962.

ILLUSTRATIONS

Fig. 0.1. Rafael Barradas, Cover design (*xilografía* [xylography]) from Guillermo de Torre, *Hélices* (Madrid: Mundo Latino, 1923); rpt. in Guillermo de Torre, *Hélices* (Málaga: Centro Cultural de la Generación del 27, 2000). [*see p. 15*]

Fig. 1.1. Carlos de Haes, *Canal de Mancorbo en los Picos de Europa*, 1876, Oil on canvas, 168 x 123 cm., Museo del Prado, Madrid, Spain. [*see p. 68*]

Fig. 1.2. Aureliano de Beruete, *Vista del Guadarrama desde el Plantío de los Infantes*, 1910, Oil on canvas, 67 x 101 cm., Museo del Prado, Madrid, Spain. [*see p. 71*]

Fig. 2.1. José Corral, *Vista panorámica de Madrid desde la torre de la Iglesia de Santa Cruz*, 1929, Photograph, Museo de Historia, Madrid, Spain. [*see p. 102*]

Fig. 3.1. Robert Delaunay, *Fenêtres ouvertes simultanément 1ère partie, 3e motif*, 1912, Oil on oval canvas, 57 x 123 cm., Peggy Guggenheim Collection, Venice, Italy (Solomon R. Guggenheim Foundation, NY). [*see p. 151*]

Fig. 3.2. Robert Delaunay, *Formes circulaires, Soleil no. 1*, 1912-1913, Oil on canvas, 100 x 81 cm., Wilhelm-Hack-Museum, Ludwigshafen am Rhein, Germany. [*see p. 153*]

Fig. 3.3. Robert Delaunay, *Formes circulaires, Soleil no. 2*, 1912-1913, Oil on canvas, 100 x 68,5 cm., Musée National d'Art Moderne, Centre Georges Pompidou, Paris, France. CNAC/ MNAM/Dist. RMN-Grand Palais / Art Resource, NY. Photo: Jacqueline Hyde. Palais. [*see p. 153*]

INDEX

Academia de Bellas Artes de San Fernando, 63-64

Alfonso VI (King of Spain), 52

Andalusia, 19, 40n, 42, 64n, 80-81

Apollinaire, Guillaume, 19-20, 23, 92n, 94, 108n, 131, 131n, 148n, 150n: works of, 134, 134n, 140n, 161n, 165, 168; orphism in, 137-38, 138n; visual metaphors of, 150-51, 167. See also *Simultaneisme*

Apostrophe, 83-84, 84n, 104n. See also *Campos de Castilla*: the apostrophe in

Arcadia. See *Campos de Castilla*: Arcadia in

Aristotle, 107

Arte decorativo de Sonia Delaunay-Terk, El, 30, 30n, 133, 133n, 140, 160, 162

Avant-garde, first (Spanish), 15n, 18, 18n, 22n, 36, 89n, 91-92, 95, 106-107, 130, 161, 165, 176, 179, 183, 188: textual architecture of, 15-16; cosmopolitanism of, 16, 22; concerns of, 16, 157-58; and Machado/*Campos de Castilla*, 17, 87-88, 88n, 89, 236; and Spanish identity, 17, 22; rebellious posture of the, 18, 22, 94, 131, 178; perspective and perception vis-à-vis subjectivity in, 18, 215, 237; textual landscapes of, 18-20, 122; perceptual simultaneity of, 20, 226; memory in, 24, 178, 237; architectonics of, 31, 234; and mimesis, 109, 162; and the Delaunays, 132-33, 143; and modern poetry, 183-84, 212; aesthetics of, 224, 226, 232. See also *Creacionismo*; *Ultraísmo*

Azorín. See Martínez Ruiz, José A.

Barbizon School, 71, 71n, 74n

Baroja, Pío, 41, 43

Barradas, Rafael, 15, 93n, 94, 94n, 116n, 136n

Beauduin, Nicolas, 92, 134n, 145n

Baudelaire, Charles, 112n, 203, 231-32

Benjamin, Walter, 23n, 112n, 232: works of, 23; memory in, 23-24, 231; film and the camera for, 121n

Bergson, Henri, 80n, 225: and memory, 32, 80, 80n, 120-21, 151, 151n, 152, 165-66, 217, 219, 232; perception in, 79, 176, 230-31, 236

Bernal, José Luis, 186

Beruete, Aureliano de, 41-42, 58-59, 59n, 61, 61n, 62, 62n, 63, 70n, 79: paintings of, 70-71, 71n, 73

Blériot, Louis, 159

Borges, Jorge Luis, 15n, 93, 93n, 94

Borges, Norah, 15n, 93n, 94, 96-97, 105n

Campos de Castilla, 45n, 89-90, 95, 159: poems of, 17, 25, 39-40, 44-45, 52-53, 53n, 54, 61-62, 65, 65n, 66-69, 72-87, 178n, 228; Arcadia in, 17, 25, 39, 76-77, 82, 87; Spanish identity in, 17, 45, 52, 55, 227; Spain's decline in, 17, 24-25, 38, 48, 53, 77, 84-85, 87, 227-28; Spain's renewal in, 17, 39, 85, 229; the countryside in, 17, 25, 37-39, 53-55, 64, 68-69, 75-76, 85; Castile in, 17, 19, 25, 38-39, 42, 45, 61, 64, 69, 82-83; the collective in, 18-19, 25, 65, 85-87, 130, 178; memory and recollection in, 19, 24-25, 65, 79-82,

NORTH CAROLINA STUDIES IN THE ROMANCE LANGUAGES AND LITERATURES

Recent Titles

THE INVENTION OF THE EYEWITNESS. A HISTORY OF TESTIMONY IN FRANCE, by Andrea Frisch. 2004. (No. 279). *978-0-8078-9283-1.*

SUBJECT TO CHANGE: THE LESSONS OF LATIN AMERICAN WOMEN'S *TESTIMONIO* FOR TRUTH, FICTION, AND THEORY, by Joanna R. Bartow. 2005. (No. 280). *978-0-8078-9284-X.*

QUESTIONING RACINIAN TRAGEDY, by John Campbell. 2005. (No. 281). *978-0-8078-9285-8.*

THE POLITICS OF FARCE IN CONTEMPORARY SPANISH AMERICAN THEATRE, by Priscilla Meléndez. 2006. (No. 282). *978-0-8078-9286-6.*

MODERATING MASCULINITY IN EARLY MODERN CULTURE, by Todd W. Reeser. 2006. (No. 283). *978-0-8078-9287-4.*

PORNOBOSCODIDASCALUS LATINUS (1624). KASPAR BARTH'S NEO-LATIN TRANSLATION OF *CELESTINA*, by Enrique Fernández. 2006. (No. 284). *978-0-8078-9288-2.*

JACQUES ROUBAUD AND THE INVENTION OF MEMORY, by Jean-Jacques F. Poucel. 2006. (No. 285). *978-0-8078-9289-0.*

THE "I" OF HISTORY. SELF-FASHIONING AND NATIONAL CONSCIOUSNESS IN JULES MICHELET, by Vivian Kogan. 2006. (No. 286). *978-0-8078-9290-4.*

BUCOLIC METAPHORS: HISTORY, SUBJECTIVITY, AND GENDER IN THE EARLY MODERN SPANISH PASTORAL, by Rosilie Hernández-Pecoraro. 2006. (No. 287). *978-0-8078-9291-2.*

UNA ARMONÍA DE CAPRICHOS: EL DISCURSO DE RESPUESTA EN LA PROSA DE RUBÉN DARÍO, por Francisco Solares-Larrare. 2007. (No. 288). *978-0-8078-9292-0.*

READING THE *EXEMPLUM* RIGHT: FIXING THE MEANING OF *EL CONDE LUCANOR*, by Jonathan Burgoyne. 2007. (No. 289). *978-0-8078-9293-9.*

MONSTRUOS QUE HABLAN: EL DISCURSO DE LA MONSTRUOSIDAD EN CERVANTES, por Rogelio Miñana. 2007. (No. 290). *978-0-8078-9294-7.*

BAJO EL CIELO PERUANO: THE DEVOUT WORLD OF PERALTA BARNUEVO, by David F. Slade and Jerry M. Williams. 2008. (No. 291). *978-0-8078-9295-4.*

ESCAPE FROM THE PRISON OF LOVE: CALORIC IDENTITIES AND WRITING SUBJECTS IN FIFTEENTH-CENTURY SPAIN, by Robert Folger. 2009. (No. 292). *978-0-8078-9296-1.*

LOS *TRIONFI* DE PETRARCA COMENTADOS EN CATALÁN: UNA EDICIÓN DE LOS MANUSCRITOS 534 DE LA BIBLIOTECA NACIONAL DE PARÍS Y DEL ATENEU DE BARCELONA, por Roxana Recio. 2009. (No. 293). *978-0-8078-9297-8.*

MAPPING THE SOCIAL BODY. URBANISATION, THE GAZE, AND THE NOVELS OF GALDÓS, by Collin McKinney. 2009. (No. 294). *978-0-8078-9298-5.*

ENCOUNTERS WITH BERGSON(ISM) IN SPAIN: RECONCILING PHILOSOPHY, LITERATURE, FILM AND URBAN SPACE, by Benjamin Fraser. 2009. (No. 295). *978-0-8078-9299-2.*

IMPERIAL STAGINGS. EMPIRE AND IDEOLOGY IN TRANSATLANTIC THEATER OF EARLY MODERN SPAIN AND THE NEW WORLD, by Chad M. Gasta. 2013. (No. 296). *978-1-4696-0996-6*

INSTABLE PUENTE. LA CONSTRUCCIÓN DEL LETRADO CRIOLLO EN LA OBRA DE JUAN DE ESPINOSA MEDRANO, por Juan M. Vitulli. 2013. (No. 297). *978-1-4696-0997-3*

ILUSIÓN ÁULICA E IMAGINACIÓN CABALLERESCA EN *EL CORTESANO* DE LUIS MILÁN, por Ignacio López Alemany. 2013. (No. 298). *978-1-4696-0998-0*

THE TRIUMPH OF BRAZILIAN MODERNISM. THE METANARRATIVE OF EMANCIPATION AND COUNTER-NARRATIVES, by Saulo Gouveia. 2013. (No. 299). *978-1-4696-0999-7*

ETNOGRAFÍA, POLÍTICA Y PODER A FINALES DEL SIGLO XIX. JOSÉ MARTÍ Y LA CUESTIÓN INDÍGENA, por Jorge Camacho. 2013. (No. 300). *978-1-4696-1000-9*

PUTTING MONET AND REMBRANDT INTO WORDS: PIERRE LOTI'S RECREATION AND THEORIZATION OF CLAUDE MONET'S IMPRESSIONISM AND REMBRANDT'S LANDSCAPES IN LITERATURE, by Richard M. Berrong. 2013. (No. 301). *978-1-4696-1365-9*

MAPPING THE LANDSCAPE, REMAPPING THE TEXT: SPANISH POETRY FROM ANTONIO MACHADO'S *CAMPOS DE CASTILLA* TO THE FIRST AVANT-GARDE (1909-1925), by Renée M. Silverman. 2014. (No. 302). *978-1-4696-1522-6*

Send orders to: University of North Carolina Press
P.O. Box 2288
Chapel Hill, NC 27515-2288
U.S.A.
www.uncpress.unc.edu
FAX: 919 966-3829